THE WILHELMSTRASSE

PAUL SEABURY

THE WILHELM-STRASSE

A Study of German Diplomats
Under the Nazi Regime

GREENWOOD PRESS, PUBLISHERS
WESTPORT, CONNECTICUT

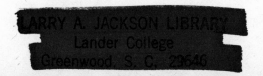

Library of Congress Cataloging in Publication Data

Seabury, Paul.
 The Wilhelmstrasse : a study of German diplomats
under the Nazi regime.

 Reprint of the ed. published by University of
California Press, Berkeley.
 Originally presented as the author's thesis,
Columbia University.
 Bibliography: p.
 Includes index.
 1. Germany. Auswärtiges Amt. 2. Germany--
Diplomatic and consular service. 3. Germany--
Foreign relations--1933-1945. I. Title.

[JX1796.S45 1976]   327'.2'0943   76-2403
ISBN 0-8371-8790-7

Originally published in 1954 by University of California Press,
Berkeley

Reprinted with the permission of University of California Press

Reprinted in 1976 by Greenwood Press,
a division of Williamhouse-Regency Inc.

Library of Congress Catalog Card Number 76-2403

ISBN 0-8371-8790-7

Printed in the United States of America

TO MY PARENTS

PREFACE

Since the end of World War II, a great wealth of information has emerged about the nature of National Socialism, its origins and antecedents, its deeds, and the men and social forces of which it was composed. We now seem far removed from these things; many of them we are inclined to forget. Much has happened, both in postwar Germany and in the rest of the world, to impair our full sensitivity to these events, and to their inhumanity and brutality.

And yet, the same passage of time has provided us with wider perspectives for comprehending them. The work which follows would have been far different had it been written in the confused months of the immediate "postwar" period. The emergence, in recent years, of voluminous documentary material (much of it produced in the Nürnberg trials), memoirs, and scholarly studies, has made it now quite apparent that little new light can be thrown upon Nazi foreign policy, or upon the once intriguing problem of "who made German foreign policy" during the Hitler regime.[1] Yet this same material has led unerringly into another aspect of German government and diplomacy: the German Foreign Office.

It is a rare occasion when a nation's diplomatic archives are opened to the scrutiny of outside contemporaries, as were those of the German *Auswärtiges Amt* and the *Reichskanzlei* at the end of World War II. For obvious reasons, such documents ordinarily remain secret for generations. True, after World War I, the publication in Weimar Germany of *Die Grosse Politik;* in Russia, of the tsarist foreign-office archives; and, in Britain and France, of selected diplomatic files gave historians an early insight into the nature of prewar European diplomacy. Understandably, the scholarship turned loose upon these materials was directed chiefly toward an exploration of the war's origins, and to controversies over the political and moral responsibility for its outbreak. These studies resulted in much information about the nature, direction, and consequences of prewar great-power imperialism and, in particular, of its economic manifestations. Yet it is regrettable that little was done with these sources to explore the internal "dynamics" of the machinery of diplomacy, or to study the diplomatic bureaucracy specifically as a phenomenon of political organization.

For students of diplomatic history, international relations, and public administration, numerous and competent studies of the foreign offices and foreign services of most Western states are today available.[2] Much can be learned from them of the workings of modern diplomatic machinery. Some were conceived, quite properly, as guides to diplomatic practice. All of them reveal much about the formal structure of Western foreign offices, about the several administrative problems arising in the conduct of foreign policy; about their personnel methods and means of advancement in service; and about the traditions and ethical standards which have prevailed in them.

Yet all these studies labor under one general and unavoidable impediment. A student of foreign-office organization is almost inevitably restricted in his access to and use of contemporary archive materials. Considerations of state security and of propriety with respect to living statesmen, prohibit his overzealous use of state documents to describe in detail the workings of modern diplomacy.

These impediments were not to such an extent placed in the way of the author of the present work. Total defeat of Nazi Germany brought in its train total exposure of its records—including Foreign Office documents. These papers, along with documents subsequently made public at trials of ministerial officials, were made available to researchers—a notably limited public. The careers and activities of German diplomats are thereby revealed to a degree seldom encountered in the study of the diplomatic service of a modern great power. For these reasons the following study may perhaps claim a candor and documentation not usually present in works of this kind.

The purpose of this work is twofold. On the one hand it is an analysis of one crucial segment of the German civil service under the Nazi regime and thus intimately connected with the whole problem of National Socialism and the Nazi state. On the other hand it deals with a wider, and perhaps more universal problem: the behavior and moral responsibility of the bureaucratic technician in modern society—a problem not unique to Germany.

"The fixed person for the fixed duties," A. N. Whitehead wrote prophetically some years ago, "who in older societies was such a godsend, in the future will be a public danger." This study focuses attention on such men: on the technicians of diplomacy in a totalitarian regime, on the forces which played upon them, on their response to them, and on the manner and reason for their behavior under a ruthless system.

In the first three decades of our century, Max Weber and

others stimulated much interest in the nature of bureaucracy in modern society, and of the "technicians" who ran the depersonalized machinery of government.[3] One aspect of this investigation centered upon the behavior and the power of the modern civil service.

Large, long-established state bureaucracies, Weber asserted, are capable of considerable independence and insulation from political leadership, and of formulating and executing their own policies regardless of the policies of that leadership. The notion that a bureaucratic establishment somehow may be reduced to a totally passive "instrument" of political leadership ignores known facts of administrative behavior of officials. The notion that a civil service should not only function as an instrumentality but also be indifferent to the question of who possesses state power, and the ends to which this power is exercised, likewise ignores the realities of bureaucratic behavior. Max Weber, in his study of bureaucracy, it is true, conceded that an administrative state apparatus *was* potentially capable of "rationalization"; that "dehumanization"— the obliteration from official behavior of "love, hatred and all purely personal elements"—constituted psychological prerequisites for a fully "rational" bureaucracy. While such characteristics doubtless constitute standards of administrative behavior, they represent merely operative norms, and ignore the potentialities, within a bureaucratic establishment, of discretionary behavior, of rule- and decision-making, where an official administrative apparatus itself may make policy. Wielders of state political power always have been conscious of the potentialities of oppositional behavior in a civil service—regardless of whether they possessed the capacity to frustrate it; and while the modern democratic state may establish legal frameworks to surround a permanent civil service and restrict its overt political activities (for example, the Hatch Act in the United States), such formal legal measures can, of course, only with extreme difficulty penetrate to the core of the political power of a bureaucracy.

The degree to which a state bureaucracy may, or may not, be pervaded with loyalty to a given political regime, or share, in broad measure, common political values with such a regime, is not easily discoverable. We may suggest certain criteria of analysis: the degree of development of an autonomous bureaucratic *esprit de corps;* the value implications of such a service ideology; the degree of economic independence possessed by dominant elements within such a bureaucracy; the sociological origins of such men; the relationship of a "bureaucratic elite" to other agglomerations of political power within a society; the nature of material and psychological rewards available to higher civil servants as consequence of compliant behavior; the relationship of substantive policies espoused by a political leadership to established or "traditional" policies of an older bureaucracy; and the degree of cultural homogeneity of a bureaucratic officialdom.[4] In all events, it is clear that, while rational administrative organization, the functional rationalization, and hierarchical ordering of a bureaucratic administration require the diminution and restriction of free, autonomous individual decision making (and the consequent establishment of fixed and official laws, rules, or administrative regulations), this very characteristic of a bureaucracy constitutes one of its greatest collective powers. The fact that bureaucratic institutions, overtly or covertly, may exercise wide discretionary powers in making public policy is today a generally recognized fact.[5]

Yet bureaucratic "neutrality"—the assertion of official disinterestedness in the making of administrative decisions—is a valid notion under specific circumstances; to assert otherwise would be to deny any prospect of rational administrative behavior at all. In a constitutional state, the administration of public law by bodies of public servants requires the existence of norms of "disinterestedness." To assume that the political or ideological predispositions of a career bureaucracy (granting a necessary homogeneity of belief systems in such an officialdom) inevitably dispose it to a specific course of political behavior regardless of its political leadership, severely misjudges the potentialities of powerful leadership. Weber, who correctly emphasized the potentialities of autonomous power in a fully rationalized bureaucratic establishment, failed to assess adequately the vulnerability of such an officialdom under certain circumstances. His antithesis of the "charismatic" to the bureaucratic personality—the former endowed with qualities of magnetic leadership and irrational persuasion—indicated his awareness of the problem presented by a gifted manipulator of men placed in charge of a bureaucratic establishment. But the techniques of extracting compliance from obdurate organized bureaucracies need not be limited merely to charisma; a bureaucracy may be reduced to hapless confusion, paralysis, and total subordination by other devices as well, and thereby abandon whatever ideological virtue it may theretofore have possessed. Nor need such devices be employed by the formal political leadership of the state. The techniques of persistent denunciation, public defamation, character assassination, private terror may, under revolutionary conditions, have a profound effect upon the character and morale of a bureaucratic establishment, and, indeed, within a relatively brief time demolish its institutional effectiveness.[6]

In dealing with the first of the two stated purposes of this study, an analysis is made of the behavior of the traditional, conservative German foreign service—the Wilhelmstrasse—in the politically violent Nazi period; an assessment is sought of the collective reactions of that bureaucracy to the varied inducements to compliance which the Nazi state afforded it; and of the techniques used by a totalitarian state to control its inherited civil service.

The burden of this narrative and analysis is not directed at any uniquely "German" problem of totalitarianism. This is

a study of the progressive disintegration of a diplomatic service; of the moral problems encountered by men of bureaucratic power—conservative or otherwise—when faced by the
terror and inducements of a revolutionary movement which
shattered the constitutional fabric of a pluralistic society.
There is much in this narrative which will appear ludicrous
and, at times, fantastic. None of it is untrue. The consequences
of the irresponsible exercise of irresponsible power are well-
known. As Trevor-Roper has said, "neither courts nor feudal-
ism are nurseries of political intelligence."[7] The examples of
grotesque personal struggles, incompetence, and confusion in
the foreign service of the Third Reich and its leadership have
their place here because they were characteristic of the totalitarian system in which they occurred. But the humor and irony
which we may see in them today should not cause us to overlook the larger and far more pervasive horror of the Nazi
state itself. If this study may claim any worth, it is not comedy,
but tragedy.

The author wishes to express his gratitude to a number of
persons whose advice and help were of value in the shaping
of this work. His chief debt is to Professor Franz L. Neumann
of Columbia University, under whose scrutiny the contours of
this book emerged; to Professors Peter Gay and Fritz Stern,
also of Columbia University, whose encouragement and enlightenment were a goad and reassurance; to Professors Raymond J. Sontag of the University of California and Gordon
Craig of Princeton, who read this manuscript in various stages
of development; to Miss Catherine Ferner, of the International
Law Library of Columbia University, whose persistent patience and help brought together most of the materials used in
the study; to Mr. Henry Sachs, of the United States Army
Document Center 7771 in Berlin, Germany, who provided
access to documentary sources on the Nazi Party; to Frau
Marta Woermann, of the Documentary Archive of the Law

Faculty of Heidelberg University, for her assistance in furnishing materials used in the defense of Wilhelmstrasse officials in the Nürnberg trials; to Dean Lawrence Chamberlain of Columbia College for his charitable and always heartening judgments and advice; to Professor Ernst B. Haas of the University of California for his critical scrutiny of this manuscript; to Mr. Max E. Knight of the editorial department of the University of California Press, for his competent assistance; and to Random House for permission to quote a passage from Archibald MacLeish's *Actfive and Other Poems*. To his wife, the author can but say that, while the ensuing pages were the product of his pen, they were wrought by him under her own standards of style and judgment to which he could only have aspired, and which sprang from a political understanding which political scientists, not uncommonly, lack.

P. S.

CONTENTS

ILLUSTRATIONS

(following page 92)

There are many such in the sand here—many who did not perceive, who thought the time went on, the years went forward, the history was continuous—who thought tomorrow was of the same nation as today. There are many who came to the frontiers between the times and did not know them— who looked for the sentry-box at the stone bridge, for the barricade in the pines and the declaration in two languages— the warning and the opportunity to turn. . . . What is required of us is the recognition of the frontiers where the roads end.

ARCHIBALD MACLEISH

I

PERMANENCE
AND
TRANSITION

In times past, the great European foreign offices took their names from their locations. Whitehall, the Quai d'Orsay, and the Wilhelmstrasse in the nineteenth century became the three great avenues of diplomacy. Whitehall, once named for the palace of the bishops of York, is a street in Westminster running from Charing Cross to Parliament Street. As a political expression it calls to mind the buildings which are situated on it: more particularly the British Foreign Office. Similarly, the Quai d'Orsay is identified with the French Ministry of Foreign Affairs, and the Berlin Wilhelmstrasse with the German Foreign Office.

Such thoroughfares, a part of the turbulent present, still echo the past greatness of their histories. The imaginative visitor of today might easily fancy that along their pavements still crowd the troubled spirits of Palmerston and Grey, Poincaré and Briand, Bismarck and Stresemann. Confronted by the imagined presence and counsel of such departed statesmen, the living servants of the state may sense in issues of contemporary moment greater historical proportion and depth.

But the diplomatic service acquires its durability, its unique traditions and rules, from other things than the masonry which gives it shelter. Institutions of men seem to persist despite the demonstrated transiency of mortar, brick, stone and steel and, even, of individuals themselves. History, which after all deals with intangibles as easily as with the tangible, will long remember and judge such institutions as groups of men, long after their geographical habitat and architectural shelters have been obliterated.

Such was the fate of Wilhelmstrasse 74–76—headquarters of the German foreign service—and its inhabitants. A visitor returning to the Berlin of 1954, chancing to turn south from Unter den Linden, one block east of the Brandenburger Tor, would have found it hard to recall even the location of these vanished gray buildings. In not too remote days, two stone sphinxes guarded the main portals of the German Foreign Office. They, too, are obliterated. A vast and silent waste marks the remains of the street of Bismarck, Stresemann, Neurath, and Ribbentrop. A waste also is the corner of Wilhelmstrasse and Voss-Strasse—the place where once the Reich Chancellery stood. In 1954, the Wilhelmstrasse—which once teemed with the traffic of European diplomacy—was but a deserted path paralleling the frontiers between East and West Berlin, casting the dust of its rubble in the eyes of too-curious passers-by. The judgment of recent history has been visited upon the diplomats of Germany.

The Wilhelmstrasse was not always the home of the Prussian diplomatic service, from which that of modern Germany sprang. Almost a century passed between 1728, when Frederick William I directed his Minister von Ilgen to establish in

Potsdam an agency to carry out Prussian foreign affairs, and that day in 1819 when the Prussian government purchased Wilhelmstrasse No. 76 from the Russian diplomat Alopaeus. This building, destined to become the administrative center of Prussian diplomacy, was used solely by the Prussian Foreign Minister Graf von Bernstorff as his personal residence from 1819 until 1832. Here, also, from 1862 to 1878, Bismarck himself lived until (in this latter year) he moved down the street to Wilhelmstrasse 77, which once was the Palais Radziwill, and which later became the Reich Chancellery. After the Franco-Prussian War, the Prussian Foreign Office (*Auswärtiges Amt*) became the Reich Foreign Office (*Auswärtiges Amt des deutschen Reiches*). After this, more buildings along the street were acquired: Wilhelmstrasse 75—once owned by the Decker publishing house—was purchased in 1877, and came to be used as a villa for Bismarck's foreign state secretaries. After World War I, Wilhelmstrasse 74 was taken over from the former Reich Office of the Interior (*Reichsamt des Innern*). Later, the Foreign Office, in its latter-day expansion, came into possession of other buildings widely scattered throughout Berlin. But the central core of its administrative apparatus remained in Wilhelmstrasse 76. At various times, other Reich agencies and ministries were located on this street—the Reich Colonial Office, the Reich Office of the Interior, the Reich Chancellery, and the Reich Propaganda Ministry. Yet the title "Wilhelmstrasse" could be claimed only by the chaste gray buildings which lined the western side of the street and housed the career civil servants of German diplomacy.[1]

"The Wilhelmstrasse," according to a pre-World War I Baedeker, "forms the western boundary of the Friedrich-Stadt. The northern half of this street is considered the most aristocratic quarter of the city."[2] The same adjective might have been applied to Imperial Germany's diplomatic repre-

sentatives and of its chief Foreign Office officials. Before
World War I, lacking an aristocratic title were only eight of
the sixty German diplomats listed in the biographical appendix to the collection of German Foreign Office documents,
Auswärtige Politik des deutschen Reiches 1871–1914. As one
quasiofficial biographer of German diplomacy later wrote:
"It must not be forgotten that, next to brains, the other two
'b's' (birth and bank account) have always played an important role in diplomacy and will continue to do so."[3]

Similar comments could be (and were) made about all
major European foreign services both before and after World
War I. John Bright—we might recall—once described the
British Foreign Service in 1858 as "neither more nor less than
a gigantic system of outdoor relief for the aristocracy,"[4] a
view equally tenable at later dates. Years later, the French
Foreign Office was criticized for its "antirepublican" character, in much the same sense.[5] Even a critic of the American
State Department, writing in 1942, could observe of the "republican" officialdom of the American diplomatic service:

> Their personal background, their schooling, their personal beliefs
> and family connections, their economic and social standing ... breed
> a disbelief in change, a suspicion of new formulations.... The insti-
> tution tends to attract—and select—men who, to begin with, might
> be expected to respond to these traditions.[6]

Certain circumstances surrounding the growth of the diplomatic service of Western Europe made this branch of state
activity much less susceptible than others to "democratization"
during the nineteenth century. Traditionally European diplomacy had been largely the affair of kings and princes and
small groups of advisers. Ambassadors were personal emissaries of their rulers to the courts of foreign princes. This
practice continued even where monarchical absolutism—as in
England—was checked and overthrown. A diplomat found
socially unacceptable at a foreign court would have been a

political liability to his sovereign. As de Callières, early in the eighteenth century, wrote of the diplomats of his time: "It is ... desirable that an ambassador should be a man of birth and breeding, especially if he is employed in any of the principal courts of Europe, and it is by no means a negligible factor that he should have a noble presence and a handsome face."[7]

The aristocratic diplomat, then, was but a representative of the political and social system in which he lived and worked, and he persisted, with this system, through the nineteenth century.

The aristocratic tradition in Imperial Germany's diplomatic service was markedly distinguished from those of the other great Western European powers. In 1871, Germany inherited from Prussia a highly rationalized, professionally trained, permanent bureaucracy, an important part of which was the Prussian Foreign Office. The prestige of this bureaucracy as a whole was enormous. Recruited not only from the aristocracy but also from the commercial and, later, industrial middle class, its personnel by the turn of the century was an amalgam of the "liberal" nationalist and conservative elements of German society. This was particularly true of the higher officialdom of the German Foreign Office. Top diplomatic posts in Imperial Germany, it is true, were filled frequently by aristocratic "amateurs," recruited by the Kaiser and his chancellors from the Junker nobility and, even to a greater extent, from the western and southern German petty aristocracy. But the Foreign Office of Prussia, and later of Germany, did not permit such amateurism to pervade its permanent diplomatic officialdom. Bismarck himself once remarked that "birth could not be an excuse for inefficiency."[8] Imperial Germany led the great powers of Europe by systematizing personnel selection methods for its foreign service,[9] and by introducing far more elaborate objective requirements for candidates than those which are customary, even today, for the British or American services.

An order of the Reich chancellor dated April 30, 1903, which remained in force through 1914, may serve to illustrate this. According to its rules, a prospective candidate for the German foreign service faced a rigorous process of selection. He was required to have a thorough mastery of English and French; evidence of adquate educational background; and it was recommended that he have successfully completed the first legal examination in one of the federal states. "Applications for admission," the order read, "are to be directed to the State Secretary of the Foreign Office. The following are to be transmitted with the application: a self-composed career statement; evidence of completed (educational) examinations; a medical statement concerning the applicant's health; and a statement of the applicant's personal property holdings."[10]

If an applicant could meet these requirements, he was permitted to undergo the first of two examinations, the so-called written and oral preëxamination, supervised by a special standing committee headed by the state secretary himself. Applicants failing this examination were not permitted a second attempt.

The successful applicant, however, was admitted to the so-called preparatory service: a probationary period, the duration of which depended normally upon the applicant's prior legal accomplishments. Thus, five years in this service were required for candidates with no previous legal training; four years, for those who had passed their first state legal examination; and only one for those who had passed their second legal examination or the examination for the higher administrative service in one of the federal states. Admission to this status as a candidate, however, conveyed no claim to final acceptance in the career service. At the end of his preparatory service, the candidate was subjected to the even more severe final examination (*diplomatische Prüfung*).

This second screening examination was far more comprehensive than the first. It comprised written and oral examinations of the candidate's knowledge of history, public law, international law, economics, finance, and commerce. In the oral examination he was subjected to questions on history and geography in both French and English. As in the earlier exam-

GRADES OF GERMAN FOREIGN-SERVICE OFFICERS IN THE HIGHER SERVICE
AND THEIR AMERICAN EQUIVALENTS
(December, 1938)

Grade	Salary group	Equivalent American title
Botschafter.....................	B 4	Ambassador
Gesandter I. Klasse.............	B 7	Minister First Class
Generalkonsul I. Klasse.........	B 7	Consul General First Class
Gesandter.....................	A 1 a	Minister
Botschaftsrat..................	A 1 a	Embassy Counselor
Generalkonsul.................	A 1 a	Consul General
Konsul I. Klasse...............	A 2 b	Consul First Class
Gesandtschaftsrat I. Klasse......	A 2 b	Legation Counselor First Class
Konsul.......................	A 2 c	Consul
Gesandtschaftsrat..............	A 2 c	Legation Counselor
Legationssekretär..............	A 2 c	Legation Secretary
Vizekonsul....................	A 2 c	Vice Consul

SCOURCE: Adapted from Erich Kraske, Handbuch des auswärtigen Dienstes, p. 48.

inations, he was judged by a board headed by the state secretary. Successful completion of this examination carried with it appointment in the foreign service as legation secretary, the lowest rung of the permanent higher officialdom, and the assurance of promotion to higher rank.

These "objective" criteria assured the German foreign service of a continuing stream of financially well-endowed, university-educated law students—an educational elite. Before World War I, a private income of at least RM 15,000 was officially required of applicants.[11] Without it a young diplomat would have been unable to survive in what was, after all, a financially exacting occupation, and one poorly rewarded. Even a higher official with rank of *Vortragender Rat* (rendered in this book as "senior embassy counselor," in rank equivalent to *Botschaftsrat*), in the early 1900's received no more than a minimum salary of RM 7,000 and a maximum of RM 11,500.[12] Subjective criteria of family origin continued to play a decisive part in the selection of diplomats. Until 1919, the job of selection of new officials lay in the hands of the powerful Foreign Office Political Division, which itself drew heavily upon the German aristocracy for its officials. The last five Political Division directors in the Imperial Foreign Office were: Prince Lichnowski, von Flotow, Count Botho-Wedel, Count Georg Wedel, and Prince zu Wied.[13] As L. W. Muncy wrote, only those candidates who passed their examinations with the highest grades "could be sure of an appointment regardless of station or connections." For the rest, familial lineage, membership in the *Studentenkorps* of one of the German universities, and personal connections were decisive.[14] As Max Weber wrote, "It is common knowledge that the student corporation is the typical method of social education for the entrants into nonmilitary governmental offices."[15]

Between 1871 and 1914 the bureaucratic institution housed along the Wilhelmstrasse grew in size and complexity. At the time of the Franco-Prussian War the Prussian Foreign Office had been, organizationally speaking, a rather simple affair. Two bureaus, both under supervision of a state secretary, were in charge of political, personnel, trade, and legal affairs. Reflecting Bismarck's intimate preoccupation with the details of diplomacy, Wilhelmstrasse 76 housed both the chancellor and the Political Division. "Technical" divisions were relegated to a smaller office farther down the street.

After 1879, however, in response to Germany's rapid overseas expansion and industrial growth, other agencies were added to the Foreign Office. In 1890, separate Trade, Legal, and Personnel divisions had grown up alongside the central

Political Division. In the same year a Colonial Division (which later became a separate office) was added. By 1914, the Foreign Office consisted of five separate offices.[16]

NEW BLOOD

Imperial Germany's collapse in 1918 produced a burst of revolutionary energy which, in the course of its first six months, seemed to portend a transformation of German society. When the reins of political power were handed to the majority Socialist leaders in November, 1918, the German civil service was, for the first time since the early nineteenth century, placed in the hands of a party committed to drastic social reform.

The catastrophes of war and defeat, in this early phase of the Weimar Republic, had widely discredited not only the foreign policy of Imperial Germany, but also the diplomats of the Wilhelmstrasse. The excesses of "secret diplomacy," revealed in Germany as well as in other great European powers, exposed the great discrepancy between public word and private deed in the prelude to the war. This upsurge of belated hostility to diplomats and statesmen was not confined to Germany. It permeated the parliaments and press of all Western powers. The utopian Wilsonian demand for the abolition of "secret diplomacy" found expression in proposals for constitutional reforms at the Weimar Constitutional Assembly. These reforms were enacted and became part of the new republican constitution. In article 35 of the constitution, the new Reichstag was given greater control over the supervision of foreign policy; a permanent Committee on Foreign Relations with investigatory powers was established, and could act even when the Reichstag was not in session.[17] The new constitution further conferred upon the German parliament discretionary power to remove the foreign minister independently of the cabinet as a whole. The power of ratifying treaties of alliance and others affecting federal legislation was given the Reichstag and Bundesrat. Through enlarged appropriation powers, the Reichstag obtained theoretically wide discretionary powers over internal administrative policy in the Foreign Office, as well as in other ministries of the federal government.

The Wilhelmstrasse, in the critical and anarchic days between November, 1918, and May, 1919, continued to function under the interim custodianship of Count Brockdorff-Rantzau as the new Republic was born. Its ranks thinned by the depredations of war and four years of greatly diminished diplomatic activity, the foreign-service personnel in April, 1919, had shrunk to 40 per cent of its 1914 size. The new Social Democratic regime, seeking to stabilize its control over its inherited civil service, found few diplomatic enthusiasts. A few younger officials, believing in the notion of German democratization, bore witness to their new loyalties by wearing black-red-gold buttons in their lapels. Most, however, continued to adhere to the vanished monarchy.[18] New political officials appeared in the office—concessions to the new times; on November 11, 1918, in fact, an order was issued to all officials of the Foreign Office calling for the creation of an elected "workers' council"—an idea regarded by most as rather "comical, something quite new and singular in the history of the Office," and was rendered moribund soon after its establishment.[19] Yet, seemingly, the birth of the German Republic portended the appearance of a new official apparatus charged with making and carrying out a "new" German foreign policy. Eduard Bernstein uttered words in 1921 which were pertinent for these early, optimistic days:[20]

The democratization of diplomacy in the long run means nothing less than the abolition of diplomacy. . . . But the direction of the whole reorganization of our foreign service must aim to place the relations of the German Republic toward other peoples upon an entirely different basis than it has been in the past. . . . We need a foreign service which, both in form and spirit, gives expression to our republican ideals.

In those days it was the conviction both of the German Social Democratic and moderate Center leadership that basic reforms should take place within the German foreign service. Bernstein's remarks were vague, but during the Weimar Constitutional Assembly other Republican leaders were more explicit. In the words of one:

We are convinced that there are men in *all* strata of our Republic who are capable of representing Germany abroad. The circumstance that these [representatives] now come from only one class must be done away with; for we no longer have any use for ambassadors intended merely for a specific stratum of foreign societies, we need them for all classes in every country.[21]

In April, 1919, Foreign Minister Brockdorff-Rantzau announced that such changes were, in fact, under consideration. Under the direction of a certain *Geheimrat*, Edmund Schüler, a complete reorganization of the German foreign service was in progress. The structure of the prewar Foreign Office was being demolished. A new, streamlined "regional" apparatus was to arise upon the ashes of the old Foreign Office divisions (*Abteilungen*). The "monopoly" which the once-powerful and exclusive Political Division once had exercised over the Foreign Office as a whole was to be broken. Brockdorff-Rantzau declared before the Reichstag: "I know that people are saying that the 'same old sluggishness' still prevails in the Foreign Office. But whoever says this has no knowledge of the changes already made or still in preparation. . . . I am firmly resolved to make changes."[22]

The year 1919 seemed opportune for experimentation in such reforms. The Socialist Foreign Minister Hermann Müller declared in the fall of that year: "The German Republic must bring new men into its top [diplomatic] posts. But that alone is not enough. Above all we must see to it—this is perhaps more important—that the basis of selection [of officials] is broadened in the future, in order that tomorrow's officials will be drawn from all walks of life."[23]

As of April 1, 1918, only 184 active higher officials remained in the foreign service, compared with 335 in April, 1914—a decrease of 61 per cent. By April, 1919, a year later, the number had dropped to about 145. Neither Brockdorff-Rantzau nor Müller aimed at a total purge of the older diplomats. "It is entirely unnecessary," said Müller in the fall of 1919, "to dismiss every diplomat who served the Reich under the *ancien régime*. . . . But it is quite obvious that whoever harbors the intent of intriguing against the Republic shall under no circumstances be appointed to any diplomatic post."[24] In October, 1919, a spokesman of the Constitutional Assembly's Central Committee was able to report, of the foreign service, that not less than 119 officials had been retired either "voluntarily" or "not quite voluntarily."[25]

Organizational plans in 1919 for the Wilhelmstrasse headquarters called for nine divisions and a special foreign-trade bureau—a structure far more elaborate than its prewar Imperial predecessor. Many German missions and consulates abroad were not restored to their prewar dimensions until long after ratification of the Versailles peace treaty. But due to the sudden expansion of the home office, a large number of positions suddenly were available to be filled by new diplomats. As the venerable Wilhelmstrasse doorkeeper commented, "The German Reich keeps getting smaller and smaller, but the Foreign Office gets bigger and bigger."[26]

The "Schüler reformers" of the Foreign Office aimed at liberalizing entrance requirements into the career service. Accordingly, after World War I new applicants no longer were required to give evidence of independent means to qualify for entrance examinations. Accepted candidates, ranked as attachés in the service, were provided with minimum stipends of RM 350 per month. Official regulations for admission procedures noted the desirability of candidates' prior nongovernmental employment, in chambers of commerce, private business, and even trade unions. "Labor attachés" replaced "military attachés" in German embassies abroad. By abolishing the invidious distinction between consular and diplomatic career services, the reforms provided greater theoretical opportunity for new candidates who otherwise might have been condemned to second-rate careers.[27]

Yet there was no sharp break with the basic principles of civil service established in Imperial Germany. The procedure for selection of candidates remained substantially as it had been. After 1919, candidates no longer were required to have completed the *Gerichtsassessor* (legal) examination, although this remained highly desirable. Postwar regulations permitted only candidates between the ages of 24 and 30. A thorough knowledge of English, French, and preferably, a third language, was necessary. The second (attaché) examination remained as rigorous as before, perhaps more so,[28] reducing the unique advantages of mere familial connections to subjective factors affecting advancement *within* the service.[29]

Legal alterations of the older Imperial civil-service code accompanied these Weimar administrative changes, and established the relationship between the Reich civil servants and the new Republic. The substance of the legal basis of the Weimar civil service was inherited from Imperial Germany, and chiefly from the first Imperial civil-service law of 1873. As before the war, the Weimar Foreign Office was empowered to choose its career officials autonomously. Appointive powers were delegated by the Reich president to separate ministries for subordinate career officials. But the professional official, once having achieved career status, received guarantees of important rights from the Reich civil-service law. Barring demonstrated incompetence, gross malfeasance of duty, or irreparable physical incapacitation, a career official was assured of at least routine promotion, periodic salary increases, and, ultimately, pensioned retirement. The aims of such elaborate regulations were, of course, to guarantee a life career for officials and to guard against arbitrary "political" interference from outside which might impair the supposedly "neutral" character of the service. Demotion, involuntary suspension, or discharge from service for any reason, were impossible without mandatory recourse to due process from administrative tribunals.

The substance of these legal guarantees was retained under the Weimar Republic, but amendments to the old law strengthened, rather than weakened, the position of the civil servant in German society. The constitution itself specified that officials of the Republic were career officials for life. The new civil-service law, to ensure the political reliability of these "servants," required an oath of loyalty to the Republic and its constitution. Moreover, legitimate political activity was sanctioned for officials. Weimar careerists, unlike their predecessors, were permitted to become active political party members, and even to stand for election without prejudicing their official status.

But if we look more closely at the effects of these changes upon the foreign service in Weimar Germany, we can see that the aim of "democratizing" German diplomacy seriously failed of its mark. True, there had been by no means full agreement within the German Reichstag of 1920, nor within the foreign service itself, on the exact objectives of the Schüler reforms. While there was much enthusiasm evidenced particularly in the Center and "liberal" parties for a streamlining of the Foreign Office and the foreign service, much of it arose from the belief that the older foreign service of Imperial Germany had been little interested in the welfare of the German business community and in the expansion of Germany's overseas trade. "Efficiency" of the new foreign service was a far more widespread desire than "democratization." The questions of bureaucratic "efficiency" and the responsible exercise of bureaucratic power are inseparably linked. Together, they constitute one of the most crucial dilemmas of modern industrial society. For, if a bureaucracy is to serve as an effective instrument of democratic policy, it must be tolerably "efficient." But a rationally organized, efficient bureaucracy, with its own *esprit de corps*, boasting of a highly competent personnel, need not necessarily be responsible to its constitutional superiors. Nor is it necessarily imbued with the same political philosophy as its constitutional superiors.

The Schüler reformers of the German Foreign Office in 1919 believed that the likelihood of such bureaucratic irresponsibility could best be diminished by two specific measures: first, the introduction of "new blood" into lower career-service posts; and second, the intrusion of "outsiders"—that is, noncareer appointees—into important posts abroad and within the Wilhelmstrasse at home.

This latter policy aroused much opposition from the right-wing parties of postwar Germany and from many career officials themselves, who viewed the infiltration of such "amateurs" as a threat to their own aspirations and to the integrity of the whole Service. The Social Democratic Foreign Minister Hermann Müller, in fact, was moved by such protests to assure the Constitutional Assembly at Weimar that "party politics" would not govern the filling of top diplomatic posts.[30] But this disavowal of intent did not quiet the parliamentary voices of the Right from inveighing against the "novel" practice of appointing nonprofessionals (and nonaristocrats) to diplomatic posts abroad. " 'I would like to know,' remarked a certain Deputy Schultz during an Assembly debate on Foreign Office reorganization, 'what would happen if people were let

into the banking or shipping business who previously had not
the slightest inkling of specialized knowledge.' ('Hear, hear!'
from the Right)."[31]
A deputy of the *Deutsche Volkspartei* played upon this
same theme during the 1922 Reichstag budget debates. " 'I
believe,' he declared, 'there is considerable reason to doubt
the correctness and propriety in these difficult times of sending men to fill diplomatic posts abroad whose entire qualifications ... consist merely of parliamentary or feuilleton
activity—or a mixture of both.' (Hoots from the Social
Democrats.)"[32]
After 1919 a number of important diplomatic posts
went to politicans and parliamentarians from the Left and
Center parties. To Paris, for example, went Wilhelm Mayer-
Kaufbeuren, a deputy of the Bavarian *Volkspartei;* to London,
Ambassador Friedrich von Sthamer, the former mayor of
Hamburg; to Vienna, Maximilian Pfeiffer, also of the Bavarian *Volkspartei.* None of these men had had previous diplomatic experience. A few Social Democrats likewise became
diplomats of their new Republic, filling secondary diplomatic
posts in Brussels, Warsaw, Berne, Riga, and Belgrade. But
despite the participation of the Social Democratic Party in
governmental coalitions, none of its top leaders obtained major
posts abroad.[33]

Experimentation with "outsiders" in the German foreign
service, so deeply resented by the careerists, proved a total
failure. In 1922, three years after the birth of the Weimar
Republic, the careerists of the Imperial Foreign Office once
more dominated the Wilhelmstrasse headquarters. The chiefs
(*Ministerialdirektoren*) of all eight divisions of the reorgan-
ized Foreign Office were experienced officials of the prewar
foreign service: Richard Gneist, Gehard von Mutius, Eugen
Rümelin, Karl von Schubert, Ago von Maltzan, Hubert Knipping, Gerhard Köpke, and Friedrich Heilbron.[34] In fact, these

division chiefs had all entered the foreign service between 1896 and 1906.[35] If the intent of the Weimar republicans had been to remove decisive power from the traditional Imperial diplomatists, this intent in no way had been realized. Those few "outsiders" who had entered the upper echelons of the Foreign Office in 1919 had disappeared. The professionals had triumphed, and their triumph was the greater because of the absence of steady ministerial leadership at the top. Between December, 1918, and August, 1923 (before the accession of Stresemann), a steady procession of foreign ministers briefly had held the reins of the Foreign Office—Ulrich von Brockdorff-Rantzau, Hermann Müller, Adolf Köster, Walther Simons, Joseph Wirth, Friedrich Rosen, Walther Rathenau, and Frederic von Rosenberg.[36] The political instability of the early postwar years was reflected in frequent cabinet changes.[37] Lacking continuity of leadership at the top, the locus of day-to-day control of the Foreign Office sank a notch lower, to the level of the newly-created post of state secretary which took the place of the Imperial undersecretary. (The former state secretaries received the title "minister.") In 1920 this office was filled by a prewar career diplomat, Haniel von Haimhausen, the scion of a wealthy industrialist family. The trend back to the older officialdom was equally apparent on lower levels of the Foreign Office. In 1921, the post of deputy division chief (*Ministerialdirigent*) had been created for all divisions. Officials appointed to these positions were intended to be "advisers," deputies, and alter egos of the division chiefs, charged with routine management of division affairs. In practice, Weimar foreign ministers came to rely heavily upon them for technical advice, frequently preferring them to the division chiefs. In the words of Herbert von Dirksen, who in 1925 was appointed to one of these posts:

They accompanied the Foreign Minister to conferences; they prepared the briefs and had direct access to the State Secretary and to the Foreign Minister; they frequently represented the Foreign Office in Reichstag committees or in the Bundesrat. Often they had knowledge of the most secret affairs without being permitted to divulge it to their immediate superiors [the division chiefs].[38]

In 1925 these deputy division chiefs, too, were drawn exclusively from the old career service—Dirksen himself, Bülow, Zech-Burkersroda, Richthofen, Horstmann, Trautmann were deputy division chiefs of the Near Eastern, League of Nations, West European, Middle Eastern, Anglo Saxon, and Far Eastern divisions.[39] Among the division chiefs themselves, in 1925, Friedrich Gaus of the Legal Division and Ago von Maltzan of the Near Eastern Division were of the "old school." The able and liberal director of the West European Division, Köpke, came from the old consular service, while the remaining division chiefs were still appointees from outside the foreign service.

But by 1929, on the top official level of the Foreign Office, the picture had changed even more. Of the six division chiefs listed in *Wer Ist's* (1928 and 1935 editions), five were career civil servants of prewar vintage.[40] The "outsiders" who had occupied important mission posts abroad had virtually disappeared. Of the fifteen most important German missions in 1929,[41] ten were in the hands of pre-World War I diplomats; three others were managed by envoys who, before 1918, had begun careers in internal Reich ministries. In 1929 only two posts—London and Berne—still remained in the hands of "amateur" Weimar newcomers, Friedrich Sthamer and Adolf Müller.[42]

This shows that the Weimar experiment of injecting "new blood" into the upper levels of the foreign service failed. Attainments on the lower levels were hardly better.

In the early (1919–1922) expansion of the German foreign service, the induction of large numbers of younger career officials on lower levels of the higher service had seemed a harbinger of gradual change in the character of the top service personnel. But this numerical expansion ceased during the catastrophic inflation days of 1923. The economic crisis brought severe pressure from the Reichstag upon ministries of the Weimar Republic for sharp reductions in government expenditures. This pressure, in turn, was reflected in personnel curtailments in Reich agencies, including the Foreign Office. The number of higher officials in the German foreign service was greatly reduced. In 1923 the post of secretary of state for economic affairs, established in 1919, was eliminated, partly for financial reasons.[43] But it became quickly apparent where the really significant personnel cuts would be made— on the attaché level, where most of the new, albeit less immediately important, faces existed. In his report to the Reichstag early in 1923, the budget committee rapporteur voiced an unfelicitous admonition to the youth of the new Germany who might have aspired to serve in its diplomatic service: "A career in the Foreign Office at home or abroad today must be described as bad, and will become even less favorable from year to year."[44]

Caught between the Scylla of budgetary liberality—with its inflationary risks—and the Charybdis of excessive parsimony, the Foreign Office reformers in the German Reichstag chose Charybdis. In 1921, even the Social Democrat Eduard Bernstein came to support curtailed Foreign Office appropriations, even though one inevitable consequence would be increased difficulties of transforming the character of the diplomatic service.[45]

The retrenchment had, of course, no immediate effect upon the composition of the officialdom in higher posts. But the closing of the Foreign Office doors to significantly large numbers of new members was symptomatic of a national problem of the time: that of satisfying the ambitions of numerous university-educated youths who anticipated careers commensurate with their training. In 1929, one observer of the German Foreign Office noted that, while an average of 200 applications for the foreign-service examination were annually received by the Wilhelmstrasse, post vacancies were averaging only fifteen per annum.[46] In 1931, Foreign Minister Julius Curtius revealed that, since 1927, the total personnel of the Foreign Office had been cut in half and Reichstag appropriations reduced 17 per cent. In fact, he declared, there were at the time only 100 more higher officials in the foreign service than there had been in 1914; yet still further reductions of personnel were contemplated by cutting down the number of *Referenten* (chiefly attachés and legation secretaries).[47] A search for new ways of economizing would continue. "Thus," he primly concluded, "it can always be said that the Foreign Office performs its work neatly and thriftily."[48]

In this way, six years after the birth of the Weimar Republic in 1919 the composition of the higher officialdom of the German Foreign Office had reverted to its traditional pattern. Four years later, in 1929, exactly half of the mission chiefs abroad were aristocrats. Almost all of them were career diplomats of the *ancien régime*. An investigation by the Reichstag in 1926 to discover whether "favoritism" still was accorded to the nobility in the selection of diplomatic officials, revealed that, of 484 higher officials then in the foreign service, 126 were of the German nobility. One Reichstag committee rapporteur was moved by this news to remark: "If I might be permitted to repeat the remark of one of my honorable colleagues in the Budget Committee, the relation of aristocratic to middle-class names in the organizational scheme of our [Foreign] Office roughly corresponds to that of a prewar field artillery regiment."[49]

Several notable spokesmen of the Center and moderate Left in the Reichstag continued to attack the undemocratic character of the foreign service. But the original demands for reform were seldom heard at this later date from the democratic parties of Weimar Germany. The Republic had failed to secure the support of its servants, and as it disintegrated under the shocks of depression and National Socialism, the control of state machinery drifted into the hands of the "experts." What was true of the diplomatic bureaucracy was equally true of other ministries.[50] The delegation of emergency powers by the Reichstag to the Brüning, Schleicher, and Papen cabinets after 1930 vastly increased the political power of the entrenched civil service. By 1932, the craving of the officials for a "strong" government (that is, a ministerial government unrestrained by parliamentary control) had been largely realized.

How loyal were the career diplomats to the Republic which they served? Some, notably such eminent civil servants as Leopold von Hoesch, who served as ambassador in Paris and London; Dr. Wilhelm Solf, ambassador in Tokyo; and Adolf Müller in Berne, unquestionably were representative of a new and liberal Germany. Many, however, found little to be said for the foreign policies of the Weimar Republic, resented the parliamentary oratory of democratic amateurs, yearned for the authoritarian constitutional arrangements of the past, and deplored the absence of unitary direction and nationalistic vigor which alone, to their mind, could break asunder the shackles restraining German "greatness." "Stresemann," one of them later reminisced, "was indeed of a higher stature than the general run of [Weimar] foreign ministers. But in the Foreign Office he was held to be too trusting in international affairs, a field in which he was not fully at home."[51] "A multitude of people," wrote Wipert von Blücher, of the Eastern Division, "cannot make foreign policy, for which but a single will is needed."[52] No exertions of these men, however, played a crucial role in the demise of German democracy. As formulators and administrators of policy, their chief concern was for a strong, nationalistically oriented political climate at home. "I never could warm up to problems of domestic policy," Ernst von Weizsäcker wrote in his memoirs, "and judged them only so far as they favored or disturbed a sound foreign policy. From my parents and from school I had been a monarchist. . . . I viewed a constitutional monarchy with a competent prince at the top as the kind of political order most suited to Germans in normal times."[53] The political coloration of the Foreign Office, like that of other crucial ministries of Weimar Germany, had recovered its Rightist complexion as consequence of the weakening of the republican coalition. While as late as 1932 the Catholic Center Party retained a certain influence in Wilhelmstrasse personnel policy, this was a consequence of its strategic pivotal role in domestic politics; the Social Democratic Party, devoid of such advantage, had no representation in the decisively important posts of the Berlin headquarters after 1920.[54]

In the twilight of German democracy, however, eminent spokesmen of the Center and moderate Left in the Reichstag raised their voices against the "plutocratic" character of German diplomatic officialdom and its threat to German democracy. Deputy Rudolf Breitscheid (SPD) and the Center Deputy Georg Schreiber drew attention, in the 1931 budget debate, to channels linking key Foreign Office posts to extreme Right-wing parties. Through these channels "indiscretions" had leaked to nationalist groups outside to arouse public protest against government policies unacceptable to the parties of German reaction. "Such indiscretions," Schreiber warned, "will only backfire on the bureaucracy itself; they undermine the very theory of a career civil service."[55] There were many high diplomatic officials who did not trouble to conceal their distaste for the Republic, and who yearned for a restoration of the Empire. Some of them—mission chiefs abroad—ostentatiously refused to honor the Republic on its Constitution Day (August 11). Such career diplomats as Ulrich von Brockdorff-Rantzau, Ago von Maltzan, and Baron Nadolny throughout the Weimar era attempted to steer official German foreign policy toward the traditional Prussian dream of an "eastern oriented" policy of close collaboration with Russia. Together with General von Seeckt and the general staff, they (and not their political superiors) were first instrumental in establishing secret ties between the German Reichswehr and the Bolshevik Red Army in 1920.[56] Brockdorff-Rantzau and Maltzan, and not Foreign Minister Rathenau, first were responsible for drafting German proposals in 1922 for a Russian-German pact subsequently negotiated and signed at Rapallo in April, 1922.[57] From that year until 1929, Brockdorff-Rantzau, as ambassador in Moscow, labored relentlessly to forge a de facto alliance between the two "pariah" states of Europe to redress Germany's power position on the European continent. Military and economic technicians were sent to the Soviet Union; German aviation and tank experts experimented within Russia upon new devices of warfare prohibited to Germany by the Versailles treaty. By terms of an economic agreement signed in 1929, German Rhineland industrialists were successful in laying open a vast external market for their industrial commodities in the Soviet Union.[58] While Stresemann labored to rehabilitate Germany in the eyes and esteem of the Western democracies, the Foreign Office career diplomats— supported politically by extreme nationalist elements in German society—labored to build a continental alliance which would restore German military and economic supremacy over Central Europe and enable her to rectify Versailles, not by patient negotiation and compromise, but by force. Aspects of this policy were subscribed to by successive cabinets (Rathenau in 1922 was persuaded to Maltzan's viewpoint on tactical grounds). But carried to its extreme, the goal of a Russian-German bloc was not one subscribed to by the Liberal and Socialist parties of the Weimar coalition. It was the foreign policy of German reaction, and it was expressed through the Foreign Office.

Our story, however, is not concerned with the diplomacy of Weimar Germany but with the diplomats who moved from this era into the totalitarianism of National Socialism. By 1932, the German diplomats had survived democracy; if not hostile, they were, by and large, indifferent to it, as they were to all questions of forms of government so long as these did not interfere with the efficient exercise of their own bureaucratic power. How these men were to fare under the coming dictatorship of National Socialism is the burden of what follows.

II

BROWNSHIRTS
AND STRIPED
TROUSERS

"What *does* a legation counselor do all day long?" Hermann Göring rhetorically inquired of a Foreign Office official in 1935. "In the forenoon he sharpens pencils, and afternoons he goes out to tea somewhere."[1]

This remark, coming from a Nazi leader in 1935, was illuminating. It was a traditional jest, made in traditional fashion. It was also, in a way, a confession of failure. Two years after the National Socialist seizure of power, German diplomacy—virtually unsullied by the incursions of "outsiders"—remained the same butt of humor as it had been before 1933. It was a new Germany in which Göring spoke; the Reichstag, the political parties of Center, Left, and non-Nazi Right, long since had fallen under the Nazi impact. German democracy was dead, its defenders cast into concentration camps or exile. In the blood purge of June 30, 1934, the revolution had devoured its own progeny, as in Robespierre's days. But all such excesses had passed by the modest gray edifices on the Wilhelmstrasse, leaving the inhabitants for the most part unscathed. Why had German diplomacy been spared those ruthless measures which, in two years' time, had transformed Germany as a whole? Baron Constantin von Neurath, who had been foreign minister under Schleicher, stayed on; so did his state secretary, Bernhard von Bülow, until his death in 1936. The seven principal Foreign Office division chiefs serving on January 30, 1933, still were in their positions two years later; all of them were career diplomats, recruited by the pre-World War I foreign service.[2] Abroad, in German missions, the task of representing the Reich was more solidly in the hands of the older aristocratic elements than during the "democratic" 'twenties; then, outsiders had been brought in at least occasionally to serve as ambassadors and ministers.

For one thing, the new rulers of Germany in 1933 could count few diplomats in their ranks, and even fewer specialists in foreign affairs, capable of taking over from the experienced careerists the difficult and technical aspects of diplomacy. The handful of ranking Nazis—such as Alfred Rosenberg, Robert Ley, Reinhard Heydrich, and Theodor Habicht—who, in the early months of 1933, ventured abroad to Geneva, Rome, London, and elsewhere, had universally made deplorable impressions as diplomats. Rosenberg, visiting London in May, 1933, as the Führer's "personal representative," had been denounced in the British press, snubbed by the prime minister, and forced to cut short his stay because of these humiliations.[3] Robert Ley of the Nazi Labor Front (his task of crushing the free German trade unions completed), attending the Geneva International Labor Organization conference in June, 1933, as an "employee representative," had his credentials rejected by the conference; under the influence of alcohol, he publicly had likened Latin American delegates to "monkeys" (*Baumaffen*), before huffily leading his delegation back to Berlin

on June 19.[4] Reinhard Heydrich, later the "hangman" of
Bohemia-Moravia, as an *SS* consultant to the German disarmament delegation in Lausanne had personally lowered the
German flag from above his delegation's hotel, substituting
the Nazi swastika.[5] Theodor Habicht, Nazi Reichstag member
and Hitler's "state inspector" for Austria, two weeks after his
appointment as press attaché in the German embassy in Vienna
early in 1933, was arrested by Austrian police for conspiring
against the Dollfuss regime.[6] Undiplomatic activities such as
these had unpleasant repercussions. Even Neurath and his
delegation to the London Economic Conference had been
booed by British crowds.[7] Such representatives lent little credi-
bility to Hitler's assertion on May 17, 1933, that Nazi Germany harbored only good will toward her neighbors. Indeed,
by the summer of 1933, they definitely must have appeared
to Hitler as liabilities.

Constantin von Neurath was a genial man; occasionally he
could be candid as well. He evidently did not, in 1933, expect
much of the National Socialist "revolution." He was a close
friend of Hindenburg and had remained in the new Hitler
cabinet at Hindenburg's insistence. In a conversation with the
British ambassador on February 4, he confided that the president "had made a point of his being retained in the new Government. . . . He had accepted on condition that he was given
a free hand and that no experiments in foreign policy were to
be tried. He knew that he had the President's full support."[8]
But Neurath was not held in high repute by many of his
colleagues, subordinates, and foreign diplomats in Berlin. His
lassitude and his indulgence in frivolities had contributed to
a facile acceptance of Hitler's *faits accomplis*. François-
Poncet, the French ambassador, found him "wanting in moral
courage," and prone to "yield to pressure." Also, Poncet observed, "he was lazy."[9] Even Weizsäcker, himself poorly
endowed with the opposite quality, judged the foreign minister

as "anything but dynamic."[10] Dirksen, Neurath's ambassador in Tokyo, recalled that he "did not possess any great zeal for work."[11] A close friend of the foreign minister was reported once to have remarked that "Constantin von Neurath does not like to stalk game; he shoots it from his station."[12] Crafty, amenable to persuasion, and well at home in the diplomatic world of Berlin, Neurath by 1935 fully had made his peace with the Nazis, going even so far as to acquire a new Dahlem residence expropriated from its former Jewish owner.[13]

For a short while in 1933, however, some officials considered resigning rather than remaining in office under the new regime. According to former Chancellor Brüning (who, early that year, discussed this problem with State Secretary Bülow), he had been informed that "almost all" leading officials were thinking about it. But Brüning had opposed the idea: "I advised Herr von Bülow strongly," he wrote, many years later, "to remain in office, and to urge these others to do likewise, for they ... together with moderate leaders in the Reichswehr, alone would be in a position to frustrate any aggressive foreign or military policies of Hitler."[14]

Had not, after all, the German diplomats survived the revolution of the Left in 1918? Kurt von Kampfhövener, an experienced career officer, dwelt upon this point in his discussions with other officials in 1933, albeit with some historical inventiveness. In Bolshevik Russia, he argued, the old tsarist diplomats had quit. Admittedly, this defection had served to impair the efficiency of Bolshevik diplomacy; but the Revolution soon found men from its own ranks to carry on the job. Thus, abdication from office had served no purpose other than that of depriving tsarist officials of any further influence. Had not the German officials of 1918–1919 been a wiser lot? They had remained, and after a trying period the Revolution had subsided and the "semi-Bolshevik" Kautsky had disappeared from the Foreign Office. In Fascist Italy, Kampfhövener asked, had not the career diplomats, by choosing to remain, survived in influence? The men of the *Ministerio degli Affari Esteri* had held their ground against the "onslaughts" of "Fascist radicals." "One had the impression," he felt, "that Mussolini, under the older officialdom's influence, had abandoned his earlier aggressive designs."[15]

Kampfhövener's historical observations were only partially correct. It was true that Trotsky's purge of the Imperial Russian Foreign Office had been thorough, and that few tsarist officials found their way into Chicherin's reconstituted *Narkomindel;*[16] but this fate was hardly of their own choosing. Kautsky, after all, had never been a policy-making figure in the German Foreign Office,[17] and it was debatable, in 1933, whether many permanent officials of the Palazzo Chigi in Rome took as sanguine an assessment of Mussolini's temperament about foreign-policy matters.[18] Yet it was a plausible line of argument; with Neurath at the helm and the conservative Bülow at his side, the German experts certainly now enjoyed chiefs more congenial than had been the Social Democrats of 1919. Moreover, in some respects, might not the climate of authoritarianism prove more congenial to "expertise" than had been that of Weimar democracy? Even after the collapse of the Third Reich, Karl Ritter (Neurath's chief of the Economic Division) was able to contrast those trying days of Weimar, when "over 60 per cent" of his time had been squandered in Reichstag squabbles over commercial treaties, with the authoritarian days of Hitler, when at least he had been left "pretty much to his own devices."[19] At least, those ceaseless parliamentary budget debates, with their demands for open diplomacy and their constant public wrangling over Foreign Office personnel matters, were now at an end.

And so, the diplomats had stayed. Few personnel changes occurred in the Wilhelmstrasse during 1933. Two officials in the United States, Ambassador von Prittwitz und Gaffron and the German consul in New York, Paul Schwarz, were removed in the spring of that year. Of the two, and, in fact, of all the German foreign service, only Schwarz was moved to disaffiliate himself publicly from the Nazi regime. "I feel honored," he told American newspapermen on April 11, "for I am the only German consul to be dismissed by Hitler as far as I know."[20] In the autumn, Otto Kiep, consul general in Chicago (executed by the Nazis in 1944), also was ousted. The German minister to Lithuania was recalled from his post in April, presumably for "racial" reasons.[21] A number of older diplomats, including former State Secretary Karl von Schubert; Hugo Simon, consul general in Chicago; and Walter Zechlin, minister to Mexico, were placed on the retired list in August, 1933.[22]

But these were only a handful of officials; and the posts vacated by them were filled by men of similar background from the career service. Not a single Nazi became chief of a mission. Freiherr Ernst von Weizsäcker, who headed the Personnel Division briefly in 1933, recalled that the Party did manage to install one of its more socially acceptable adherents, the Prince Josias zu Waldeck und Pyrmont, in his division. Waldeck, an *SS-Gruppenführer*, *Freikorps* officer, and renegade *Stahlhelm* member, had been attached to Himmler's personal staff.[23] But the prince had been neither a perceptive nor a persistent man. Within a few months, swamped by the weight of documents and lacking any executive power, he resigned. An *Alter Kämpfer* did not feel at home among stacks of paper.[24]

Göring's comment to Paul Schmidt had been a contemptuous one. But if it sprang from one disdainful of the working methods of diplomacy, it came also from one well aware of the diplomats' limitations; Göring's image of "typical diplomats" was that of cookie pushers. But Hitler's conceptions were less charitable. In 1935 he reportedly observed to Hermann Rauschning: "I told those Father Christmases that what they were up to was good enough for quiet times, when they can all go their sleepy way; but not good enough for creating a new Reich."[25] The pre-Ribbentrop Foreign Office, Hitler once remarked to his associates, had been a veritable "intellectual garbage dump," composed of the refuse of incompetent rejects from other walks of life.[26] Diplomatic reports of the Foreign Office had been "miserable"—always with the same import, "that we should do nothing. . . . One day the business had been so stupid that he had inquired of the gentlemen how anything would ever be done if we did nothing."[27]

Even though Hitler's views on foreign policy before 1933 had been explicit, he had been ill-versed in the mysteries of diplomacy. Who, around him, had not been? With all its venomous attacks upon the Versailles *"Diktat,"* upon Stresemann's and Brüning's policies of peaceful change, National Socialism's foreign policy before 1933 had been chiefly a propaganda weapon for seizing internal power. But now, how was this policy to be implemented? In early 1933, Nazi Germany seemed diplomatically isolated; the attempt at fulfillment of Hitler's maximal program, if undertaken unilaterally and without recourse to diplomacy, would have had catastrophic results. Yet there were no Bismarcks among the early Nazi leaders equal to such diplomacy. Hitler himself had no acquaintance with the outside world; his only excursion outside his homeland and Germany before 1933 had been to France as a corporal in World War I. Goebbels had no foreign experience; Roehm and Himmler, none. Alfred Rosenberg, the Aryan mystic, could claim some knowledge of Russia and the former Baltic provinces, but little of Western Europe. There were few in the ranks of National Socialism who possessed any awareness of political conditions abroad. Consequently they were forced to rely heavily upon the ministerial bureaucracy.

But Hitler had little intention of becoming dependent upon it. During his first few years as chancellor, he carefully nur-

tured auxiliary instruments of diplomacy, responsible to himself alone or to Party formations, as counterbalances to the
Wilhelmstrasse.

A nucleus of a Party foreign office already existed before
the Nazis came to power. In May, 1930, the Party established
in Hamburg the Foreign Division of the National Socialist
Party (*Auslandsabteilung der NSDAP*), to serve as a kind of
clearing house for dealing with Party members abroad.[28] After
1931, this organization rapidly began to integrate Party members and groups abroad into local cells (*Stützpunkte*) and
local groups (*Ortsgruppen*) in order to rationalize administrative control over their rapidly growing membership. These
local groups were established in German communities abroad
where, along with other German cultural and civic associa-
tions, they competed for the loyalty of Reich citizens and
Volksdeutsche alike.

By 1933, the Foreign Division had grown to considerable
proportions. Its local groups existed in all major foreign countries. One year after Hitler's seizure of power, it claimed to
have more than 350 such groups throughout the world. Such
was its importance to the Nazis that in October, 1933, the
Foreign Division was placed under the direct supervision of
Rudolf Hess, deputy to the Führer. (Hess at the same time
was given authority over all matters "relating to Germanism
beyond the frontiers" of the Third Reich.) Simultaneously,
many of its local groups were elevated to the status of country
groups (*Ländergruppen*). In February, 1934, the organization was given the more elaborate title of *Auslandsorganisation der NSDAP* (usually abbreviated to *AO*) and soon
thereafter was given a place in the Party administrative hierarchy under the name *Gau Ausland*. Rudolf Hess appointed
Ernst W. Bohle as Gauleiter. In 1937, the *AO*'s headquarters,
with its administrative apparatus of more than 700 employees
and officials, was shifted from Hamburg to Berlin.

As time went on, the functions of the *AO* widened. In 1933, it assumed control over Party members in the merchant marine; in October, 1935, an *AO* "occupational unit" (*Fachgruppe*) was set up within the foreign service, under control of a "local-group leader" (*Ortsgruppenleiter*) subordinate to Bohle. Finally, on January 30, 1937, Bohle was appointed chief of the *AO* in the Foreign Office. Soon thereafter he acquired the official title of "state secretary" in the Foreign Office, with primary responsibility for Foreign Office treatment of all questions concerning German citizens abroad. However valuable its work of Nazification abroad might have been, Bohle's *AO* was only an auxiliary instrument. While it was to have considerable influence over German foreign policy in countries enjoying significant German minorities, as will be discussed later, it was of secondary importance elsewhere. It had no broad policy-making powers outside its limited sphere of activities; its leader, Bohle, was at no time a close confidante of Hitler, nor did he enjoy great renown among the older and established Nazi chieftains.

Of greater promise, however, was the Foreign Policy Office of the National Socialist Party (*Aussenpolitisches Amt der NSDAP*, usually abbreviated to *APA*) which Hitler established on April 1, 1933, to serve as an advisory body. The *APA* was largely the scheme of Alfred Rosenberg, the Party's chief racial philosopher—author of *The Myth of the Twentieth Century* and other works, and editor of the *Völkischer Beobachter*. Of all Party leaders, Rosenberg perhaps was the most violent opponent of Bolshevism and advocate of a German-led European coalition against Russia. Born in a petit-bourgeois Baltic German family in Reval, Rosenberg had spent his early childhood and student days in Talinn, Moscow, and St. Petersburg. His first wife, also a Balt, was a "binational," educated in both the German and Russian traditions. Since the early 'twenties he had been a Nazi and, as chairman of the Party's foreign-affairs committee in the Reichstag, was its leading "expert" on international affairs. Now that the Party had come to power, Rosenberg envisioned himself as the prospective foreign minister of the Third Reich.[20]

The creation of *APA* was announced in the German press on April 1, 1933, and on April 4 the reading public of Germany was given a clear idea of its intended functions. On that day, the *Völkischer Beobachter* diplomatically touched upon this subject:

> We would not be deprecating the present worthy assistance of other groups ... in our Führer's Cabinet if we were to say that the National Socialist revolution, in all areas, represents a new and unique *Weltanschauung* which exclusively corresponds to the future needs of our young Germany and which, for this reason, on occasion can determine its final form. ... In the area of foreign policy as well, the *NSDAP* since its creation has brought forward a unique and clear purpose which, through all the years of serious political crises, has been demonstrated to be correct.[30]

It added: "With the creation of the *Aussenpolitisches Amt der NSDAP*, the particular desires and the unique aspirations of National Socialism will find expression within the area of foreign policy."[31]

On the same day Rosenberg unveiled to journalists a fuller picture of the new agency. One of its purposes, he said, would be "to make the German people aware that foreign policy is not a matter for a small caste, but the concern of the entire nation."[32] Since the seizure of power, he continued, there had been no central Party agency which could act as spokesman for National Socialist views on foreign policy. This situation had caused frequent and regrettable misunderstandings. Now, the *APA* would assume this role; its specific tasks would include the entertainment of the ever-multiplying numbers of foreign visitors to the Reich; the observation of "developments" abroad; and, especially, the surveillance of activities of "various personalities." "In general terms," he declared, the *APA*'s sphere of work "would include the handling of the problems of the eastern and Danubian areas, of German equality, and the training of younger personalities who might some day be called upon to participate in the determination of Germany's destiny in foreign policy."[33]

Rumors of impending changes in the Foreign Office, on this same day in Berlin, reached such a widespread audience that "informed sources" on the Wilhelmstrasse were moved to deny that, as consequence of Rosenberg's new appointment, Foreign Minister Neurath had requested to be retired from his post.[34] Hitler now had placed a watchdog at the door of the Foreign Office. But how sharp were its teeth? In Party circles, the *APA* came to be known as *"Apparat Nr.1."* Its structure was remarkably similar to that of the Foreign Office itself; it consisted of geographic (*Länder*), foreign-trade, press, cultural, and administrative divisions.[35] A host of Party "experts" on foreign matters, doubtless anticipating that the *APA* soon would become the successor to the official Foreign Office, sought employment in it.

But imminent events were to disabuse Rosenberg of his hopes. A diffident administrator and a poor tactician, Rosenberg proved to be no match for his rivals on the Wilhelmstrasse. Early in May, 1933, he embarked upon a visit to London as Hitler's personal emissary, to sell National Socialism to the Baldwin government, Whitehall, and the British public.

The mission was of the greatest importance. Hitler, in *Mein Kampf,* had dwelt forcefully upon the compatibility of the British Empire and the new Germany which he would some day lead. His reasons were simple. Imperial Germany's failure before 1914 to secure an alliance with Britain against Russia had had disastrous consequences. An eastward Teutonic expansion—at Slavic Russia's expense—to conquer the "living space" necessary for Germanic "survival," would only have been possible with a strong protective alliance with England. "With England alone," he had written in Landsberg prison, "could one begin the new Germanic invasion. . . . To gain [her] favor, no sacrifice should have been too great."[36] Part of that sacrifice, of course, would have been German renunciation of overseas colonies, commerce, and a large naval establishment. But such sacrifices would amply have been recompensed by infinitely greater economic and geographic rewards in the East. This policy, of course, had been ignored by Imperial Germany's rulers; the Empire had floundered into a disastrous alliance with the "racially corrupt" Austro-Hungarian Empire. Together, the two states of Central Europe had gone down to defeat in the war.[37]

This disaster—to Hitler—had merely confirmed the correctness of his conviction, and its viability for future Germanic adventures in foreign policy. British statesmen of the early 'twenties had recognized the folly of permitting France to destroy Germany, for such success would have but upset the European power balance which Britain traditionally had sought to preserve. "Whoever undertakes ... an estimate of the present *possibilities of an alliance* for Germany," he had written, "must reach the conviction that the last practicable tie remaining is only *English* support."[38] The historic mission of Germany in the East, to gain "the soil and territory to which it is entitled on this earth," once more required this guarantee.

Impressive as such Machiavellian argumentation might have been to British conservative circles (where the possibility of a German bastion against Bolshevik Russia found much congenial reception), the initial excesses of the Nazi regime had done little to engender sympathy in the British public as a whole. With Germany diplomatically isolated, in early 1933, English friendship was vital to Hitler's future plans. Rosenberg's task it was to engender such sympathy.

This diplomatic mission proved, however, to be the first and last which Alfred Rosenberg undertook for the Third Reich, and a most catastrophic one. Arriving in the British capital on May 8, 1933, Rosenberg was coolly and unceremoniously received by Sir Robert Vansittart at the Foreign

Office ("at the request of the German Embassy," as the London *Times* guardedly observed next day).[39] On May 9, visits once more were "arranged through the German Embassy,"[40] this time with Foreign Secretary Simon and Lord Hailsham. On May 10 Rosenberg laid a ceremonial wreath—decorated with the Imperial German colors and swastika ribbons—at the Cenotaph.

But this swastika tribute to Britain's war dead was snatched from the monument next day, in a widely publicized act by members of the British Legion, the members of which termed it a "desecration." And on this same day, at a hostile press conference in the Carleton Hotel, Rosenberg awkwardly lectured the assembled reporters (in German) on the glories of National Socialism and lightly shook off questions about Nazi racial policy and persecutions. By this time his efforts to see the prime minister (the chief object of his mission) had come to naught, and he hastily departed next day, 48 hours earlier than anticipated.

Soon after his departure, the London *Times* commented editorially upon Rosenberg's trip. "His visit," the paper declared, "will hardly be regarded as a success even by those who were responsible for it." Rosenberg as diplomat had failed; he had "no previous knowledge of our country, could speak no English, and was palpably unacquainted with the British temperament."[41]

As a sequel to this debacle, Rosenberg's position toward the Foreign Office and his other rivals in the field of foreign policy totally collapsed. Funds for his *APA* were drastically curtailed by the Party treasury. In a fashion, it did manage to survive through the 'thirties, justifying its mean existence by accumulating vast newspaper-clipping files, sponsoring occasional beer parties for visiting dignitaries, indulging in fanciful projects, and from time to time inflating its insignificant undertakings in lavish reports prepared for the chancellor. But its occasional ventures into the Wilhelmstrasse's orbit were ruthlessly crushed.[42]

Although by 1937 many Foreign Office officials privately evinced dismay at the disintegration of their own power and at the implications of impending Hitlerian adventures which they could but little influence, it was also true that the new regime had reaped for them many harvests which Republican Germany had not. Weimar Germany's brief experiment with the Geneva League, for men like Neurath, Bülow, and Weizsäcker, had been at best a discomforting experience, repugnant to men whose distrust of open parliamentary proceedings was matched by an aversion to traffic with lesser breeds on a level of juridical equality.[43] Hitler's decision to withdraw Germany from the League, and from the Disarmament Conference, had met with their favor.[44] Likewise, the unilateral denunciation of the Versailles arms-limitation clauses in 1935 had been a happy day for them as well; Hitler had but fulfilled, by unilateral fiat, what months of earlier, fruitless negotiations at Geneva and Lausanne had not. True, there had been indications that Hitler's aggressive foreign policies would not match the prescribed Bismarckian pattern: Hitler's ambitious efforts, in 1934, to break the French-Eastern alliance system by coming to terms with Poland, had caused some concern to nationalist diplomats like Baron Nadolny, who feared the possibility of Soviet realignment with France. Similar apprehension had arisen over the subversive activities of the Nazi Party in Austria in the summer of 1934, culminating in the assassination of Chancellor Dollfuss, grounded in the suspicion that such adventures would alienate Fascist Italy. The palpitations aroused by Hitler's "Saturday surprises," especially the reoccupation of the Rhineland, had proved unwarranted; the results of this particular measure were hardly uncongenial to the diplomats. Far from diplomatically isolating Germany, Hitler's aggressive measures rapidly had reaped friends in unexpected quarters; the London Naval Agreement of 1935, the Anti-Comintern Pact of 1936, and the rapprochement with Italy during 1937, betokened a drastically altered set of "objective conditions" with which Nazi Germany would have to deal. The central European territorial aspirations of the Nazi regime—including the truncation and destruction of Czechoslovakia and the "settlement" of the Polish Corridor question—were shared by Hitler's diplomats; only caution and a sense of timing distinguished their approach to these "historical tasks" from that of the Nazi leadership. Yet the close relationship of influential Foreign Office officials with prominent professional militarists during this time bred joint dismay over the consequences of a premature war, in which German arms would ill match the combined forces of the Western democracies and the Soviet Union.[45]

III

THE
MOBILIZATION
OF DIPLOMACY

On February 2, 1938, Baron Constantin von Neurath cele-
brated his sixty-fifth birthday, and the fortieth anniversary
of his career in public service. This was a day of ceremonies
for the German foreign minister. It began early in the morning with a gathering of his family. His daughter was there,
with her husband, State Secretary Georg von Mackensen.[1]
Neurath's son, a career officer, had come with his wife from
Brussels for the occasion. At eleven o'clock, the entire membership of the Foreign Office gathered in the house of the
former Reich president (now taken over by Neurath) on the
Wilhelmstrasse, to convey their best wishes to their chief.
The oldest official in the service, Ambassador von Bergen,
formally expressed their sentiments: "Your untiring and
ceaseless pursuit of duty at all times and at all of those posts
which you have so successfully held in the past forty years,

shines as a great example to all of us."² Gauleiter Bohle of the *AO* also spoke kind words on behalf of the Party. At noon, the Berlin diplomatic corps, led by its doyen the Papal Nuncio Monsignor Orsenigo, likewise paid respects to the foreign minister and presented him with a silver bowl filled with orchids.³

The foreign minister's long service to his country had earned him many friends, and large numbers of letters and telegrams arrived on that day. So many, indeed, were they that next day he was moved to announce in the newspapers that it was impossible for him to answer them all personally.⁴

Among those who sent greetings was one to whom Neurath's anniversary had particularly heartening significance. The German press had not mentioned the fact that retirement from the foreign service was customary at Neurath's age; but Joachim von Ribbentrop was fully aware of this, and his wire of congratulations had its own reasons. Forty-eight hours later, on February 4, Neurath was removed from his post. Ribbentrop—then ambassador to the Court of St. James—at the age of forty-four became foreign minister of the Third Reich.

Adolf Hitler was kind to his retiring minister and gave him to know that great missions were still in store for him. In a published letter, Hitler wrote:

On the occasion of the completion of the first half-decade of National Socialist government, you once more have requested to be allowed to retire. I am not able to grant your request, since I cannot spare your indispensable services even in view of your recent sixty-fifth birthday and the fortieth anniversary of your service. In the five years of our common work your advice and your judgment have become indispensable. As I now relieve you of your duties in the Foreign Office and appoint you President of the Secret Cabinet Council, I do so in order to keep at the highest level of the Reich an advisor who has loyally stood by my side during these five trying years. To thank you for this today is my most heartfelt need.⁵

The wish might have been sincere, but the honor was as empty as it was unanticipated. The Secret Cabinet Council, a sinecure, never met, and passed into oblivion the day it was born.⁶ While it is not clear whether Neurath actually had wished to be retired, it was less his own removal than Ribbentrop's appointment as successor which was his heaviest cross to bear. Years later, in captivity, the former foreign minister could still express wonder at Hitler's ungracious act:

Q. How did it happen that Ribbentrop finally got the job of Foreign Minister instead of someone else?

A. That's a question which has been put to me several times, and I can't answer it. I don't know. I can't understand it, especially because on the 14th of January [1938] when I asked Hitler to be relieved from my office, he said to me, "But I will never make this Ribbentrop Foreign Minister." And forty [sic] days later he was in. Nobody can tell me how it would be. I can't understand it.⁷

Neurath's sixty-fifth birthday had been antecedent to this change, but hardly its cause. The governmental shakeup of February 4, of which his resignation had been a part, included several other diplomatic posts. Franz von Papen in Vienna, Herbert von Dirksen in Tokyo, and Ulrich von Hassell in Rome likewise were removed from their posts. But the significance of Hitler's acts of that day lay not so much in the diplomatic as the military sphere of Reich power. It was directed primarily at the Reich War Ministry, the officers' corps, and the German army as a whole.

Behind the newspaper headlines of February 5 announcing Neurath's resignation, the removal of General von Blomberg as war minister, Hitler's own assumption of direct control of the entire Wehrmacht, Keitel's appointment as chief of a reconstituted Supreme Command (*OKW*), and Fritsch's removal as commander-in-chief of the army, lay a hidden struggle for power over the Third Reich's military machine. In this struggle, the army's general staff had come off second best. A brief explanation of this struggle is necessary here, for its significance in the next few months was to be great.

In broad measure, the German general staff, like the Foreign Office, until this time had enthusiastically supported Hitler's major policies of a "revision" of Versailles. It had welcomed the reintroduction of compulsory military service in 1935, the reoccupation of the Rhineland in 1936, the limited military adventures in Spain in 1936, and the rearmament program which, by late 1937, was in full swing. Briefly, in the revolutionary situation between January 30, 1933, and June 30, 1934, the Reichswehr had been faced with the unpleasant possibility of being swallowed up in a new Nazi mass army, swelled by the incorporation of units of Ernst Roehm's mass paramilitary organization, the *SA* brownshirts. But this threat had not been realized. The Hitler purge of June 30, 1934, while it had eliminated General Schleicher, had also put an end to Roehm's military aspirations—and to his life. It had symbolized Hitler's willingness to compromise with the leadership of the German army. By 1937, the *SA* no longer was a threat to the German army. The officers' corps of the now-expanding Reichswehr continued to be the object of veneration from a military-minded German people. The reintroduction of conscription in 1935 presented the army once more with the prospect of indoctrinating the youth of Germany with the ideals of Prussian military tradition—the ideals of Moltke, Schlieffen, Scharnhorst, and Frederick the Great.

Some of the leadership of the officers' corps, it is true, had made common ideological cause with the National Socialists. Blomberg, as war minister, the aged Field Marshal von Mackensen, and a few ranking generals of the army had espoused the official racial and political doctrines of the Nazi state. But the army remained in the new Germany much what it had been in the old—a conservative force, politically and socially reactionary, now a survival of Prussianism in a new, petit-bourgeois state. Like the Foreign Office bureaucracy, it remained an area of state power relatively aloof from the radical elements of the Party. While amenable to practical coöperation with its National Socialist masters, it had by no means been "coördinated" (*gleichsgeschaltet*) into the "movement" itself.

But if Roehm and the *SA* had failed to realize their dream of Nazifying the German army, a new threat to the army had emerged from another source by 1937: Himmler's *SS*. Originally, in 1929, Himmler's *Schutzstaffel* had comprised only 280 men, a select, racially elite corps of the Party whose purpose was to "protect the Führer." It had grown, by 1937, to the dimensions of an army of 210,000 men. In January of that year, it included three armored regiments, the *Leibstandarte Adolf Hitler, Deutschland*, and *Germania*, plus two or three independent divisions. The strength of these Party armored units by no means was great enough to challenge the Reichswehr, and therefore did not satisfy Himmler. His proposal, early in 1937, to develop within the *SS* special armored units to police German's borders against incursions of "communists, saboteurs, and adventurers" (a proposal which, if realized, would have considerably expanded the *SS* as a whole), was opposed by General von Fritsch, as commander-in-chief of the army.

The continued existence of the German army as an autonomous satrapy in the Third Reich seemed incompatible with Himmler's own plans, for various reasons. In his endeavors to challenge its authority, Himmler during the course of that year had found allies—first Göring, and then Hitler himself. While Göring's own hostility to the army leadership stemmed perhaps more from his personal ambition to control it than from ideological convictions which moved Himmler, Hitler's mistrust of the army in 1937 sprang chiefly from other, more substantive considerations. While the army leadership until that time had approved and abetted his successful "revisionist" policies, there was growing evidence that its leadership, including Blomberg, Fritsch, and Beck (chief of the army general staff) did not concur in Hitler's plans for future military conquests in eastern Europe.

These plans had been revealed, in part, by Hitler to his military and diplomatic chiefs in a conference on November 5, 1937. Hitler envisaged a general program of forcible German expansion in eastern Europe, which could not be delayed beyond the years 1943–1945. Such a program, Hitler had reasoned, was essential for Germany's economic and political survival. The "living space" in the East was required not only for German colonization, but for economic exploitation. The first targets of German arms would be Austria and Czechoslovakia, and such undertakings might involve the prospect of an international conflict as early as the summer of 1938.

Neither Neurath nor Blomberg had concurred with the Führer's views in this conference, for strategical as well as tactical reasons. In the fall of 1937, much of Hitler's assessment of the international situation sprang from a belief that tensions, arising from the Spanish Civil War, between Italy, Britain, and France in the Mediterranean would result in war. With the Western powers thus engaged, Germany's hands might be freed for her "necessary" Eastern adventures. Neurath and Blomberg both had discounted the prospect of such a war. And, furthermore, while they did not mention it, it may be assumed that the possibility of Western intervention in a conflict between Germany and Czechoslovakia was present in their minds. But the generals had reasons for far deeper dislike of Hitler's program than merely tactical ones. Both, as representatives of conservative Junker thought, shared with Seeckt an affinity for close Russian-German collaboration, harbored deep aversions to an alliance with Italy, and believed that a strong Germany might be able to come to an understanding with "conservative" forces in Britain.

It was not, therefore, a coincidence, that the purge of February 4, two months after the Führer conference, included on its rolls the names of the three conservative military and political leaders who had voiced strong objections to Hitler's plans. The immediate causes of Blomberg's and Fritsch's dismissals were, perhaps, far more dramatic than Neurath's. Blomberg, by marrying a "commoner" of dubious prior profession, had violated the unwritten social code of his officer corps, and thus was the easier for Hitler to remove. Fritsch, subjected to character assassination by Himmler's Gestapo, accused of homosexual proclivities (a crime under German criminal law), likewise was removed before the charges against him could be refuted. He, like Blomberg, vanished into obscurity.

Thus Hitler had seized direct control of the army and of the Foreign Office. Five years after the Nazi seized power, five months before the Sudeten crisis was to reach its peak, and five weeks before the invasion of Austria, the decks of the Nazi ship of state were being swept clean for action. Hitler was prepared to embark upon a program of ruthless expansion and, if obstructed by diplomacy, to involve the Third Reich in a major war.[8] Hitler's new foreign minister for this trying period would be Joachim von Ribbentrop.

Ribbentrop was born on April 30, 1893, in Wesel am Rhein, son of a minor Imperial army officer, Lieutenant Colonel Richard Ribbentrop. The family had produced a long line of minor Hannoverian military figures, one of whom reputedly fought beside Blücher at Waterloo.

Joachim was the youngest of three brothers. In youth he was in delicate health, inheriting a frail constitution from his mother, who died of tuberculosis nine years after his birth. It was this physical handicap which doubtless diverted him from following his father's career. After attending the *Kaiserliches Lyzeum* in Metz (where his father then was stationed), the young Ribbentrop was sent abroad to study, in London and Grenoble. Several years before World War I, he made his way to Canada; there the pleasant, attractive young man remained for four years, employed variously as bank clerk, timekeeper, and small-scale wine importer. When the war broke out, Ribbentrop returned home, enlisted in the Torgau

Hussar Regiment No. 12, and served, apparently with some distinction, on the Polish-Russian front,[9] and, later, with the German War Ministry's mission in Constantinople.

After the collapse of Turkey in 1918, Ribbentrop returned to Germany and, if his own report be true, served briefly as aide-de-camp with the War Ministry delegation at the Versailles peace conference.[10] The war over, he went next year to Berlin, where he established himself as a job-lot wine merchant. With singular fortune, he met and married the daughter of Otto Henkell, the German champagne manufacturer.

Within the next few years Ribbentrop acquired wealth and repute in this trade. His firm, Schöneberg und Ribbentrop, became the German agency for French chartreuse, Meukoff brandy, Johnny Walker Scotch whisky, and Pommery and Greno champagnes.

The purveying of wines and liquors proved to be Ribbentrop's vocation, but not his avocation. In recent times and in most Western countries, there have hovered about the diplomatic life of great capitals those financially well-endowed social entertainers, content to move in the periphery of official life and to partake of its splendor, if not of its responsibilities and power. Such, evidently, were the Ribbentrops of the 1920's. Financial success spurred his social ambition. On May 15, 1925, under circumstances which he later unsuccessfully sought to camouflage (even in his SS files), Ribbentrop was adopted by a distant spinster relative, Gertrud von Ribbentrop, the daughter of a lieutenant general in the Prussian army who, it appears, was knighted in 1884. Joachim Ribbentrop immediately changed his name and that of his firm to "von" Ribbentrop.[11] His Dahlem villa became known for its dinners and receptions; his gifts of choice wines to German and foreign diplomats established a proper reputation for affable generosity.

Conviviality flourishes on champagne, and Ribbentrop, its purveyor, remained aloof from the acrimonious domestic pol-

itics in the Germany of the 'twenties. The early Ribbentrop
was by no means a Nazi. On occasion he affected monarchist
leanings. Certainly he held no public or private brief for the
anti-Semitism espoused by the Nazis; considerations of rationality and decency aside, many of Ribbentrop's business
associates and friends were Jewish. Few of his customers at
that time could have been Nazis. How was it, then, that he came
to enter the circle of Hitler's advisers?

Ribbentrop was known, among his associates, to harbor
fashionable antipathies to Bolshevism; during the mid-
'twenties, as an auxiliary service to his foreign business
friends, he undertook to publish and circulate periodic bulle-
tins on the internal political and economic state of the Reich.
His business trips abroad brought and kept him in touch with
various public personalities in Britain and France; he could
claim an amateurish knowledge of the political affairs of
Western Europe.

According to one reliable observer, Ribbentrop was brought
to Hitler's attention by one Vicco von Bülow-Schwante.[12] This
person, a black sheep of the prolific and prominent Bülow
family, had been cashiered from the German diplomatic service in 1919 for misconduct. He knew certain leaders of the
Nazi Party, notably Rudolf Hess. He met and befriended Ribbentrop in the late 'twenties. Through Hess, according to this
observer, Bülow-Schwante met Hitler, and the latter, "by way
of conversation happened to mention that he had no gift for
languages nor anybody at his disposal who really could read
Le Temps or the *Times* to him."[13] Ribbentrop's linguistic abilities were considerable, though not flawless; Bülow-Schwante
drew Hitler's attention to them, also showing Hitler copies of
Ribbentrop's privately printed news letters. Hitler was apparently impressed with these evidences of Ribbentrop's acumen
and his proper awareness of the "growing danger of Bolshevism." The two men finally met, according to Ribbentrop, at
the Führer's Berghof in Berchtesgaden, on August 12, 1932.[14]

In the ensuing months Adolf Hitler was a frequent visitor to the Dahlem home of the Ribbentrops, although this friendship was not widely known. Hitler himself was much of a newcomer to Berlin life; the ways of the cosmopolitan world here were unfamiliar to him. But at the Ribbentrop's he soon became initiated into the etiquette of upper bourgeois life; under Frau Ribbentrop's tutelage, he learned appropriate table manners.[15] Their home became a link between the Ribbentrop's parvenu segment of upper Berlin society and the Nazi Party. Here, indeed, Hitler later negotiated with Papen in the last critical days of the Schleicher cabinet, to strike his infamous bargain which brought him, finally, to power as chancellor of the German Reich on January 30, 1933.[16]

Several impressions emerge from this brief portrait. Ribbentrop, unlike all of Hitler's other chief collaborators before 1933, was not an *Alter Kämpfer* of the "movement." He did not even join the Party until 1932, and even then did not publicly admit to the fact.[17] Compared with the other Party leaders who soon were to become his peers in Hitler's court—Göring, Hess, Goebbels, Frick, Rosenberg—Ribbentrop was an upstart. Where, after all, had he been during the early street battles and sufferings of the Party? As late as 1935 his name was conspicuously absent from the Party's quasiofficial Who's Who, the *Deutsches Führerlexikon*. He was not an ideologist, like Rosenberg, whose passionate espousal and elaboration of Nazi irrationalism made up for lack of organizational capacities and physical "activism." Ribbentrop's snobbish affectation of monarchist sentiments, his pretense of aristocratic forebears, his close association with Jewish friends and business associates; all these things could have done little to endear him to the Party's leadership.

An explanation for Ribbentrop's admission to Hitler's circle must be found in those qualities which were not shared in like degree by others of the "men around Hitler." His linguistic abilities, his wide travels abroad as student, tourist, and salesman, had by 1930 conferred upon him a breadth of superficial foreign experience and contacts unknown to the parochial Party chieftains about him. There were other, more subjective elements. His capacity, later to be perfected, of flinging "thunderbolts of flattery" at Hitler "without turning a hair"; his mawkish aping of Hitler's ideas; his persistent antechamber lobbying in Hitler's various headquarters, are traits adequately described elsewhere.[18] Ribbentrop by 1933 was Hitler's own man; so he was to remain throughout the course of the Third Reich's history.

"Freiherr Joachim von Ribbentrop has good looks, a frank smile, charming manners and fluent English and French." In this fashion, an anonymous English acquaintance of Ribbentrop began an article on him in 1936.[19] The champagne salesman of Weimar Germany had risen fast in the intervening years. By now he was well known outside Germany on the European continent and in England, possibly more so than in his home country itself. It was he, and not Alfred Rosenberg, whom Hitler in 1933 had selected to be his chief adviser on foreign affairs. In 1934 he became Hitler's commissioner for disarmament questions; in 1935, ambassador at large (*Botschafter zur besonderen Verwendung*), a title until then unknown in German diplomacy. Following the death of Ambassador Hoesch in 1936, he was appointed Hitler's ambassador to the Court of St. James.[20]

Other honors fell to Ribbentrop in these years. He was appointed to the Reichstag in 1933; he became *Gruppenführer* and later *Obergruppenführer* in Himmler's *SS*. But even more important than these sinecures, he became organizer and chief of the Nazi Party's *Dienststelle Ribbentrop*, attached to the staff of Hitler's deputy, Rudolf Hess.

Ribbentrop performed his early roving commissions with singular vigor and dispatch. As Hitler's alter ego, he frequently traveled abroad, cutting through the troublesome red tape of the Wilhelmstrasse bureaucracy. On occasion, even some of his most important visits to foreign capitals took place without the prior knowledge of the Foreign Office, or of its mission chiefs. Ribbentrop took his orders directly from his Führer, not from the diplomats. His friends, confidants, and acquaintances were scattered throughout England and France. Some of them, like Fernand de Brinon, were holdovers from Ribbentrop's days in the wine business. Others—Lord Rothermere of the *Daily Mail*, Philip Conwell Evans, Pierre Flandin, Sir Ian Hamilton—were newly made acquaintances, drawn to him because of his close connection to Germany's new ruler.

In the days before his appointment to London, Ribbentrop was the mystery man of German diplomacy. But even to those to whom he was not a mystery, his genial appearance, affability, and informality stood in sharp contrast to the formal stiffness and punctuality for which Germany's diplomacy habitually was noted. The claptrap of Nazi ideology which had proved the downfall of Rosenberg the diplomat, concerned him but little. He was his prince's secretary, not his court philosopher; and Hitler, still considering himself misjudged by many in the outside world, had much need of new friends, not only in offices of state, but in the worlds of trade, industry, the press, and in the villas, hunting lodges, and country estates of the Western world which Ribbentrop claimed to know so well.

To say that Ribbentrop, the "amateur," was disliked by the career diplomats would not be an adequate measure of their estimate. They viewed him with contempt. He was a social climber; he was irresponsible; his official reports to Hitler, in their eyes, were monuments of stylistic and substantive turgidity; his exaggeration of minor personal diplomatic feats were both deplorable and ungentlemanly; his oversimplification of complex political issues alarming and (they believed) transparently naïve.[21] But far worse, he was an upstart competitor for their job; and for this latter transgression,

Ribbentrop won the undying enmity of the Foreign Office bureaucracy and their expectation of his early downfall.

And yet they misjudged their man. Ribbentrop did not go the way of Alfred Rosenberg. Early in 1933, he was established by Hitler in his own special *Dienststelle Ribbentrop* (sometimes referred to as the *Büro Ribbentrop*) across the street from the Foreign Office, in the former office of the Prussian minister president. This *Dienststelle*, liberally sustained by funds from Hitler's personal treasury, the *Adolf Hitler Spende*, was endowed with a working capital of RM 20,000,-000. It swiftly grew from a small staff of 15 men in 1934, to 50, and finally became a swollen establishment of more than 300 retainers (*Gefolgschaftsmitgliedern*)[22] to assist Ribbentrop in his new tasks.

Ribbentrop staffed this quasiofficial apparatus with an array of young diplomatic novices, aristocrats, some deserving Party functionaries, and many personal friends. None of them were then prominent men; but among them were to be found such later figures of Nazi diplomacy as Otto Abetz, Heinrich Stahmer, Baron von Steengracht, Martin Luther, Horst Wagner, and Walter Hewel—aspiring diplomats, who soon found this establishment amply rewarding to their impatient ambitions. This was a different "trout hatchery"[23] than that of the Foreign Office. The laurels of a diplomatic career in the regular Foreign Service—even for those carefully selected candidates fortunate enough to be admitted—were hard to come by; only after years of patient and obscure labors could one rise to official prominence. But the recruitment and promotion methods of the *Dienststelle*, arbitrary and unbureaucratized, were unfettered by such rigid, long-established routine procedures.

In addition, the *Dienststelle* inherited the confiscated libraries and files of Professor Mendelssohn-Bartholdy's once reputable *Hamburger Institut für Auswärtige Politik*, and drew upon the research department of the now Nazified *Deutsche Hochschule für Politik* in Berlin and Karl Haus- hofer's Munich *Geopolitisches Institut*.[24] These technical facili- ties rendered the new ambassador relatively independent of technical advice from the Foreign Office.[25]

Until 1938, the *Dienststelle* was under the technical direc- tion of Dr. Hermann von Raumer, nephew of Hans von Raumer, treasury minister under Stresemann. As did his chief, Raumer entertained great ambitions for his organization. He would develop a small "general staff" here, capable of dealing with the most important foreign-policy issues, unencumbered by the troublesome, complex bureaucracy of the Foreign Office. As one of Raumer's associates later wrote, he conceived the *Dienststelle* to be a kind of "paradiplomatic" agency, undertaking such tasks as the Foreign Office was unsuited for.[26]

Whether or not Raumer aspired to supersede the old For- eign Office, the *Dienststelle* and its chief soon assumed a seri- ous role in Reich policy. It was Neurath who guided the first faltering steps of Nazi diplomacy on the international stage; but Ribbentrop and his bureau became entrusted with special diplomatic tasks in the wings. As special commissioner for disarmament questions, he toured the capitals of the Locarno powers in 1934 to sound them out on Hitler's rearmament proposals. In May and June of 1935, as ambassador at large, he negotiated with the British government the Anglo-German Naval Agreement, guaranteeing to Germany 35 per cent parity in tonnage in all categories of naval vessels (except subma- rines),[27] an unexpected triumph which served greatly to en- hance Ribbentrop's reputation as a diplomat with the Führer. In 1936, it was he who represented the Reich at the League Council meetings after Germany's invasion of the Rhineland.

The Anglo-German Naval Agreement of 1935, far more favorable to Germany's now quite remilitarized aspirations than Hitler had ever dreamed, raised Ribbentrop's prestige to new heights. Correspondingly, however, opposition to him

grew within the Foreign Office itself. State Secretary Bernhard
von Bülow, concerned lest the new ambassador irreparably
short-circuit the complex lines of his own policies, appointed
a junior foreign-service officer, Erich Kordt, as liaison with
Ribbentrop's staff, to assist him in his work, but in reality also
to serve as an informer on his activities.[28] Foreign Minister
Neurath adamantly resisted efforts to have Ribbentrop elevated to higher office. When, in 1936, both Ambassador Hoesch
in London and State Secretary Bülow in Berlin died within
a few weeks of each other, Neurath prevented Ribbentrop's
appointment as state secretary by threatening to resign if this
came to pass. Ribbentrop, as consolation, was appointed to
succeed Hoesch in London.[29]

This London assignment came as a bitter disappointment to
Ribbentrop; he never viewed it—despite contrary assertions—
as his chief occupation. He delayed his departure for England
until late fall, 1936, almost 90 days after his appointment had
first been announced, in order to fortify his *Dienststelle* against
anticipated vicissitudes during his long absence from Berlin.
Even after his arrival in London on October 26, he spent the
greater part of his fifteen-month tenure either in Berlin or in
Berchtesgaden, in attendance on the Führer. Between November 25, 1936, and November 26, 1937, he made no less than
eleven trips between London and Berlin. Disturbing questions
raised in the British House of Commons inquired whether
Ribbentrop's domestic enterprises in Berlin were compatible
with the duties of a diplomatist accredited to the Court of St.
James. "Is not the position of German Ambassador in England
a full-time job?" inquired one Liberal M.P. of Foreign Secretary Eden—a question upon which the latter refused to comment.[30] The interior of the German embassy at Carleton House
Terrace—a classic example of Georgian architecture—was
torn apart and remodeled along appropriate lines of monumental National Socialist severity to accommodate Ambassador von Ribbentrop; a retinue of *Dienststelle* officials was

established in London to assist him. But the ambassador's chief diplomatic and political aspirations lay elsewhere. His protracted negotiations with the Japanese government, culminating in the Anti-Comintern Pact of 1936, were handled by him in Berlin, without the participation of the Foreign Office. He continued his peregrinations of other European capitals on behalf of the Führer, earning from *Punch* magazine the sobriquet of "the Wandering Aryan." Indeed, on the eve of his departure from London as foreign minister in early February, 1938, the London *Times* was moved to comment editorially, upon the fruits of his mission, that "his term as Ambassador has been too brief and too broken to make any positive impression."[31]

Published German diplomatic documents and British state papers reveal little of the ambassador's reception in London. But for Ribbentrop this London interlude coincided with a drastic change of heart about England. He had arrived in London in October, 1936, remembered in British conservative circles as architect of the 1935 Anglo-German Naval Agreement. Coinciding with a transitory diminution of hostile German colonial propaganda, his arrival led the London *Times* to auger his mission well. It was preceded, the *Times* had declared, "by the knowledge that he [Ribbentrop] was recently instrumental in having the German colonial campaign shorn of its more irritating features."[32]

The new ambassador lost no time in proclaiming himself the disciple of an anti-Bolshevik coalition of the great Nordic peoples. In his first major London speech at Grosvenor House in December 15, Ribbentrop extolled German leadership in the struggle against the Communist International, her need for colonies and for "self-sufficiency." But a war between England and Germany "must never be repeated," for it would, he warned, "mean the unavoidable victory of world revolution, bolshevism, and the destruction of everything dear" to Germans and Englishmen alike.[33] Upon his hosts—and upon himself—he privately impressed the great personal sacrifice which his "chosen" task of building Anglo-German friendship had entailed. As he told Winston Churchill one day in 1937, he had spurned Hitler's offer to make him foreign minister, in order that he might, instead, come to London.[34] After the war his claim was more modest but equally inaccurate. The Führer, he reminisced, had offered him the post of "undersecretary" in the Foreign Office (presumably the job of state secretary) which he had rejected. "I told the Führer I thought it would be well worthwhile, by going over to London and trying to find out whether it wasn't possible, after all, to get this alliance."[35]

The thought of an Anglo-German alliance—drawn from the intellectual arsenal of *Mein Kampf*—was as much of an *idée fixe* with Ribbentrop as his later obdurate Anglophobia was to be. And the unresponsiveness of phlegmatic British officialdom to it was something which the champagne salesman never was fully able to comprehend. His terms were characterized by extreme simplicity: a permanent Anglo-German naval parity agreement along the lines of the 1935 agreement; joint "guarantee" of the Low Countries; Germany would agree, as he told postwar interrogators, to "guarantee" the British Empire. For her part, Britain would "recognize" Germany as a "strong power in Europe"; as he told Winston Churchill, the future of the Third Reich lay in Eastern Europe, and, in return for British help there, Germany was prepared to "stand guard for the British Empire in all its greatness and extent."[36]

Although the later events of Munich were to demonstrate that powerful forces of appeasement in Britain held to this way of thinking, Ribbentrop by the fall of 1937 had convinced himself of the malevolence of the "British Empire" and, furthermore, of its evil intentions toward Germany. The impatience of Ribbentrop the salesman wore through the thin veneer of persistence of Ribbentrop the diplomat. His efforts to "sell" his novel and revolutionary plan to the skeptical

Lord Vansittart (then permanent undersecretary of the British Foreign Office) at the Olympic Games in Berlin in the summer of 1936 came to naught. "I was trying to induce him," Ribbentrop told a postwar American interrogator, "win him over to come to this Anglo-German arrangement. . . . It was like speaking to a stone wall. He didn't move at all."[37] Attempts to revive the previous project of a state visit for Hitler to London were similarly unsuccessful. His notable diplomatic *faux pas* at a court reception in 1937—when Ribbentrop gave the Nazi salute to the king—produced a violent reaction in the British press and among the British public; his activities as German representative on the London Non-Intervention Committee—established ostensibly to prevent the spread of the Spanish Civil War to other quarters—did little to endear him to British officialdom. Ribbentrop interpreted the abdication of Edward VIII as the triumph of elements in the British "ruling classes" hostile to the Third Reich.

Indeed, by Christmas, 1937, the German ambassador was convinced that his mission had failed. Sunk in deep depression, and fearful lest his London tenure and its attendant failures might mark his demise as Hitler's chief diplomat, Ribbentrop retired in a blue funk to the upper reaches of the Carleton House Terrace embassy to write, in haste and confusion, the swan song of his mission. His memorandum to Hitler, preserved in the documents of the war-crimes trials, urged that Hitler abandon further attempts to seek agreement with the British. The British government would tolerate no change in the status quo of Eastern Europe. Since the abdication of Edward VIII, all chance of peaceful reconciliation was gone. The abdication had been manipulated by Prime Minister Baldwin for fear that the king would not "collaborate in policies hostile to Germany." Outwardly, Ribbentrop wrote, German diplomacy now should appear to seek an understanding with England, but secretly it should seek to develop close connections with Italy and Japan. "Every day in the future,"

Ribbentrop concluded, "when our political efforts are not fundamentally determined in full awareness that England is our most dangerous opponent will only be of profit to our enemies."[38] This posture of violent Anglophobia was to be maintained by Ribbentrop throughout the remaining course of his career—a far more hostile position in this matter than that taken by any other prominent member of Hitler's entourage. What measure of personal rancor, of frustration, had entered Ribbentrop's mind during this London exile? No documents fully can explain this; nor could the "objective" political situation in Britain at the time do so either. Lord Halifax, visiting Berlin in December, 1937, ostensibly to indulge his boar-hunting proclivities with Hermann Göring, had presented a picture of British policy far more pliable than that depicted in Ribbentrop's memorandum. The "frank smile" and "charming manners" Ribbentrop once had shown in England were now transformed into the grim features of an ambitious man determined on a far different course, and aware that his own personal success was contingent upon an extreme espousal of Hitler's own views. His ambassadorship was nearing its end; an avowed enemy of Great Britain was to become German foreign minister.

FROM POACHER TO GAMEKEEPER

During and after the Austrian crisis of early 1938, the German Foreign Office underwent a refurbishing to meet the demands of its new, "activist" chief. Earlier, the Carleton House Terrace embassy in London—its structural and its human components—had been renovated from top to bottom to accommodate Ribbentrop the ambassador. Now, the Berlin Foreign Office headquarters awaited similar happenings.

Unlike many of his predecessors, Ribbentrop chose not to live in the Wilhelmstrasse quarters reserved for the foreign minister, preferring instead to remain—while he was in Berlin—in his more secluded and spacious Dahlem villa on Lenze Allee. His considerable real-estate holdings elsewhere, and his known inclination for following Hitler about, betokened an administration which might not be too intimately linked to the Wilhelmstrasse. During the past few years, he had acquired a 750-hectare estate, equipped with a private golf course, in Sonneburg, near Berlin; a horse-breeding farm at Tanneck bei Düren, near Aachen; and a house near Kitzbühel, available for mountain chamois hunting. Later, as consequence of the union with Austria, he was to acquire Schloss Fuschl, a castle on a small lake near Salzburg, within short motoring distance of the Führer's Berchtesgaden chalet.[39] In these places, remote from Berlin, much of his later diplomacy was to be conducted. After the war had begun, his chief headquarters were to be in a railroad car in the van of the Führer's train. But for the moment, early in 1938, Ribbentrop was in Berlin, and turned his attention to the Wilhelmstrasse establishment.

The new foreign minister might easily have brought with him to the Foreign Office a new set of directors drawn from his own *Dienststelle* or from Party agencies. But he did not. One of his first administrative acts was to align himself with the Wilhelmstrasse officialdom. His *Dienststelle*, of such assistance to him in the days of his "antechamber diplomacy," now became expendable. His retinue of amateur specialists was, for the most part, dissolved, and its members left uncomfortably and resentfully to attach themselves to other Party agencies. A few favorites, it is true, were transferred to the Foreign Office at this time, but only after they had passed the prescribed attaché examination.[40] The *Dienststelle's* gifted administrative chief, von Raumer, briefly remained with Ribbentrop as adviser on Japanese matters; but soon was removed after a bitter personal clash with his chief.[41] For the moment

Ribbentrop had no desire to feud with the career bureaucracy; in fact, he turned to it when he came to fill the most powerful posts in the Foreign Office. Some more astute diplomats had anticipated this. Dirksen, with commendable candor, recalls having received news of Ribbentrop's appointment not without some relief. "Ribbentrop as foreign minister," he later wrote, "would be a 'hard nut'—about that I had no doubt. But just as a poacher, when appointed gamekeeper, often becomes a useful member of society, so, I reasoned, Ribbentrop would become susceptible to reason and good counsel."[12]

Neurath's son-in-law, State Secretary von Mackensen, had resigned shortly after Ribbentrop's appointment. To succeed him, the foreign minister selected Ernst von Weizsäcker, a choice most congenial to the career bureaucracy. A former naval officer, Weizsäcker was, strictly speaking, not a "proto-type" career official. Like Neurath, however, he was the son of a distinguished retainer of the Royal Württemberg court. Originally he had chosen a career in the Imperial navy, but this ambition had come to an abrupt end in 1918 when both Empire and navy collapsed. At the age of 38, Weizsäcker looked for another career. Through a series of fortunate circumstances he entered the postwar German diplomatic service, but without the usual stint of university training. He was transferred from the fleet to the Hague as naval attaché in 1919, and there met Richard Gneist (later personnel chief of the Foreign Office), with whose encouragement he entered the service. Cautious and conservative, given to monarchist and nationalist sentiments, Weizsäcker rose steadily in the Foreign Office bureaucracy. By 1938 he had accumulated a number of posts to his credit: minister to Norway, minister to Switzerland and, finally, director of the Foreign Office's Political Division in Berlin. A confidante of the late State Secretary Bernhard von Bülow, Weizsäcker as state secretary seemed to many of his colleagues a highly satisfactory appointment.[13]

Why had Ribbentrop chosen him? The new foreign minister

doubtless was fully aware that the post easily could have been filled by a "reliable" Party official. In his memoirs, written ten years later, Weizsäcker refrained from offering any explanation for Ribbentrop's act, observing only that "Ribbentrop probably would not have chanced to select me for the post . . . had he known my opinion of his political ideas."[44] But another Foreign Office diplomat and friend of Weizsäcker was more candid in his own recollections:

Ribbentrop shrank from appointing a high Party functionary [as state secretary] since he feared that, if he did so, a rival might develop. For this very reason he viewed with mistrust even the State Secretary for Germans Abroad, Ernst Wilhelm Bohle. . . . Thus it did not harm Weizsäcker in Ribbentrop's eyes if he had had trouble with Bohle's organization. . . . One day Ribbentrop asked me what I would think if he were to appoint Weizsäcker State Secretary. . . . I replied, "There is no better choice. He will be no simple subordinate, but he has been an officer and knows how to follow orders." Ribbentrop creased his forehead in statesmanlike folds. "So—he can obey. Then please ask him to have lunch with me today."[45]

The foreign minister made further concessions to the careerists. Erich Kordt, whom Bülow had loaned to Ribbentrop as a liaison officer in 1933, became chief of the new foreign minister's official secretariat (*Büro Reichsaussenminister*, usually called *Ministerialbüro* or *Büro RAM*). Kordt was given wide discretionary powers to select his own subordinates. Ernst Woermann, Ribbentrop's discreet and competent embassy counselor in London, was appointed director of the Political Division, replacing Weizsäcker. Neurath's six other division chiefs and five of their deputies continued in their posts.[46]

But aside from these new appointments, no immediate changes were in store in the Foreign Office. Key personnel in foreign missions remained substantially unaffected. Herbert von Dirksen was recalled from Tokyo in this February "purge," but he soon found himself chosen to fill Ribbentrop's place in London; General Eugen Ott, the Tokyo military attaché and one-time friend of the murdered General Schleicher, succeeded him as ambassador to Japan—an appointment calculated by Ribbentrop to please more the military elements in Japan than his own Party at home. In Rome, the son-in-law of Admiral Tirpitz, the future conspirator Ulrich von Hassell, a strong opponent of the flourishing Rome-Berlin Axis, was removed in order to assuage the feelings of Mussolini. But in his place, a career diplomat, Georg von Mackensen, was sent. No other changes occurred.

The Foreign Office speedily took on the appropriate manifestations of National Socialist severity. One day after taking over, Ribbentrop, in his brusque drill-sergeant fashion which was to become more characteristic in future years, assembled his officials for review in the inner court of the Wilhelmstrasse office, and paraded before them with outstretched arm, taking their salute in return. New directives flowed from the foreign minister's pen; by command, the black "Republican" frock coat, customary ceremonial dress for post-World War I German diplomats, was discarded for more martial garb—a dark-blue uniform with gold buttons, arm insignia, oak-leaf clusters and dagger, designed by a prominent Berlin tailor under the watchful eye of Frau von Ribbentrop. Officials of the higher grades found this new costume so richly adorned with spun silver oak leaves on their lapels that they came to be called, among themselves, "men behind foliage" (*Menschen hinter Blättern*). SA troops mounted guard over Wilhelmstrasse buildings. New security regulations were introduced by Ribbentrop, who warned that "careless talk and negligence of duty in the future would be ruthlessly stamped out by the Supreme War Lord."[47]

In the preceding five years, Foreign Office officials as a group had not remained entirely aloof from the Nazi Party. Even before Ribbentrop's advent, many of them already had applied for and acquired Party membership. As of December

1, 1937, under Neurath's regime, at least a third of the 92 higher foreign-service officers then stationed in Berlin are known to have been admitted.

MEMBERSHIP OF HIGHER WILHELMSTRASSE OFFICIALS IN THE NAZI
PARTY AS OF DECEMBER 1, 1937[48]

Joined before entry into Foreign Office 7
Joined after entry into Foreign Office 26
    Total number of Party members 33
Not Party members 37
    Application for membership rejected 1
    No information 21
                                                      —
            Total 92

Of Neurath's eleven chief Wilhelmstrasse officials (as of December 1, 1937)—his state secretary, his division chiefs, and their respective deputies—at least five had joined the Party.[49]

This state of affairs, if continued, was likely to prove embarrassing for Ribbentrop. Not enough of his bureaucrats were Party members; aside from Gauleiter (and state secretary) Bohle, his bête noire, not one prominent diplomat early in 1938 belonged to Himmler's SS.[50] "Aesthetic considerations" alone were enough to make Ribbentrop sensitive to the need for immediate outward evidence of Party spirit in his new office, if it were to figure in high state counsels, receive the confidence of the Führer, and enhance his own standing in the Party.

Ribbentrop began his missionary work. In April, 1938, he approached Himmler to request that his two chief career officials, State Secretary Weizsäcker and Division Chief Woermann, be admitted to the SS. The affair was ticklish; only since the previous December had Woermann been a Party member, and Weizsäcker's own date of admission was April 1, 1938. Outside of their official line of duty, neither had been markedly active for the Party, and the bestowal of high SS rank upon such "inactivists" was somewhat irregular. Yet the central headquarters of the SS quickly granted the foreign minister's request. On April 13, 1938, a Himmler adjutant dispatched an interoffice memorandum to *SS-Obersturmführer* Tiefenbacher:

Dear Tipferl!

Please telephone *SS-Hauptsturmführer* Spitzy and tell him he may notify *SS-Gruppenführer* von Ribbentrop that the *Reichsführer-SS* is in agreement with his proposals concerning Weizsäcker and Woermann. Weizsäcker will be accepted in the *SS* as *SS-Oberführer* and Woermann as *SS-Standartenführer* on 20 April....

Heil Hitler!

Yours, Rudi[51]

Ribbentrop's gratitude for this "expeditious settlement" was transmitted next day to the *SS* personnel office.[52]

Woermann's testimony at the Wilhelmstrasse trial, ten years later, sheds light upon these events:

A. In October, 1937, Ribbentrop [then still ambassador in London] asked me why I wasn't joining the Party. I said nobody had asked me to, so he said that nobody was ever asked to join the Party. The next day, the *Landesgruppenleiter* [of the *AO*] appeared and asked me whether I would join the Party, and so I did.

Q. So you joined the Party. Did that make you a convinced Nazi?

A. No. Sometimes I tried very hard to become one, but I didn't succeed, especially after I got to know Ribbentrop better, and then the doubts which I had before were confirmed.

Concerning his entry into the *SS*, Woermann continued:

I was still in London after Ribbentrop became Foreign Minister, and one day I was called by Brueggelmeier, who has been mentioned here several times, in the Minister's office. He told me the Minister would like me to get this well-known uniform, and was I prepared to do so. I asked him what he meant, and he said, "the black uniform." I asked what this was all about, and he said that Herr von Weizsaecker and, in fact, a large number of officials ... had been asked to take the same step, and so I said I would.[53]

Woermann's testimony here is not exactly correct, for, as a matter of fact, only he and Weizsäcker, of the higher career officials, had been tapped for this singular honor. In fact, it would appear that there were distinct limits to Ribbentrop's eagerness to establish close affiliations between his diplomats and the SS. He intervened for these two men, and for several of his minor adjutants attached to his personal staff. But no other prominent career official received like attention.

Undeniable advantages lay in incorporating a small number of conservative career officials into Himmler's dreaded SS. Henceforth, at Party conclaves and other such ceremonies, there could be an "outward and physical sign" of what might pass for an "inner and spiritual" devotion to the Party which, after all, had been somewhat lacking in Neurath's time, and future evidence of which might help silence some of the more strident Party criticism of the diplomats' "conservatism" and "passivity."[54] Further, the nominal attachment of Weizsäcker and Woermann to Himmler's SS Central Headquarters would give useful Party rank to Wilhelmstrasse spokesmen in their future dealings with Party agencies. The link between the Foreign Office and the powerful Himmler apparatus was forged, albeit discreetly, by the foreign minister himself.

The spring and summer of 1938 would have proved to be trying seasons for Ribbentrop to engage in any major overhauling of his service, had he so desired. With February and the Austrian *Anschluss*, the tempo of Germany's diplomatic activity had measurably quickened, and little opportunity was left for such administrative enterprises. If, at this crucial moment, Ribbentrop had allowed his attention to be diverted from such matters, the "great lines" of Hitler's foreign policy might easily have slipped through his fingers, leaving both him and the Wilhelmstrasse diplomats as sideline spectators.[55]

To his consternation, the new foreign minister had found himself in just such a situation on March 12, 1938. For, when

Hitler's *Anschluss* of Austria was carried out, Ribbentrop was far from the center of the stage, in London, taking leave of his ambassadorship. The Austrian affair was in the hands of Hitler, Göring, Papen, and the infamous Seyss-Inquart. Neurath, in Berlin, once more was temporarily in charge of the Foreign Office during Ribbentrop's absence; and it was while Ribbentrop was lunching with the British Prime Minister and Whitehall officials that word came through the British Foreign Office of the entry of German troops into Austria.

Winston Churchill has recalled that Ribbentrop, outwardly untroubled, dallied over his lunch, engaging in light conversation, delaying the departure of Chamberlain and Cadogan who, evidently excited, wished to return to their offices. Churchill interpreted this as a stalling device, which might be true;[56] but Ribbentrop himself was equally taken aback by the news, if privately and for different reasons. Until then, his own role in the whole Austrian affair had been negligible. And now, as foreign minister, he was left out of this triumphant event. Ribbentrop's "signature" was to be affixed, next day, upon the Law for the Reunion of Austria and Germany, signed at Linz; but this was a mere formality, because he was still in London at the time.[57]

As a matter of fact, no top-level Foreign Office official was present at Linz on this "historic" occasion. Once more, in characteristic fashion, Hitler had acted without consulting his foreign minister. On March 16, acting State Secretary Mackensen in Berlin directed the following memorandum to Legation Counselor Clodius of the Foreign Office Economic Affairs Division, through Division Chief Wiehl:

> The Foreign Minister asked Herr von Weizsaecker in Vienna, whether and in what form the Foreign Office participated in bringing about the Law for the Reunion of Austria and the Reich, which had been countersigned by the Foreign Minister. Herr von Weizsaecker replied that nothing was known to him of any participation of the Foreign Office. The Foreign Minister then spoke to the Minister of the Interior [Frick] about the matter and expressed his regret that

his Department had not been consulted. Reichsminister Frick replied that this view did not correspond to the truth, that on the contrary, the Foreign Ministry had participated, Counselor of Legation Clodius having taken part in the conversations in Linz.

To Ministerialdirektor Wiehl with the request that, in the name of the Foreign Minister, he ask Counselor of Legation Clodius for a written statement as to whether and by virtue of what order he was in Linz and took part in the conversations.[58]

Clodius's memorandum in reply noted that his participation had been largely at his own initiative, approved by the state secretary; while at Linz he had played but a minor role. "There could be no doubt," he wrote, ". . . that it was merely a matter of my personal opinion in this question and that I was certainly not acting under orders from the Foreign Ministry."[59]

These humiliating developments of March, 1938, the foreign minister resolved never to have repeated. A past master at back-door diplomacy, Ribbentrop now was to turn violently upon his unofficial competitors in an attempt to reassert the "competence" of the Foreign Office. In this struggle, Ribbentrop could make a strange alliance with his career diplomats. They as well as he stood to lose much if matters were torn from the hands of the Foreign Office. Ribbentrop the gamekeeper, as Dirksen had predicted, proved a far different person from Ribbentrop the poacher. Weizsäcker, writing in his memoirs in 1949, bore witness to the vigor with which his superior, now Foreign Minister, took up the shotgun in defense of his new preserve: "As vigorously as Ribbentrop the unofficial collaborator of Hitler once had shoved aside the Foreign Office, Ribbentrop now defended his competence against all influences of irregular foreign policy advisers."[60]

Ribbentrop's energetic zeal was now directed against Bohle's *AO*, Goebbels's Propaganda Ministry, Himmler's police apparatus, Hess's Party Chancellery, and Rosenberg's minuscule *APA*. The more dramatic consequences and circum-

ANNUAL EXPENDITURES OF REICH MINISTRIES AND OTHER AGENCIES IN THE FISCAL YEARS 1934-1939, IN MILLIONS OF REICHSMARKS[61]

Agency	1934	1935	1936	1937	1938	1939 (estim.)
Reich President	1.2	192.3	154.9	259.8	623.2	476.4
Reichstag	7.2	7.1	7.8	7.7	8.9	18.2
Reich Chancellery	33.1	(united with Reich President since 1935)				
Foreign Office	42.8	46.8	47.0	49.4	58.0	80.8
Interior Ministry	58.5	385.8	540.4	1,040.0	1,609.5	2,107.5
Propaganda	26.1	40.8	35.0	53.3	70.7	95.1
Economics	260.4	254.5	334.5	429.6	1,019.8	967.1
Labor	1,509.0	1,911.0	1,252.5	874.3	1,423.0	1,448.9
Army, Navy, *OKW*	1,310.5	1,735.7	3,596.4	5,014.7	1,221.3	20,500.0
Justice	13.5	465.6	480.1	501.0	545.7	630.9
Food and Agriculture	221.6	261.4	315.9	579.9	1,019.3	1,598.7
Transport	228.6	294.2	384.6	431.9	499.0	495.7
Supply	1,257.7	1,377.6	1,363.2	1,440.0	1,515.0	1,746.3
Accounting	2.6	3.1	4.2	6.1	6.5	8.1
Aviation	642.3	1,035.7	2,224.7	3,257.7	6,025.9	*
Finance	449.9	472.7	497.8	591.9	695.5	808.6

* Amalgamated into *OKW* budget after 1938.

stances of this fascinating jurisdictional squabble must await later treatment. In 1938, as the foreign minister prepared to deal with these competitors, organizational changes began to germinate in the Wilhelmstrasse, which gradually, and then with great swiftness, were to change measurably its character and role within the Third Reich.

Under Neurath's more or less complacent regime, the Wilhelmstrasse and its establishments abroad had not shared in the generally vast bureaucratic expansion enjoyed by most other ministries of the Third Reich. Budgetwise, Nazi Germany's outlay for its diplomacy had been extraordinarily modest. Among the twelve chief Reich ministries in 1934, the Foreign Office took tenth place in its expenditures, absorbing approximately RM 42,800,000, or about .5 per cent of the total Reich fiscal outlay in that year. (The Propaganda and Justice ministries had spent less.) Four years later, in 1937, immediately before Ribbentrop took over, diplomacy had become the Third Reich's least expensive ministerial commodity, costing annually only RM 49,400,000 and absorbing less than .3 per cent of the German government's total expenditures. The Propaganda Ministry, since 1934, had tripled its expenditures, the Interior Ministry requirements were 27 times their 1934 levels. But during the same period Neurath's expenditures had increased less than RM 7,000,000, or about 15 per cent.

This budgetary passivity was as much a reflection of the cautious personnel policies employed by Neurath, as it was a barometer of Hitler's faith in traditional means of diplomacy. The dimensions of the Foreign Office had remained relatively unchanged. As a matter of fact, when Neurath had earlier dissolved the regional (*Länder*) groupings and restored the Foreign Office to its pre-World War I form (involving restoration of the old Political Division as the central core of the Wilhelmstrasse), considerable economies of personnel had doubtless been achieved.

During the first half of 1938 the lines of Ribbentrop's long-range personnel plans emerged—indistinctly at first, but later with considerable clarity. With a green light from the Reich Finance Ministry, the Foreign Office's 1938 expenses rose about RM 9,000,000, or 18 per cent, over their 1937 levels (and, in 1939, were to go still higher—an additional RM 23,000,000, an increase in one year of almost 40 per cent). Within the scope of these additional allowances, considerable changes were made possible.

Evidence of such plans appeared first in the Wilhelmstrasse's Personnel, Press, and Cultural divisions.

Division Chief Curt Prüfer, the career head of the Personnel Division, survived only the first months of Ribbentrop's tenure and was transferred, late in 1938, as ambassador to Brazil.[62] As his successor, Ribbentrop appointed his first Nazi division chief, Hermann Kriebel. This official, an "old China hand" and for many years consul general in Shanghai, had, for a careerist, a long and active Party affiliation; he had joined the Party in 1928, and carried the SA rank of Obergruppenführer.

Under Kriebel's brief tenure,[63] two other key positions in the Personnel Division went to active Nazis. Hans Schroeder, before 1935 a minor consular official, a Party member since March, 1933, and former Landesgruppenleiter of the AO in Cairo (1934–1936) became deputy director.[64] Besides Schröder, however, a new and more ominous figure now entered the Personnel Division: Heinz Bertling. This former Freikorps officer and now SS Sturmbannführer was loaned, on February 8, by Himmler to Ribbentrop, and attached to a new section of the division.

With this latter appointment, it was the foreign minister's intention to breed, within the foreign service, a younger group of activist officials, a "Ribbentrop generation," which ultimately would supplant those career officials upon whom he now, uncomfortably, depended. The diplomats of tomorrow

were to have little in common with those of yesterday. Plans
for a new Foreign Office Training School (*Nachwuchshaus des
Auswärtigen Amtes*) were drawn up by an old Party terrorist
and wheel horse, Freiherr Manfred von Killinger. A house on
Von der Heydt-Strasse in Berlin was purchased and refur-
bished to accommodate it.[65] Here, selected physical specimens
from the Hitler Youth and other affiliated agencies would
receive training in the arts of fencing, horseback-riding, box-
ing, and foreign languages. In Killinger's plan, an early-
morning program of sports and political indoctrination would
be followed by a parade of these new diplomats to the Wilhelmstrasse, where from 9:15 A.M. until 1:00 P.M. they would
employ themselves variously in the anterooms of leading officials.[66] The traditional but now antiquated university training
of diplomats would be a thing of the past; and, as it went, so
would the "academic bureaucracy" in the Foreign Office itself.
On February 8, 1939, this training school was placed under
the command of *SS-Sturmbannführer* Bertling.[67]

Ribbentrop's creatures at this time were also installed in
other corners of the Wilhelmstrasse—the so-called *Referat
Deutschland*, the Cultural and Press divisions, and Ribbentrop's own *Büro RAM*. The events in *Referat Deutschland* and
the Press Division are discussed in the following sections.
(The *Büro RAM* is taken up in the next chapter.)

The strange fortunes of Vicco von Bülow-Schwante (the
young career foreign service diplomat who was cashiered in
1919 because of professional misconduct) serve to illustrate
the gradual transformation of the Foreign Office's relations
with internal Reich and Party agencies in the mid-thirties.
Bülow-Schwante after a lengthy and humiliating absence from
the foreign service, found favor with the new regime, and was
appointed protocol chief of the Foreign Office in 1933. His
enjoyment of close relations with a few high Party functionaries, with Ribbentrop himself, and his familial relationship

to Neurath's State Secretary Bernhard von Bülow, coupled with his polished personality, proved rewarding assets for all concerned. In this post he remained until the spring of 1938 when, accompanying Hitler on a state visit to Rome, he committed a protocol error which prompted his reassignment to Brussels as German minister.[68]

Added to the strenuous duties of protocol chief, Bülow-Schwante held another less publicized Foreign Office post. As head of the *Referat Deutschland*, he acted as liaison between the Foreign Office and Party agencies within the Reich. Such ticklish diplomatic problems as arose in consequence of Party persecution of Jews, the dissemination of Party propaganda through German missions abroad, and collaboration with the Gestapo and Himmler intelligence services, were within his domain. A small agency, *Referat Deutschland* in 1938 consisted of Bülow-Schwante, one senior legation counselor, and three minor officials. However, despite its modest staff, this agency was not a wholly passive clearing-house. The zealous efforts of Bülow's deputy, Dr. Emil Schumberg, from 1935 onward, to press upon Foreign Office and Gestapo officials plans for a new "police order" in Europe met with some limited success. Under the auspices of *Referat Deutschland*, guided tours were arranged for impressionable visiting police chiefs from the Balkans through such unique institutions as Dachau and Sachsenhausen. Secret technical agreements were concluded, through it, between the Gestapo and the police of Italy, Yugoslavia, and Finland. Schumberg assiduously pressed for an elaborate anti-Soviet political-police organization of European states, "under German leadership," so that Berlin might become "the center of a police defense alliance [*Abwehrfront*] of civilized European states against political criminality," particularly since such an arrangement would lend credence to Germany's claim that Europe was being "protected against Bolshevism by National Socialism."[69]

Bülow-Schwante's removal as chief of *Referat Deutschland*,

however, was the removal of a man who was closely related to the traditional conservative leadership of the Foreign Office. As protocol chief he was succeeded by an affable, hearty former legation secretary, Freiherr von Dörnberg, a close personal friend of the new foreign minister. But in filling Bülow-Schwante's vacated post as chief of *Referat Deutschland*, Ribbentrop reached outside of the regular career service, to employ a certain ominous acquaintance, an unscrupulous man with an imposing name: Martin Luther. Luther was to give new intensity and direction to the work of the office which he inherited.

An obscure tradesman from Berlin-Zehlendorf, Luther had drifted into the Ribbentrops' circle of neighborhood acquaintances in the early 'thirties. Outside of his business hours at that time, Luther had occupied various minor local governmental and Party positions chiefly concerned with the collection of money; as local chief of the Party's relief organization (*NSV Hilfskasse*), he had paid periodic visits to the Ribbentrops' home to solicit contributions. In this capacity he had first come into contact with Frau Ribbentrop. Through her, he developed a friendship which was to prove most fruitful. At first, Luther, a jack-of-all-trades, was entrusted with the redecoration of the Dahlem villa, then, with the enlargement of the Ribbentrops' private stables. In 1936, when Ribbentrop went as ambassador to London, Luther accompanied him, to assist in the remodeling of the Carleton House Terrace embassy building.[70]

Luther had an untiring zeal for work and a facility for making himself indispensable. When Ribbentrop became foreign minister, Luther acted, unofficially, as Ribbentrop's private expert on Party matters in the *Dienststelle Ribbentrop* (which still remained organizationally separate from the Foreign Office); and when Raumer resigned, Luther moved in to take his place, as chief *Referent* of the *Dienststelle*.

The task of transferring Martin Luther from the *Dienststelle* into the regular Foreign Office, however, was beset with obstacles. Prüfer's Personnel Division raised strong objections.[71] But Party difficulties were far more important. Luther, it appears, had recently been indicted on charges of embezzlement in connection with his Party work in Zehlendorf; a trial was pending before a Party court in Berlin. Had this resulted in Luther's expulsion from the Party, it would have been legally impossible for him to enter the Reich civil service. Ribbentrop thus undertook to divert the course of justice; he intervened with Martin Bormann, the deputy of Rudolf Hess, to have the case speedily and favorably terminated. On August 23, 1938, Bormann wrote to the Supreme Party Court in Munich: "Legal proceedings are pending before District Court 2 against Party Member Luther (No. 1010333). I am particularly interested in seeing that this trial is carried through most speedily, since the future employment of Party Member Luther must immediately be decided upon. At present the trial has been postponed until mid-September 1938 due to the delay in preparing the case [*wegen vorübergehender Verhinderung des Sachbearbeiters*]. If necessary, there is always the possibility of entrusting the case to another judge on the Party District Court."[72] The trial was called off several weeks later.[73]

Shortly after the Sudeten crisis, Luther, now absolved of his sin, entered the Foreign Office as senior legation counselor. For a brief period he acted as chief of the new *Referat Partei*. Here he handled much of Bülow-Schwante's former business—liaison with Party agencies (other than the *AO* and the *SS*), participation of Foreign Office officials and foreign dignitaries at Nürnberg rallies, and visits abroad by prominent Party and state dignitaries. Temporarily, the more complex activities of *Referat Deutschland,* such as Jewish questions, anti-Comintern affairs, international police and *emigré* matters, remained in the more experienced hands of *Geheimrat* Hinrichs, Bülow-Schwante's subordinate.[74]

The second area of the Wilhelmstrasse where Ribbentrop installed his own friends in 1938 was the Foreign Office's Press Division. Here, too, a career man was replaced by another Ribbentrop favorite and "activist," as the foreign minister sought to gear his ministry into the rapidly developing schemes of the Führer.

In the early days of Nazi Germany, Ambassador Aschmann's Press Division of the Foreign Office had quickly slipped into obscurity. Its once reputable voice—in Weimar days—as the chief spokesman for Reich governmental agencies to foreign news correspondents, long since had been drowned out by the strident tones of Goebbels's Propaganda Ministry, where more imaginative minds had undertaken to embellish and purvey domestic news to the outside world.

In May, 1933, Goebbels, flushed with success, had pressed Hitler to abolish Neurath's press agency and to merge its remnants with his own newly established Propaganda Ministry, as its Foreign Section. Neurath had opposed this proposal with unaccustomed vigor. At a ministerial conference on May 24 of that year, he insisted that the Foreign Office required an agency to collect and disseminate news from abroad, to maintain contact with foreign press representatives in Berlin, and to assist the political offices of the Wilhelmstrasse in their work. Faced by Neurath's adamant attitude, Hitler had compromised: the foreign press activities of both Goebbels and Neurath, he decreed, henceforth would coexist. *"Promi"* (as the Propaganda Ministry was known) would handle the "aggressive" aspects of foreign propaganda (as, for example, the combating of "atrocity stories" abroad). The Foreign Office would continue respectably to embellish and publicize "official" government policy—it would "restrict itself to its traditional activities."[75]

Like most compromises between aggressive, expansive agencies and antiquated ones, the agreement at best merely retarded logical developments. On June 30, 1933, a Hitler decree sheared off from the Foreign Office the tasks of controlling news services and "enlightenment" in foreign countries; art; art exhibitions; moving pictures and sports, and bestowed them upon Goebbels's young and hungry ministry. The Foreign Office's authoritative daily press conference continued to drone on under the direction of a senior official, but the focus of journalistic interest in Berlin shifted to the halls of the Propaganda Ministry. Press attachés in missions abroad were also placed under the control of Goebbels.

Now Ribbentrop, harboring the ambition of becoming the peer of Goebbels in the arts of propaganda, soon found these circumstances intolerable. Dependence upon the Propaganda Ministry for publishing and extrapolating upon his oral emanations and diplomatic triumphs was not long to be continued. He soon found pretext for launching an administrative attack. During the Sudeten crisis, the Foreign Minister complained of the inadequacy of foreign press analyses supplied him by his own Press Division. Division Chief Aschmann was summoned to Munich and ordered to create immediately a new news-analysis agency (*Nachrichtenbeschaffungsapparat*). A young "activist" propaganda expert, Paul Karl Schmidt (not to be confused with Paul Otto Schmidt, Hitler's interpreter and, later, chief of Ribbentrop's *Büro RAM*), was appointed to take charge of it.

At the age of 27, Schmidt became the Foreign Office's youngest senior legation counselor. A former Nazi party worker and student agitator, he, as Luther before him, entered the Foreign Office via the *Dienststelle Ribbentrop*. Now, as Aschmann's deputy, he was groomed to replace his non-Nazi superior and to wage battle against the Foreign Ministry. In 1939, the long-time chief of the Press Division relinquished his post to Schmidt. An amiable old school friend of Ribbentrop, Rudolf Likus, likewise with no previous diplomatic experience, emerged as special consultant on propaganda matters. Schmidt's Press Division swelled to great proportions. By 1941, it was composed of 14 sections, including area desks and functional agencies which directly competed with the Propaganda Ministry's agencies.

Open conflict, according to Erich Kordt, broke out between the two ministries in the summer of 1939. During Ribbentrop's absence from Berlin, the Propaganda Ministry evicted by force Ribbentrop's Radio Section officers in Berlin-Charlottenburg, and blockaded the personnel after some of Ribbentrop's orderlies had "retaken" the Radio premises. On orders from Goebbels, electric and telephonic wires were cut off from the building.[76] The ensuing tempest in a teapot, involving the two ministers, was brought to Hitler's direct attention. In September, yielding to Ribbentrop's importunings, the Führer promulgated an arbitral award delineating the frontiers between the satrapies of Goebbels and Ribbentrop. The decree was a substantial defeat for Goebbels. Henceforth, the foreign minister was authorized to make known his "wishes and instructions" to Goebbels and to appoint liaison officers within the Propaganda Ministry. For his part, Goebbels was ordered to accept and duly broadcast or publish the written outpourings of Ribbentrop's inventive mind. "Once and for all," Hitler's ukase concluded, "I forbid differences of opinion to be brought to my attention without both gentlemen reporting to me about them together."[77]

THE NADIR OF NEUTRALITY

Between 1933 and 1937 certain legal changes were wrought in the structure of the Third Reich, which affected the German civil service in general, and the foreign service in particular.

After World War II some former German diplomats urged that their profession, while subordinated to the Hitler regime, bore no integral connection with National Socialism; that the diplomatic service served more permanent national interests than those of the Third Reich. Thus, Foreign Office State Secretary Ernst von Weizsäcker sought to draw a distinction between service of the German nation and of the Hitler regime: "As a civil servant, one does not serve a constitution, but the Fatherland. One serves whichever government and constitution is given the country by the people."[78] In similar vein, Paul Otto Schmidt wrote in his memoirs: "Governments came and went, foreign ministers changed, but for German diplomatists such events signified no change in their fundamental task: to represent the Reich abroad."[79]

The German foreign service, as an integral part of the Reich civil service, was subject to uniform Reich law which took, in the main, the form of the civil-service law of 1873 and of its subsequent modifications and amendments.

Under the Weimar Republic no radical changes took place in the statutory basis of the German civil service. The basic legislation which the Weimar Republic inherited from Imperial Germany laid great stress upon the career principle of public service. It spelled out, in considerable detail, principles governing the selection, promotion, retirement, discipline, and dismissal of all career public servants. The principle of patronage, the proffering of public administrative offices as reward for political service, was alien to this system.

The fact that the old Imperial laws governing the civil service were carried over into the Republican era made it virtually impossible for the parties of the Republic—the Social Democrats, Democrats, and Catholic Center—to develop a genuinely Republican civil service. The fact that the coalition of these three parties, which was formed in 1919–1920, failed thereafter to retain or regain a durable working majority in the Reichstag, made it impossible for a militant reform of the civil service to be achieved. The civil servants of Imperial Germany were carried over into the new era; existing civil-service laws made it impossible to remove them except by action taken by disciplinary courts composed of other civil servants and judges of equal or of higher rank than the official being tried. Dismissals from service were rare. Similarly, civil-service laws which required that a civil servant, in the event of his removal from one post, be transferred to another post of equal or of higher rank, made it virtually impossible to remove top officials from top posts in their ministries, since there were usually few posts of equal rank outside.[80]

Thus, the Weimar Republic's federal civil service preponderantly was drawn from the *ancien régime*. A certain leeway for political reform was made possible by the fact that specific top ministerial posts—that is, those of state secretary, undersecretary, and division chiefs—were regarded legally as "political" posts, the incumbents of which were not to receive the same civil-service protection which accrued to holders of lower ministerial positions; they could be removed without cause by their political superiors. The efforts of the Left and Center parties of the Weimar Republic to fill such positions with "outsiders,"—noncareer officials—thus were all too frequently denounced by Rightist parties; the charge of violating principles of civil-service "neutrality," was raised against them. In the German Foreign Office, efforts to reform the service through the appointment of such "outsiders" proved, as we have seen, a total failure. By 1926, all such "political" posts were in the hands of career civil servants anyway, and only a few ambassadorial posts abroad were held by noncareerists.

The legal basis of the German civil service was somewhat changed only a few months after the Nazi seizure of power. The Law for the Reëstablishment of the Professional Civil Service, of April 7, 1933, and a supplemental law of July 20,

1933, set new criteria under which officials could be removed or retired from service.[81] According to these laws, officials could be discharged or retired who (1) since 1918 had attained the legal status of officials (*Beamten*) without conforming to prescribed ministerial rules of entry; (2) were of "non-Aryan" descent; (3) had been members of the Communist Party; (4) after the Nazis had come to power, had been active as "Marxists," that is, as Communists or Social Democrats.

While these decrees established new norms for the removal of officials, they contained reservations providing wide discretionary interpretation by the various Reich ministries. Thus, for example, the mandatory "non-Aryan" removal clause did not apply to veterans of World War I, to officials who had entered service before August, 1914, and to officials fortunate enough to obtain special dispensation from the Reich minister of the interior. Furthermore, mandatory discharge of officials with prior Communist affiliations did not apply to those who, before January 30, 1933, had joined a "party or organization" which supported the "government of national revolution." Neither law seriously affected the basic career principle, nor changed the principle of decentralized (that is, ministerial) autonomy in personnel selection and promotion.

Later decrees, however, did do so. On September 24, 1935, a Hitler decree prescribed the active participation of the deputy to the Führer (Rudolf Hess) in the appointment of such higher officials as by law were appointed by the Führer and chancellor himself, namely, officials within or above the salary group A 2 c. Henceforth, the Party Brown House possessed a veto power over the selection and promotion of ministerial officials.

These early laws represented but a transitional stage in the development of Nazi civil-service policy. They were chiefly designed to speed up an initial purge of overtly hostile anti-

Nazi elements; to let down barriers to deserving Party functionaries; and, finally, to subdue latent "disloyal" elements.[82] Many higher German foreign-service officials, as late as 1937, still considered their official status within the government of the Third Reich "nonpolitical." But such a view corresponded neither with their real earlier status in Imperial Germany nor the Weimar Republic, and it did not, in 1937, correspond with their status in the National Socialist state. We must momentarily digress and explore this myth of "nonpolitical" status as it relates to the problem of a state bureaucracy.

It is important to distinguish between the formal, legal notion of "neutrality" for a civil service (a notion indispensable to the idea of a rationally organized state bureaucracy) and the very real value content which the notion of "neutrality" implies in a "political" sense. Policy predispositions are a characteristic of any relatively homogeneous and tightly organized bureaucracy. It is, for example, customary for the officialdom of policy-making state agencies to couch its stated policy preferences in a frame of reference of a "national interest." Indeed, the task laid upon policy-making and executing agencies of assessing claims and aspirations of conflicting groups makes it imperative that some such theoretical standard exist. So far as externally formulated, objective, and rigidly defined rules or regulations circumscribe bureaucratic discretionary powers of decision making, we may say that the concept of formal neutrality is indispensable. The official's decisions must be made *sine ira ac studio*, disinterestedly, dispassionately, and in accordance with objective rules. However, when such rules or regulations (or policy decisions) are made within the bureaucracy itself or are subject to wide discretionary interpretation by its officials, the question of the political predispositions of the bureaucrat becomes of crucial significance. It is naïve to conceive of an ideally "rationalized" bureaucratic machine—bloodless, dehumanized, its personnel wholly divested of ideological bias; nor may we realistically imagine such a service which neglects to develop, within its own ranks, an assertedly autonomous *esprit de corps*, an ideological focus of loyalty.

The invocation of a "domestically-disinterested national interest," transcending particularistic aspirations of organized power groups within a society, is customarily associated with the concept of administrative or bureaucratic "neutrality," and presupposes a higher level of reality where policy decisions are made, and a frame of reference which is wider than particularistic groups can command, precisely because they are particular. The policy maker may rationalize the act of administratively vetoing particularistic claims, or the act of advocating others, in the field of foreign policy, by invoking "higher" claims of national security, national economic welfare, national territorial aspirations, and so forth. The fact that such an act of vetoing—as, for example, an administrative decision denying certain domestic producers more effective governmental protection against foreign competition—actually may benefit other sectors of the population (as, in our example, consumers and importing firms) does not in itself rule out the possibility that other, assertedly transcendent, considerations entered the mind of the bureaucrat in making his decision. Such "transcendent" considerations may prove decisive—diplomatic relations with certain important exporting countries; considerations of international economic stability, and so on.[83] We may thus admit that the bureaucrat, by invoking the concept of a "national interest," is justified in so doing, because his strategic position in the decision-making process, and his statutory authority, requires him to balance and weigh frequently incompatible claims; requires him, as it were, to operate on a higher, or at least qualitatively different, level of reality.

If, then, we may grant that the idea of a "national interest" is, at least, a professional tool which the higher civil servant finds indispensable for making decisions, we must still beware of certain pitfalls which now beset us. How "disinterested," under any circumstances, can a higher official be? Institutionalized political biases within a bureaucracy itself frequently make it exceedingly difficult to distinguish between a concept of national interest closely linked to the particular interests of that bureaucracy itself (for instance, the theories of sea power and national interest elaborated by Captain Mahan, or Admiral von Tirpitz, and the American, or German, naval bureaucracy before World War I), and a concept of national interest to which such institutional interests may be relatively disinterested. Bureaucratic institutions may become sufficiently wedded to the sponsorship or perpetuation of specific substantive policies (for example, a "navy second to none") that they themselves may become deeply involved in the domestic pluralistic struggles which they may claim to transcend. Institutional attitudes or predispositions may persist as decisive elements in bureaucratic policy making, long after the original impetus to their formation has disappeared. Armies— bureaucracies of violence—normally will be disposed to justify their continued existence or enlargement, regardless of whether an objective need for their maintenance is demonstrable. Likewise, to our present point, spokesmen for diplomatic bureaucracies have been known to put forward claims to the perpetuation or the adoption of substantive policies, for the purpose of augmenting, or at least maintaining, their own power, influence, or establishment. The existence of a deep-rooted *esprit de corps* within bureaucratic establishments may, therefore, be closely tied to the espousal of specific substantive policies—regardless of their objective merits.

We would err, however, in asserting arbitrarily that such attitudes are exclusively, or even primarily, attributable to the unique nature of a bureaucracy itself. A powerless bureaucracy, dominated by external forces, may accept specific policies imposed upon it (and concerning which it might have the gravest reservations) merely as a condition of its own survival. The policy predispositions of higher officials in a bureaucracy may be decisively affected by the fact that they share values with other important strata of society. A bureaucracy lacking a minimal degree of social homogeneity in its personnel, or wanting any long-established vested interests, *may* prove an extremely tractible instrument in the hands of a powerful "political" leadership superimposed upon it.

But we should bear in mind, when analyzing the claim of political "neutrality" advanced by higher officials of the German civil service, and, particularly, of the German Foreign Office, that the notion of formal neutrality served frequently to disguise real political predispositions; that, objectively, this claim served as a device for conserving political power for the Foreign Office and provided a rationale for its policy preferences and autonomous aspirations. The National Socialist Party, in *Gleichschaltung* and legal reorganization of the German civil service, sought to destroy, once and for all, the myth that the traditional carriers of state power were non-political and "neutral"; and that the Party sought to reshape the civil service as a whole into a legal and ideological framework which accorded the Nazis the monopoly of determining what the "national interest" was to be.

This new ideology, in the early days of the Nazi regime, attacked the "nonpolitical" myth of the German civil service from two points: first, it proclaimed the political unity of the state, the Party, and the people; second, it assigned to the Party the "leadership," or "political-dynamic" role in society, and to the state (and, specifically, to the civil service) a mere politically static expression of this leadership. This theory, as developed by the Nazi legal philosopher, Carl Schmitt,[85] requires a brief description here, because it found ultimate expression in the German civil-service law of 1937, and because it marked a sharp break with the legal tradition and with the previously hostile attitude evidenced by the Nazi Party leadership toward the bureaucracy of earlier days.

To Schmitt, the National Socialist system had reconciled the antagonisms between state bureaucracy, the extra-state political organizations (parties) and the German people which, he asserted, had existed in the "pluralistic" party system and society of the Weimar Republic.

Before 1919, Schmitt declared, the Hegelian view of the state as the "realm of objective reason" required that the Prussian, and, later, the Imperial German officialdom be much more than a passive, neutral apparatus. In theory, this officialdom had been an independent power in the state. This Hegelian ideal, to Schmitt, had been partially realized in nineteenth-century Prussia and Germany; here, the dominant Prussian officialdom had developed, in its internal credo, the belief that the state, manned by trained and incorruptible officials, stood "above" burgeois society and was, hence, able to serve the totality of the nation's interests.

But this theory required that the German bureaucracy be not merely an efficient, smoothly functioning machine, but, far more important, *the* caste of political leadership (*politisch führende Schicht*). In this respect, said Schmitt, the officialdom had failed. Instead of exercising leadership, it had sought to realize its mission in routine technical administrative and judicial activities. The "dynamism" Hegel had foreseen for it failed to appear. The German civil service became enmeshed in a "so-called positivism" of "neutral" activities; it implemented directives emanating from society rather than assuming positive leadership itself. Consequently, being "neutral," it was unable to "recognize the enemies of the state." Worse still, after the collapse of the Empire in 1918 and the establishment of the Republic, German officialdom had come to view its chief function as that of arbiter between the organized party and class interests of a divided, "pluralistic" society. It could no longer stand above society, but only stand *between* the classes of society.[86] "Neither the neutral officialdom nor the pluralistic [Weimar] system . . . fulfilled their state tasks nor developed political leadership themselves. Thus they failed."[87] On January 30, 1933, the Hegelian *Beamtenstaat*—which had identified civil service with ruling class—demonstrated its bankruptcy, and was replaced by a new system. "On this day," Schmitt proclaimed, ". . . one could say that 'Hegel died.' "[88]

But this new "system," despite its ideology, the Nazi legal philosopher declared, had "redeemed" the German civil service. In the new trinity of state, party, and people, Carl Schmitt asserted, the officialdom could finally discover its real mission. No longer would it have to regard itself as a "politically irresponsible" instrument, a neutral arbiter in the meaningless struggles of a divided, pluralistic society. The Party itself was to maintain a monopoly of political leadership; but the German civil servant, in Schmitt's words, could still be a *Volksgenosse*—a very member incorporate of this trinity, endowed with new, positive responsibilities and new opportunities for constructive action. Being at the same time a *Parteigenosse*, the civil servant could, furthermore, become a member of that militant, dynamic organization which was to bear forward the state and people—the Nazi Party. As Hitler himself had intimated earlier at the Nürnberg Party Congress in 1934, National Socialist theory now rejected the concept of the all-powerful "totalitarian state." The state was to be merely the instrument of the people, controlled by the dynamic "movement" in their behalf.[89] This new role of the German civil service was summarized by Schmitt in rhapsodic metaphor: "Distinct, but not divided; allied, but not intermingled, the three great balance wheels must operate side by side, each according to its inner laws, and all in accord with the political limits set by the Movement itself."[90]

Several aspects of this "revisionist" Nazi theory of bureaucracy bear examination. Carl Schmitt explicitly assumed a

THE MOBILIZATION OF DIPLOMACY

theoretical harmony between the Party and the state bureaucracy. But the achievement of this harmony depended upon
the state official having a dual conception of himself; he no
longer could be merely an official, he would have to consider
himself a *Volksgenosse* first, and *Beamter* second. In the
National Socialist system he was to be guided by two general
criteria: first, those established by the state through its laws,
directives, and decrees governing his official behavior; and,
second, those established by the Party and exercised either
directly upon the individual official in his capacity as a
Parteigenosse (if he happened to belong to the Party), or
indirectly, through Party-inspired state laws which also governed his official behavior. What, however, if the directives
conflicted? It was clear that the official's dilemma theoretically
was easily resolved; the National Socialist official's loyalty
was first to the Party, and second to the state. The bureaucracy,
a pillar of two preceding regimes, henceforth was to stand as
one of two "positive" pillars of the Nazi state, rather than be
torn down as an anomalous survival of the past. Schmitt's
theory now welcomed the bureaucracy into the fold of the
New Order; if it behaved itself, there it could remain. As
Hermann Neef, the *Reichsbeamtenführer*, was to write later,
in 1942: "If the baiting of the career civil service—as it was
carried on in earlier days by the Marxist, Liberal, and Center
press—has ceased, we owe this to National Socialism alone."[91]

The civil-service law of 1937 gave legal expression to Carl
Schmitt's theory of the redeemed bureaucracy. It finally destroyed the conception of political neutrality. The German
civil service, the law's preamble read, "is linked to Führer
and Reich by ties of public service and loyalty."[92] The official
was to be the executor of the will of the Party as expressed
through the state. The state demanded from him unconditional
obedience; in return, it guaranteed to him his life career,

with its manifold benefits. An oath prescribed for every official explicitly bound him in this relationship: "I swear that I will be true and obedient to the Führer of the German Reich and People, Adolf Hitler, and that I will observe the laws and conscientiously fulfill my duties of office, so help me God."[93] In fulfilling these obligations the civil servant "at all times" was bound without reservations to intercede for the National Socialist state. He was required to bring to the attention of his superiors any incidents which might endanger the existence of the Reich or the Party. The civil servant's relation to the Party was legally recognized to affect his qualifications to assume, or remain in, office. It was not specifically mandatory that an official be a Party member. But any official who, at the time of his appointment, had been excluded or expelled from the Party—without this being known in official quarters—could not remain an official; his appointment would be nullified. Remunerative employment outside the civil service was denied to all officials unless it was officially approved; but the holding of unpaid office in the Party or in its auxiliary formations required no permission from the civil service. In fact, Party activity under certain circumstances could be taken into account in determining the pensionable time of service for retiring officials.

Thus, to an extent, Party and governmental activities were "coördinated" (*gleichgeschaltet*). Officials holding the posts of *Reichsleiter*, *Gauleiter*, *Kreisleiter*, and *Ortsgruppenleiter*, and officials of corresponding rank in the *SA*, the *SS*, and the *NSKK* (National Socialist Motorists Corps) could be removed from office only with approval of the deputy to the Führer. Finally, the Party, through the deputy to the Führer, retained its previously acquired power of review over ministerial nominees for appointment and promotion in the higher civil service.

The Nürnberg racial laws, under the 1937 civil-service law, were applied without exception to all members of the Reich

civil service. Only persons of "German" or "related" blood
were legally entitled to become civil servants. If an official
married, his spouse likewise was required to be of "Aryan"
ancestry, although exceptions were admissible for "mongrel"
(*Mischling*) spouses. Should an official, however, choose to
marry such a *Mischling,* advance permission from the minister
of the interior and the deputy to the Führer was required.

But beyond these provisions the status of the German civil
servant remained substantially as it had been under the Weimar Republic. What personal security the official may have
lost against political intervention from the Party or the state
itself, he could make up for by intensifying his own exercise
of the "Führer principle" within his own area of authority.
The bargain between the National Socialist Party and the German civil service was, after all, a reciprocal one; for his loyalty, the official stood only to gain by the privileges and life
career bestowed upon him by the Führer.

The breach in the hitherto unassailable walls of the civil
service, however, had been made. As the *Reichsbeamtenführer*
observed: "It is not the task of the ministries and other [state]
authorities alone to see that the best officials serve: this is also
an affair of the Party and of the People itself."[94] Beyond these
words lay a veiled but omnipresent threat. If the "antagonism"
which Schmitt's theories allegedly had exorcised continued to
persist; if the bureaucratic "dynamism" necessary to attain
the Party's goals did not appear, then, in Hitler's words,
"Problems which the formal bureaucracy proves unfit to solve,
the German nation will assign to its *living* organization in
order to fulfill the necessities of its life."[95]

IV

"WHERE WILL YOU FIND A TALLEYRAND?"

At Nürnberg in 1947, his memory refreshed by interrogations, former Ambassador Karl Ritter[1] managed to recall the following from his wartime experiences—a conversation with State Secretary Weizsäcker shortly after the Nazi attack upon Poland:

> I was in his office for one reason or other and at that time he abruptly criticized Ribbentrop. I said to him, "For one thing, Ribbentrop deserves credit—as long as he intended this war, his political preparations abroad were better than those of the last war." I said this in order to get Weizsäcker to talk. But Weizsäcker replied, "What political preparations abroad? That's a row!" ... He felt that the war should have been much better planned in a political way, and much more elegantly. A war against Britain and the United States is always a bad war.[2]

After 1936, in his grand design for *Götterdämmerung*, Hitler had dispensed with the advice—if not the acquiescences—of his career diplomats. As we have seen, his regard for the sensibilities of foreign missions in Berlin, for public opinion abroad, and a host of other considerations doubtless had made Hitler aware of the peacetime utility of keeping his correct, conventional, and urbane diplomats in their posts, as shock absorbers between the outside world and the grim realities of Nazi power and purpose.

But the Foreign Office was not to be a major policy-making organization. The Anglo-German Naval Pact of 1935; the decisions to reoccupy the Rhineland; the 1936 Anti-Comintern Pact with Japan; the gradual shift of German policy from support of Nationalist China to support of Japan in 1937–1938; and the decision to seize Austria—these major policy departures were the work of Hitler and a close coterie of "amateur" advisers.[3]

After such *faits accomplis*, of course, the appropriate Foreign Office divisions and missions had swung into line to implement and defend them. In 1936, for example, although the Legal Division of Dr. Friedrich Gaus was not consulted before the remilitarization of the Rhineland about legal aspects of this flagrant breach of Locarno, Gaus was given the task of preparing necessary briefs for Ribbentrop to present before the League Council, justifying it.[4] Ample evidence exists today to show instances in which Foreign Office representatives abroad disagreed with policies which they saw taking shape. In 1937 both Ambassador Trautmann (in Nanking) and leading Foreign Office officials had voiced grave reservations about the likely consequences of abandoning Nationalist China to support the maximal claims of the Japanese government in the Far East.[5] In the same year, Hassell, in Rome, had counseled against an Italian-German *rapprochement*. But the advice of these technicians, when in disagreement with Ribbentrop's and Hitler's own policies, were of little weight.

The nightmare of events which lay between the Austrian *Anschluss* of March, 1938, and the September, 1939, attack upon Poland should have demonstrated conclusively to Hitler's diplomats their meager control of his designs and "political preparations" for war. For it is clear that many of them, like Weizsäcker, shared the German General Staff's profound fears of a two-front war involving Britain, France and, possibly, the United States.

Weizsäcker did not dissemble such views before his chief during the Sudeten crisis. Not that the state secretary could have been considered a "pro-Czech," which he was not. As his own memoirs testify, Weizsäcker considered Benes, in his vigorous defense of Czechoslovakia's 1919 borders, an "international reactionary," "Certainly one of Adolf Hitler's chief trail blazers," "the tragic consequences of [whose] works for his country and for Europe he himself must have sensed in his last days."[6] The possibility of a "structural disintegration"[7] of Czechoslovakia in 1938 under economic pressure was not unacceptable to him and, as he recalled later, Munich had been "the last happy day of my life."[8] What Weizsäcker had feared was a military attack upon the Czech state so long as that country's integrity was guaranteed by the Western powers.

He and Ribbentrop had argued vehemently about this in May, 1938, during the "week-end crisis" of that month, when the foreign minister—who then, like the Führer, was bent upon war—had suggested that the Czechs be "provoked" into measures which would justify a German invasion.[9] And in counsels of moderation Weizsäcker persisted throughout that summer. True, Weizsäcker's Foreign Office (since 1935) had financially supported and nurtured the Sudeten Party in Czechoslovakia,[10] but as Erich Kordt has correctly noted, the disagreement between Ribbentrop and the "old Foreign Office" was not so much over the fate of Czechoslovakia, but over the question of "whether England would go to war as the result of another German aggression."[11] Of this probability, the leading Foreign Office officials were fully certain. And they were aware, as well, of Hitler's determination, on May

BEFORE . . .
The Wilhelmstrasse and Wilhelmplatz in the early 'thirties. Left, the Chancellery;
right, the Propaganda Ministry; left center (adjoining the Chancellery), buildings of the Foreign Office.

AFTER . . .
The Wilhelmstrasse after the war. In the foreground (corner left) the Chancel-
lery. The big portals and other architectural changes had been made by Hitler;
Voss-Strasse at the left (*Photo: Wide World*).

BARON ERNST VON WEIZSÄCKER
State Secretary in the Nazi Foreign Office, after his release from the U.S. War Crimes Prison at Landsberg, 1950 (*Photo: Wide World*).

BARON CONSTANTIN VON NEURATH
Nazi Foreign Minister, 1936 (*Photo: Interworld Press*).

GERMAN DIPLOMATS, 1939
Conference in the Foreign Ministry. Left to right: Ambassador Kriebel, Councillor Heinburg, Undersecretary of State Gaus, Ambassador Clodius, State Secretary Weizsäcker, Councillor Dr. Schmidt. In the foreground, Undersecretary of State Woermann (*Photo: Interworld Press*).

RECEPTION AT THE CHANCELLERY, 1938
Left to right: *SS* Chief Himmler, Luftwaffe General Milch, Foreign Minister Ribbentrop, Commander in Chief General Keitel (*Photo: Interworld Press*).

RIBBENTROP AND AIDES IN PARIS, 1938
The Nazi Foreign Minister (left), as he leaves the Elysée Palace after calling on President Lebrun on the occasion of the signing of the Franco-German peace declaration (*Photo: Wide World*).

THE NAZI FOREIGN OFFICE IN A RAILROAD CAR
Conference in Ribbentrop's special railroad car during the Polish campaign, 1939. To the right of Ribbentrop, Undersecretary of State Gaus; left, Hewel and Dr. Schmidt (*Photo: Interworld Press*).

RIBBENTROP HOLDING COURT WITH NAZI PARTY MEMBERS
A conference in the Grand Hotel, Nürnberg; photo originally from Ribbentrop's album (*Photo: Wide World*).

28, to launch such aggression; Walter Hewel, Ribbentrop's liaison officer with Hitler, had told Erich Kordt of this, and Kordt himself had wasted no time in telling Weizsäcker.[12] Indeed, they had anticipated it because on April 25, Weizsäcker had dispatched detailed instruments to mission chiefs abroad, ordering them on a wartime footing.[13] It was at this time that Weizsäcker evidently formulated his own strategy for "preventing war." In conversation with Erich Kordt's brother Theo—newly appointed embassy counselor in London—the state secretary urged that the London embassy spare no effort to elicit powerful warnings from the British to Hitler, in order that the Führer would not view British protests as "bluff."[14] This Theo Kordt did do; in the spring of 1938, the London embassy was kept in touch with Berlin by occasional visits of Erich Kordt. And Dirksen's dispatches to Berlin dwelt upon the possibilities of British intervention.

From London, Paris, and other capitals of Europe came the reports of German diplomats that Britain and France would honor their commitments to Czechoslovakia. But they met with a cold reception from the foreign minister. On May 24, in response to a cable from Dirksen in London, the foreign minister dismissed (as "astonishing" and as "mere threats") Halifax's remarks therein reported about the possible outbreak of a general war. And in this view he persisted, during the summer months which followed, finally ordering that reports from missions abroad disagreeing with his personal views on the question henceforth were to be ignored.[15]

On July 21, 1938, as the crisis intensified, the state secretary and his chief once more aired their differences. "Ribbentrop," wrote Weizsäcker in a memorandum after their meeting, "today enjoined me to see that the Foreign Office maintained an unwavering attitude on the Czech question. . . . If necessary, he said, we would allow a major war to break out with the Western powers, and we should win it." "I said," Weizsäcker recorded, "that even when it was our task to fool foreign coun-

tries, it was not our duty to fool ourselves. I did not believe
that we would win this war ... nor did I believe in our powers
of endurance."[16]

Yet, in opposing Ribbentrop's means for destroying Czechoslovakia, Weizsäcker found himself accepting his ends. As
the memorandum noted, the state secretary had gone on to
urge that "the structural disintegration of Czechoslovakia
[could] be accelerated by economic pressures; that military
operations by Germany now would involve no element of surprise, since everyone now anticipated them."[17] When on August 19, the two men discussed the matter still further, and
Ribbentrop revealed the Führer's determination to settle the
Czech question "by force of arms" no later than mid-October,
Weizsäcker noted that he "opposed the whole theory." A German attack, in his opinion, should be delayed at least until
"the British lost interest in the Czech matter and would tolerate
our action." But such eleventh-hour advice was lost upon the
foreign minister. Hearing it, he tartly reminded Weizsäcker
of his subordinate position—he was subordinate to Ribbentrop, Ribbentrop to Hitler, and "the Führer alone to the German nation."[18] "If I had not yet reached the stage of blind
belief in the question under discussion," Weizsäcker wrote,
"then he desired of me, in a friendly manner and urgently,
too, that I should do so. I should certainly regret it later if I
did not succeed in doing so."[19]

But as a flattering afterthought to this rebuke, the foreign
minister had news to convey to his state secretary. Ribbentrop
and his Führer were going to move into Czechoslovakia "at
the head of the first Panzer division." He would see to it that
Weizsäcker, not Neurath or anyone else, would deputize for
him in Berlin in his absence.[20]

If Weizsäcker's proffered advice was ignored, so were the
reports coming in from German embassies abroad, particularly those from London and Washington. Like the foreign
diplomats in Berlin, they were isolated from the far-distant

Bavarian eyrie where Hitler's plans were maturing. In the summer, Dirksen returned from London bearing a personal letter from Chamberlain to Hitler, which cautioned the latter to moderation. The ambassador cooled his heels for weeks before he succeeded in delivering it. This and other appeals from London to the Führer over his foreign minister's head brought storms of protest from Ribbentrop. Through Undersecretary of State Woermann, the British Ambassador Henderson was given to understand that "the Minister had been greatly upset" and "hoped that such a course would be avoided in the future."[21] Henderson's own efforts to convey to Hitler a correct report on the state of British public opinion also came up against the stone wall of Ribbentrop. Weizsäcker, whom Henderson approached on the matter, refused to handle it upward except through his superior. "Will it then . . . get any further?" Henderson anxiously asked. The state secretary merely retorted, "I must be loyal to my chief."[22] Henderson, in an exasperated dispatch to Foreign Secretary Halifax inveighed against the ring of silence which, he felt, Ribbentrop had built around his master. "How," he wrote on August 23, 1938, "can one play chess with a man who insists on moving his knight like a bishop?"[23]

Uniformed German diplomats whom the British ambassador met during the Nürnberg rally early in September had been candid to the point of indiscretion. "One noteworthy aspect of Nuremberg," Henderson reported to the British Foreign Office, "was the black pessimism of all members of the Ministry of Foreign Affairs. . . . To some of my colleagues their language about [Ribbentrop] was violent to the point of danger to themselves."[24] "Some of them," he wrote next day, "talked a lot of treason to my colleagues. Weizsäcker . . . blackly pessimistic."[25]

The state secretary had been less loyal to his chief than even the credulous Henderson supposed. For now, as clouds of war assembled over Central Europe, Weizsäcker determined upon a final act of despair and disobedience. As the deadline for Hitler's attack neared, he secretly dispatched a message to the British legation in Switzerland, calling for immediate and forceful British action. Carl Burckhardt, the Swiss historian and League commissioner for Danzig, carried it in a frantic nonstop auto race from Berlin to Berne. On September 5, 1938, the British minister there conveyed it to the British Foreign Office in veiled phrases:

Important informant just arrived from Germany and who asked that his name should not be mentioned tells me he heard from highly placed personages (one at Berlin) that Herr Hitler has decided to attack Czechoslovakia in about six weeks. . . . Personage at Berlin who was in despair said that only hope of peace is for Prime Minister to send a letter through intermediary to Herr Hitler beginning with remarks calculated to please him such as reference to his desire for a peaceful settlement but ending by saying that if Czechoslovakia were attacked England would support her with all forces at her command.[26]

The full importance of this *détente* was apparently discounted by British policy makers in London. Several days later, Burckhardt's remarkable story came to the attention of another British diplomat in Switzerland who relayed it immediately by special messenger to London, with the following remarks:

After talking with Burckhardt this afternoon, I took the opportunity of asking Oliver Hardy, who rang me up, whether George Warner's telegram of last Monday (which I had not seen) had been given really serious consideration. He said that it had been taken into consideration with other elements in the situation. . . . I therefore feared that a great deal of background had been omitted and I asked whether any further details would be of interest. He assured me that they would. Hence this letter which in view of its interest and urgency I am sending by special messenger tonight. For you will agree that it is quite unprecedented that a very high official of the proved loyalty of Burckhardt's interlocutor should take a step of this kind.

Yours ever,
R. C. Skrine-Stevenson[27]

Had it been "taken into consideration with other elements in the situation"? Published documents of the British Foreign Office reveal nothing more of it than these two dispatches. When we today look back upon the course of diplomacy in the summer of 1938, this small but remarkable event seems lost in the greater happenings of Bad Godesberg, Berchtesgaden, and Munich which followed. Voices of moderation and appeasement were momentarily to stay the march of Hitler's armies. But they were those of foreign statesmen, not of Foreign Office officials. On September 9, Henderson was instructed to give a new warning to Hitler; but he demurred. "All are convinced," he wrote, that such an action would likely "be fatal to prospects of peace."[28] Weizsäcker's self-chosen anonymity, in his *démarche*, doubtless did not lend strength to his proposals, but we may doubt whether stronger evidences would have proved more effective. Similar activities of Embassy Counselor Theo Kordt in London, to impress British statesmen of the existence of "political and military circles in Berlin" opposed to war proved equally ineffectual.[29] At this juncture, indeed, greater responsibility must be placed upon the government of Neville Chamberlain than upon the incipient *fronde* which the Czech crisis had coalesced in German military and diplomatic circles. We are, however, entitled to note the words of the Italian ambassador in Berlin, Attolico, who remarked to Carl Burckhardt in November, 1938, in connection with the strange events of the past summer, and Weizsäcker's part in them:

The Germans are not given to conspiracy. A conspirator needs everything they lack: patience, knowledge of human nature, psychology, tact.... To fight conditions like those prevailing here, you need to be persevering and a good dissembler, like Talleyrand and Fouché. Where will you find a Talleyrand between Rosenheim and Eydtkuhnen?[30]

In the uneasy months of the winter 1938–1939, as Hitler prepared for the final liquidation of the Czech problem, a pall of gloom descended over the Wilhelmstrasse. Weizsäcker, having had the "last happy day" of his life at Munich,[31] was no longer happy. Hassell, the ousted German ambassador to Italy, as he roamed through the corridors, offices, and drawing rooms of his Wilhelmstrasse colleagues at this time, has preserved a picture of this in his *Diaries*. On October 10, hardly a month after ink had dried on the Munich Pact, Hassell wrote:

As Weizsäcker has told me, Hitler had again expressed himself to the effect that the Czech problem must be liquidated within a few months. Weizsäcker was deeply distressed over Hitler's methods and about Ribbentrop. . . . He said he simply could not imagine how this business could go on much longer.[32]

On December 10, words of similar dismay came from another Wilhelmstrasse source to Hassell's receptive ear:

Lunched yesterday with Plessen.[33] He gave a fantastic picture of conditions in the Foreign Office, where, under the insane leadership of Ribbentrop, everybody's nerves are beginning to snap. The new diplomats, for instance, are to be schooled in Party training camps, which means that they will be without any knowledge.[34]

Still another talked treason to Hassell. On December 16, once more at the Foreign Office, he met with Dr. von Hentig of the Political Division, who

rightly pointed out that all this complaining was useless. The situation is so threatening that one must begin to prepare for action. But how? That is the big question. There is no chance of creating an organization. The one positive approach in this direction, which has already been made, is the surveillance of the entire Party through the Intelligence Service [*Abwehr*] of the Army.[35]

The Hassell narrative, to be later resumed, was doubtless colored by a bitter animosity on his part, lending significance to what were then only faint rumblings of discontent. Hassell's talks with the state secretary were sufficient to convince him—the former ambassador to Italy—that his own advice was to be no longer of consequence in higher Reich affairs. As a matter of fact, he wrote, as Weizsäcker had consoled him on December 15, there was little possibility that Ribbentrop would ever get around to receiving him for a formal report on his long since completed Rome mission. "Ribbentrop had still not received Ambassador Trautmann, who returned almost a half a year ago from China."[36]

Ambassador Dirksen in London shared this fate when still chief of mission. His visits to Berlin were punctuated by incidents of similar ostracism. Although he, together with Weizsäcker, Gaus, and others, was summoned to Hitler's Berchtesgaden conference with Chamberlain in September, 1938, he was not consulted and remained in his hotel while Hitler and Ribbentrop conferred with Chamberlain and Sir Horace Wilson. Although several junior Foreign Office men participated, Dirksen was isolated from Hitler and Ribbentrop and took no part in the fateful exchange of correspondence between the British and German participants at the later Godesberg conference. "The rest of us," he wrote, were left "waiting in great tension for the results."[37]

Ribbentrop's suspicions of the corrupt temerity, decrepitude, and malevolence of the British Empire amply were confirmed by Munich; henceforth, the advice of his successor at the Court of St. James had even less effect on Ribbentrop's own views. Dirksen found himself virtually ignored, receiving no instructions from Berlin outlining Hitler's intentions toward Britain. After the Nazi occupation of Prague in March, 1939, Dirksen's warnings from London that the era of appeasement had ended in Britain made no impression on Ribbentrop. When the ambassador was recalled to Berlin that month, he found the foreign minister totally disinclined to see him; only at his insistence did Ribbentrop finally receive him as he departed for London the first week in May. The "ring of silence" which Ribbentrop, with Hitler's toleration, had built around his master, had grown to more ominous proportions as time went on.[38]

"WHAT NOW?"

It was a Foreign Office interpreter, Paul Otto Schmidt, who, on September 3, 1939, received the British ultimatum which marked the beginning of World War II for Germany. Schmidt's chief, Ribbentrop, had declined to see Ambassador Henderson that morning, with the result that the British official, arriving at Wilhelmstrasse 76 punctually at 9 A.M., had found only Schmidt, a subordinate technical official, awaiting him in the foreign minister's office. Schmidt's recollection of these few moments of German history bear repetition here. As he carried Henderson's message down the Wilhelmstrasse to Hitler's office in the Reich Chancellery and, standing in front of the Führer's desk, commenced to read aloud its contents, Schmidt alone of all Germans momentarily possessed documented proof of Ribbentrop's first gross diplomatic miscalculation—England *was* going to war to honor her Polish guarantee. Schmidt recalled:

As though turned to stone, Hitler sat there and gazed in front of him. He was not, as some later maintained, disconcerted, nor did he fly into a rage, as still others would have believed. He sat completely quiet and motionless. After a while, which to me seemed an eternity, he turned to Ribbentrop—who, as though benumbed, had remained at the window. "What now?" he inquired of his foreign minister, with a look of rage in his eyes ... Ribbentrop quietly replied, "I assume that the French will bring us a similar ultimatum within the hour."[39]

Statesmen, held responsible for the policies they engender and develop, invariably come to symbolize them as well. In September, 1939, Joachim von Ribbentrop symbolized the diplomatic revolution which had thrown together the two great totalitarian dictatorships, Nazi Germany and Soviet Russia, into temporary but close alliance. But in the gloomy months of the *Sitzkrieg*, the German foreign minister had another reputation in many circles. Had it not been he who insisted that the Western powers would capitulate before Hitler's demands on Poland? Whether history will remember him as "Hitler's shadow" or bestow upon him greater eminence (and, hence, responsibility), many of the retinue of Hitler's court came at this time to believe that it was Ribbentrop's England policy which had lured Hitler into his great "mistake." Ribbentrop's awkward attempts, after September 3, to "explain" Britain's honoring of her Polish guarantee as consequence of her foreknowledge that Italy would not honor hers to Germany, did little to endear him to Mussolini and Ciano,[40] and still less to Party dignitaries at home. Early in the *Sitzkrieg* winter of 1939–1940, his State Secretary Weizsäcker was privately to whisper that one price of a negotiated peace with Britain and France would have to be Ribbentrop's dismissal; and later in the war this view was to be shared by Goebbels, Himmler, and Bormann.[41]

This rebuff to Ribbentrop's intuition was joined, however, by other headaches in the coming days of total warfare. Even in a police state it might be said that diplomacy enjoys its maximum institutional autonomy in times of peace, when not merely brute force, terror, and espionage, but negotiation, compromise, and agreement have their meaning and place. But not so in times of war. The vast apparatus of terror in the Third Reich—which already was grown to maturity when Ribbentrop became foreign minister—the army, Himmler's *SS*, and security police, were instruments uniquely attuned to aggressive expansion and war.

This was not, however, exactly so with the Foreign Office. As war spread, the functions of diplomacy would hardly become useless, but they could not be expected to expand automatically. Had the German Foreign Office failed to be geared into Hitler's plans for German military expansion, had it merely preserved its traditional role as an instrument for negotiations, it might only too easily have become a mere

appendage of other, more powerful, centers of Reich authority
and might thereby have risked institutional extinction.

In September, 1939, Ribbentrop completely dominated his
diplomatic machinery. In the peripheral wings of the Wilhelmstrasse, new and reliable subalterns now held sway; in
the traditional core divisions, its leaders were safely "an-
chored" in the *SS;* those who had cast doubts upon their chief's
undertakings were debilitated by their demonstrated failure
to modify or sabotage Ribbentrop's policies, and seemingly
content to retain the vestiges of their remaining power and
importance. The Führer might have doubted the reliability of
his diplomats, but the foreign minister, on the eve of World
War II, reposed sufficient confidence in them. On the evening
of September 3, as the lights again went out over Europe, a
special Foreign Office train pulled out of the *Anhalter Güter-
bahnhof* in Berlin, bearing the foreign minister, his staff, and
the interpreter, Paul Otto Schmidt, to points east.[42] Weizsäcker
remained behind as caretaker of the home office, as Ribbentrop had pledged in July, 1938. There was much to be done;
for, with the outbreak of war, a series of administrative reor-
ganizations were necessary to assure the Foreign Office a niche
in the wartime Reich.

The war mobilization of the German foreign service had
begun in March, 1938, when its missions abroad, under instructions from Weizsäcker, had been placed on emergency
footing. Similar changes took place in the Berlin headquarters.
On July 25, 1938, a special office (*Pol I-a*) in Woermann's
Political Division, was established to centralize all matters
pertaining to mobilization in the Foreign Office. The war accelerated these changes. On October 7, 1939, Ambassador
Ritter was given authority for the Foreign Office over all questions concerning economic warfare, blockade, contraband,
black lists, economic relations with neutral states, and German
property abroad. Ritter was directly subordinated to Ribben-

trop. A new *Referat*, called *Pol I-m*, also under Woermann, was set up to handle Foreign Office liaison with the *OKW*, under Legation Counselor von der Heyden-Rynsch. New wartime bureaus were established in Gaus's Legal Division to handle matters concerning prisoners of war, civilian internees, military law, and damage claims by neutrals. The Information Division established special desks to deal with propaganda for the front, economic propaganda, and countermeasures against enemy propaganda.[43]

Along with these measures, the Nazification of the Foreign Office proceeded apace, to mobilize the "spiritual resources" of the diplomats. By August, 1940, after two years of Ribbentrop's zealous missionary work on behalf of the Party, most of his diplomats had gotten around to applying for membership. Of the entire 120 above the rank of legation secretary diplomatic officials in the "higher service" stationed in Berlin in the summer of 1940, at least 71 already were Party members; and of these, 50 were career officials who had been in the foreign service before 1933. While full data is lacking, 22 of the 120 were not Party members at that date; but 11 of these already had applied for membership and had been rejected by the Party itself.[44]

In broad measure these figures serve to suggest the extent of the Foreign Office's Nazification at this time. By far the larger part of Nazi members of the Wilhelmstrasse in 1940 were career officials who had sought Party membership, rather than Party favorites "injected" into the diplomatic service by Hitler. Of the nine division chiefs of that date (Woermann, Wiehl, Gaus, Kriebel, Luther, Twardowski, Altenburg, Schmidt, and Dörnberg), all but Gaus, Ribbentrop's legal wizard, were career officials turned Nazi. As of this summer date, shortly after the war's beginning, we may say that the Nazi Party decisively had triumphed over the "nonpolitical" principle once so cherished by the German foreign service.[45]

After the war State Secretary Weizsäcker and others in-

sisted that this "voluntary" acceptance of Party membership
was indispensable not only for the survival of the older bureaucrats, but for their retention of power against the more
"radical" elements which Ribbentrop brought with him into
the Foreign Office in ever increasing numbers.⁴⁶ But even if
this consideration were present in their minds at the time, the
events of 1939–1940 demonstrated its lack of realism. For,
with the war, the Foreign Office began to undergo a profound
upheaval of its internal hierarchical structure, which was to
make it of little consequence in terms of policy making
whether any "moderates," with or without Party cards, remained to do any obstructing.

For one thing, after September 3, 1939, the top of the Foreign Office organizational chart—the *Büro RAM*—broke
loose from the Wilhelmstrasse and, as we have noted, en-
trained to accompany the Führer on his military excursions
across the European continent. While, before the war, Ribbentrop's antechamber activities in the Reich Chancellery and in
Berchtesgaden had kept him away from the Foreign Office
for long stretches of time, his absence now became the rule
and not the exception. Ribbentrop was not, of course, the sole
member of Hitler's court to abandon Berlin for the railroad
caravan. Where the Führer moved in his *Führerzug* during
the first months of the war, two other trains followed—the
OKW-Zug, bearing his military advisers, and the *Sonderzug
Heinrich*, named for one of its occupants, Himmler. This latter
special train housed, in addition, Minister Lammers of the
Reich Chancellery and Ribbentrop. A gradual estrangement,
as we shall see, which occurred between the foreign minister
and Himmler was to make these quarters too small for both
men before long. Ribbentrop later acquired a train in his own
right—the *Sonderzug Westfalen*. From these trains, and from
other advanced headquarters, Ribbentrop was to reign over
the Foreign Office at long distance, as absentee owner; his own
Büro RAM was to become a little Foreign Office.⁴⁷

The Foreign Office staff of adjutants and advisers who accompanied Ribbentrop on these journeys lived in a *Mitropa* sleeping car, worked in antiquated wooden dining cars, and acted as his eyes and ears. They were in constant telegraphic and telephonic contact with the home office, receiving incoming diplomatic cables and other dispatches, and transmitting back the foreign minister's incessant and occasionally insolent orders of the day.

The system was anything but efficient. As one of Ribbentrop's adjutants wrote after the war: "It was often impossible for the *Referenten* on [Ribbentrop's] staff to inform the Political Division [of intended measures] because Ribbentrop demanded that members of his personal staff carry out his instructions immediately, so that it was impossible to contact the central office in advance." All important incoming telegrams to the Foreign Office were dispatched both to "field headquarters" and to appropriate divisions in Berlin.

If certain matters did not seem important enough [to the Political Division, for example] to secure Ribbentrop's opinion or decision, the Division took the necessary steps as, for example, in the case of instructions to foreign missions. . . . But now it happened afterwards that Ribbentrop, from field headquarters, gave an answer . . . either directly or through a member of his personal staff, without the knowledge of the Berlin main office. Thus a foreign representative [might] receive with respect to the matter two separate and often contradictory orders.[48]

In his field headquarters Ribbentrop had surrounded himself with a team of newly recruited adjutants, for the most part drawn from his former Party *Dienststelle*, and largely unfamiliar with the workings of the main office in Berlin. For a while, the experienced Erich Kordt had been with him, but early in 1941 Kordt was transferred to the German embassy in Tokyo. As the August, 1940, organization chart indicates, the men of the *Büro RAM*, the foreign minister's official secretariat, presented a most varied array of nondiplomatic backgrounds and talents. There was, for one, Walter Hewel, Ribbentrop's liaison officer with Hitler. An early Nazi, he had taken part in the 1923 Hitler *Putsch*. Vigorous and adventurous, he thereafter had wandered abroad, to spend the greater part of a seven-year exile on a British plantation in the Dutch East Indies. In 1936 he returned to Germany to work in Bohle's *AO*, from which he shifted, in 1937, to Ribbentrop's *Dienststelle*. Franz Sonnleithner, attached to Ribbentrop's office as legation secretary, was a former Austrian policeman, twice imprisoned and once convicted of high treason by Austrian authorities for subversive activities before 1938. After the *Anschluss*, he came to Berlin, and joined the *Dienststelle*. Rudolf Likus, an old school friend of Ribbentrop, was a veteran of Baltic anti-Bolshevik battles with the *Freikorps* in 1919–1920, a participant in the 1920 Kapp *Putsch;* he also was an early (1922) Nazi. During the 'twenties he had held various editorial positions on obscure Nazi journals. By 1939, on his own merits, he had risen to become an *SS Oberführer*, and entered the Foreign Office as legation counselor via the *Dienststelle*. Baron Gustav Adolf Steengracht von Moyland, a young, tractable scion of a minor Rhenish noble family, had been picked up by Ribbentrop in Berlin in 1936 to accompany his *Dienststelle* staff to London. He did not enter the Foreign Office until 1938.[49]

Beyond these man, a group of five "adjutants," all trusted Ribbentrop men with *SS* rank and no previous diplomatic experience, made up the staff of the pocket Foreign Office. It would be incorrect to say that these men were the exclusive coterie of Ribbentrop's advisers. On occasion, career specialists were summoned from Berlin to attend when particular aspects of policy were under discussion. Friedrich Gaus and Karl Ritter were such occasional visitors; but their stay was usually brief and when their tasks were finished, they returned home.

A second structural change of significance in the Foreign

Office coincided with this one: the birth and speedy matura-
tion of a new division—Martin Luther's *Abteilung Deutschland*.

Luther's first task when he entered the Foreign Office in 1938
had been as chief of the so-called *Referat Partei*, which chiefly
was concerned with liaison between the diplomats and Party
authorities other than elements of Himmler's *SS* and the *AO*.
From this post Luther scrambled rapidly up the ladder of
the Foreign Office hierarchy. Entering the Foreign Office in
1938, as senior legation counselor, Luther by 1940 was a
division chief and minister first class. On May 7, 1940, Ribbentrop elevated him to the position as head of a new division
which would handle Foreign Office liaison with all Party and
SS agencies.[50] From this time until his arrest and imprison-
ment in February, 1943, Martin Luther handled such activities as collaboration with Himmler's central administrative
agency—the *RSHA* (*Reichssicherheitshauptamt*)—and the
Gestapo; international police collaboration; arrangements for
diplomatic journeys abroad; and assassination plans.[51] On
May 21, 1940, the sphere of influence of *Abteilung Deutschland* (which superseded *Referat Deutschland*) further was
widened when it was given control of the entire technical apparatus of the Foreign Office's Information Division, acquir-
ing authority over all matters related to the printing and distribution of Foreign Office publications.[52]

Abteilung Deutschland's offices were far removed from the
central Foreign Office's buildings on the Wilhelmstrasse, actually on Rauchstrasse below the southwestern corner of the
Berlin Tiergarten. Whatever considerations might have
prompted this physical isolation, it proved to be a judicious
arrangement for Luther. The new director had little desire to
subordinate his activities to the state secretary's scrutiny.
Participation of other departments and divisions in matters
assigned to Luther's area of jurisdiction increasingly came to
be done by telephone. The new division chief from Rauch-

strasse seldom attended the daily directors' conference. Directives to the new Rauchstrasse headquarters came with great
frequency directly from the foreign minister's *Büro RAM*,
by-passing the state secretary's office. After mid-1941, a tight
veil of secrecy hung over its activities; incoming communications for the Foreign Office from the Gestapo, *SS*, and *RSHA*
were forwarded directly to Luther without first being sent to
the state secretary's office and then distributed to interested
divisions, as had been standard Foreign Office procedure in
the past.[53] Thus, Luther and his associates were given discre-
tion in determining what matters should involve interdivisional
consultation, and which should not. For some time, Weizsäcker managed to keep within *Abteilung Deutschland* a
trusted observer of its activities, one Hans Bernd von Häften.[54]
But the state secretary's control of Luther's affairs was never
great, and Luther flourished in his own autonomous sphere.

Like Ribbentrop's intimates, Martin Luther's chief collaborators on the Rauchstrasse came not from career service of
Neurath's time, but from *SA*, *SS*, and *Dienststelle* employment. Hans Kramarz, a young former *Dienststelle* functionary
and Party member since 1931, had entered the Foreign Office
in 1938 along with Ribbentrop. Walter Buettner, a former
mining-engineering student and *SA* agitator, later propaganda
speaker in the Party *Gau Sachsen*, also had been with Ribbentrop's *Dienststelle*. Werner Picot, a Party, *SA*, and *SS*
member, had had his diplomatic apprenticeship in the *SA*
where, before 1935, he engaged in Party counterespionage
work. Rudolf Likus, Ribbentrop's one-time schoolmate, likewise became attached to Luther's office, serving as his chief
deputy for liaison with Himmler. Beyond one other functionary, Franz Rademacher, only Hans Bernd von Häften (a
relative of the Bismarck family) could properly have been
considered an "old Foreign Office hand."

The activities of these men will be discussed in some detail in the next chapter, as *Abteilung Deutschland* was to flourish in the atmosphere of greater terror to come; its emissaries and directives were to spread over the entire occupied continent of Europe, in implementing the German foreign minister's new ancillary diplomacy of human deportation, extermination, and spoliation. As these activities came to bulk larger in the volume of Foreign Office work, so was the measure of Luther's shadow cast more ominously over other divisions of the Foreign Office, increasingly dominating the character of their work and committing them more deeply to the measures which he and his chief espoused and demanded.

Abteilung Deutschland was not the only new division to be created at this time. Two more—the Information Division and the Radio Division—were added shortly after 1939, to be new agencies for Ribbentrop's propaganda diplomacy. They, too, were staffed predominantly with enthusiastic Party men, and they also pushed deep into the work of older divisions. But in the eyes of many older Wilhelmstrasse diplomats, Luther's *Abteilung Deutschland* was to become the evil and omnipresent symbol of their absent foreign minister, a "tumor" in the body of German diplomacy.[55]

Yet, in one sense, the coming of the war provided a reprieve for the Foreign Office officialdom. In deference to greatly swollen military manpower requirements, Ribbentrop's and Bertling's plans to flood the lower Wilhelmstrasse echelons with Aryan Nazi novices was shelved for the moment.[56] The activities of the Foreign Office training center were sharply curtailed, and its commandant, Bertling, returned to his other *SS* duties in 1941. Ribbentrop, who displayed little propensity at any time for "raiding" other agencies for high-level personnel, was thrown back upon his permanent bureaucracy, and became beset with fears of losing them either through resignation or premature retirement. Even when Ribbentrop, in a fit of displeasure, ordered his state secretary to pare the Wilhelmstrasse staff by over a hundred officials during the French campaign in May, 1940, the foreign minister quickly relented. Weizsäcker was able neatly to squash his chief's enthusiasm by threatening to quit, himself, if the purge went through.[57] Thereafter, Ribbentrop was to insist rigidly upon no wartime resignations, labeling such requests "desertion."[58]

V

THE LIQUIDATION OF DIPLOMACY

In the spring and summer of 1941, the flood tide of German military aggression pushed into the Balkans and the Russian plains. In rapid succession, Poland, Denmark, Norway, the Netherlands, Belgium, France, Greece, and Yugoslavia had toppled under the onslaught of German arms, in a series of military successes which were as unexpected to most of Hitler's diplomats as to his generals. By late autumn of 1941 German armies ranged from the Pyrenees in the West to the upper reaches of the Volga in the East.

But as Hitler's armies advanced, Ribbentrop's diplomats retreated. The rupture of diplomatic relations with immediate or future victims of German occupation measurably reduced the geographic scope of German diplomatic activity. In August, 1940, less than a year after the war's outbreak, the Third Reich still had maintained diplomatic relations with over forty states. But two years later, in August, 1942, while Germany exercised hegemony over the European continent and North Africa, she maintained diplomatic relations with only twenty-two states, many of which were now Hitler's own creatures, hostages, or satellites—Vichy France, Greece, Croatia, Serbia, Slovakia, Hungary, Rumania, Finland, and Denmark. German diplomats remained in only ten neutral states. Correspondingly, the diplomatic corps in Berlin shrank also and was reduced for the most part to a court of vassal emissaries whose continued presence, for the German government, was largely a matter of form, toleration, and convenience.[1]

This rapid curtailment of normal diplomatic activity, while it meant a sharp reduction of the Foreign Office's influence in high-policy matters, by no means reduced the volume of its work. Indeed, German diplomacy rapidly adapted itself institutionally to the policies of other Reich agencies which now were of greater significance in the prosecution of total war.

For one thing, the Wilhelmstrasse retained its previously recognized right to be consulted on any major policies developed independently by any coördinate internal Reich authorities which affected Germany's foreign relations. Thus, for example, Himmler's *Reichssicherheitshauptamt* maintained close consultation with the Foreign Office on such problems as the deportation of political prisoners from occupied areas to Germany;[2] the execution of hostages;[3] the assassination of prisoners of war;[4] and the conscription of *Waffen-SS* "volunteers" outside the Reich.[5] Foreign Office representatives participated in interdepartmental conferences dealing with subjects such as the conscription of foreign manpower;[6] the extraction of produce and resources from occupied areas;[7] the disposal and regulation of slave labor within the Reich;[8] and the staging of propaganda trials.[9]

Secondly, in some occupied areas of Europe the Foreign Office maintained the right of day-to-day participation in relations with local constituted authorities. Thus, Wilhelmstrasse representatives in France, under the supervision of Ambassador Otto Abetz in Paris, served as negotiators for internal Reich authorities in their dealings with the Vichy government. In Denmark, Ribbentrop's representative, Ambassador Renthe-Fink, acted as "plenipotentiary of the German Reich with the Danish government," and, in 1943, was replaced by Dr. Werner Best, whose enlarged powers, as "plenipotentiary in Denmark," were the equivalent of a *Reichskommissar* in other occupied areas, and enabled him to assert authority over all representatives of Reich civilian agencies in that country.[10]

Thirdly, Wilhelmstrasse representatives closely collaborated with Reich military authorities in field operations. Besides assisting the *OKW* (Supreme Command of the Armed Forces) in preinvasion technical planning, and in diplomatic preparations, Foreign Office specialists were designated to accompany army units into operational theaters, to advise and consult with military chiefs. Thus, diplomatic detachments accompanied army units into the Balkans and Soviet Union in 1941, to engage in propaganda and informational activities.[11] Foreign Office area specialists assisted the *OKW* in technical planning for Operation *Marita* (the invasion of Greece) in 1941.[12] Diplomatic missions in satellite East European countries negotiated agreements with Hungary, Rumania, and Bulgaria to permit transits for German troops in 1941 and after. A special Foreign Office detachment (*Sonderkommando*) under the direction of Legation Secretary Kuensberg accompanied army forces into the Low Countries, France, the Balkans, and the Soviet Union,[13] to sequestrate "objects of art," government archives, libraries of scientific institutes, and other useful spoils of war. The Foreign Office's Legal Division, besides advising the *OKW* on matters concerning military law, rules of maritime commercial warfare, and The Hague Convention, also retained exclusive authority over foreign-policy matters concerning prisoners of war.[14]

Beyond these activities, the Foreign Office independently engaged in subsidizing and encouraging "private" international propaganda organizations, the exchange of students from satellite and neutral areas to study in German schools, and carried on its radio and press propaganda begun before the war.[15] This was, then, to be the role of the Wilhelmstrasse in Hitler's New Order. But in the occupied areas of Europe, despite Ribbentrop's continued skirmishes to secure or to regain a voice for the Wilhelmstrasse in policy making, other voices—more strident, and backed with greater power—exacted greater attention. The disappearance of Poland (so far as Reich policy was concerned) as a sovereign state in the autumn of 1939 had entailed the exclusion of the Foreign Office from any direct responsibility for occupation matters.[16] In Norway, in 1940, Hitler's violent displeasure over the failure of Wilhelmstrasse diplomacy to win King Haakon for support of a Quisling government had provoked the Führer to withdraw permanently Foreign Office representatives from Oslo. After 1940, no high-ranking Foreign Office representative was attached to the military government in Belgium; in the Netherlands, while SS-Brigadeführer Bene functioned as a Wilhelmstrasse representative, he was in fact subordinated to the Reichskommissar Seyss-Inquart. Only in Denmark and in France, where considerations of form and propriety created special circumstances, were Foreign Office mission chiefs Renthe-Fink and Abetz officially designated as Reich plenipotentiaries in dealing with local authorities.[17]

Yet perhaps the most substantial curtailment of Foreign Office powers attended the invasion of Russia in June, 1941. In this, as in previous decisions, Ribbentrop contributed to his own demise. The foreign minister—whose sudden enthusiasm for Nazi-Soviet collaboration in 1939 was described by his envious Italian counterpart, Ciano, as "imprudent and vulgar"[18]—rapidly switched his tune after Hitler's personal

decision to attack Russia was apparent. Although the two diplomats Weizsäcker and Schulenburg continued to evince grave
doubts about the consequences of such an enterprise,[19] Ribbentrop quieted his earlier views and expressed, in a memorandum to the Führer in April, 1941, his conviction that Hitler
alone was capable of solving this "historical mission."[20]

Ribbentrop's enthusiasm for Operation *Barbarossa* was,
however, to be dampened within a short time. As it turned out,
Hitler's plans for the administration of the conquered Russian
empire left no room whatever for the Foreign Office. On April
21, 1941, the Füher entrusted to Ribbentrop's archrival, Alfred Rosenberg, the creation of a new agency, the Ministry
for Occupied Eastern Areas (*Ministerium für die besetzten
Ostgebiete—"Ostministerium,"* for short), which was to be
charged with the management of civil affairs in occupied
Soviet territories and the Baltic states.[21]

Up to this time, as we have seen,[22] Rosenberg had been for
the most part ignored in the dispensation of offices in the
Third Reich. All other Nazi paladins had firmly ensconced
themselves in both party and state positions of power. True,
he was still editor of the *Völkischer Beobachter;* he was the
guardian of National Socialist ideology; and he was yet chief
of the Party's *Aussenpolitisches Amt.* In the field of foreign
affairs, he had been frustrated at every turn. His *APA* had
shrunk to the dimensions of a newspaper-clipping house. In-
activity provided ample opportunity to nurse his grievances.
Shortly after Ribbentrop's appointment as foreign minister,
Rosenberg had written a bitter letter to Hitler, complaining
of the choice and of his own exclusion from the hastily improvised (but congenitally moribund) Secret Cabinet Council.[23]
Thereafter, extensions of Rosenberg's powers were ambushed
by the new foreign minister and his career Foreign Office
associates.[24]

When the war began, however, more promising vistas opened to the Baltic theoretician. Early in 1939 his *APA* came in touch with the Norwegian fascist leader, Vidkun Quisling, and undertook close collaboration with him. Quisling's most promising stalwarts were brought to Germany and entered into a special training program in Rosenberg's Foreign Policy Training School of the Party (*Aussenpolitisches Schulungshaus der NSDAP*)[25] in Berlin. Late in the year, Rosenberg succeeded in arranging for Quisling an audience with Hitler himself—a meeting which proved portentous for all parties, and which resulted in Rosenberg's assuming temporary but considerable influence over the course of German policy in Scandinavia.[26] In the spring of 1940, as German armies overran the Low Countries, Rosenberg was given charge of a minor spoliative expedition, the *Einsatzstab Rosenberg*—a special Party military team which looted "Jewish" art treasures, libraries, and cultural institutions in the Low Countries and France. It was a minor task, but Rosenberg fell upon it with great administrative zeal.

Far greater spoliative duties were in store for him, however, in 1941. Rosenberg's new appointment on April 20 portended an enormous curtailment of Foreign Office activities in Eastern Europe, and a massive enlargement of his own. Even before the Russian invasion began, Rosenberg evinced no inclination to permit Foreign Office participation in the future affairs of his new phantom empire.

Early in April, Ribbentrop hastily had formed, within the Wilhelmstrasse, his own Russia Committee.[27] His own "specialist" on Soviet matters, Georg Wilhelm Grosskopf, was busied with the construction of hypothetical Foreign Office branch agencies. When the time came, these would be spread through Ruthenia, the Ukraine, the Caucasus, White Russia, the Baltic states, and Great Russia itself. But Rosenberg totally rejected this bid for direct Wilhelmstrasse participation in Russian affairs.[28] On June 19, only hours before the first *Panzer* division was scheduled to move eastward, Rosenberg served final notice upon the Foreign Office—Ribbentrop's and Grosskopf's plan for on-the-spot Foreign Office consultants and observers in Russia was summarily rejected. Instead, the foreign minister was to release large numbers of his Russia specialists and place them at Rosenberg's disposal. As Grosskopf reported to Ribbentrop on that day:

> Reichsminister Rosenberg particularly emphasized that, in so far as the determination of future political conditions in the Eastern area was concerned, he had the express mandate of the Führer. . . . At the present time this mandate was unlimited, and he intended to shape political conditions according to his instructions. Thus he could admit of no influence whatsoever to the Foreign Office. At such time as independent states with their own governments were formed there, the Foreign Office naturally would enter into its own rights.[29]

Judiciously husbanding his new prerogatives, Rosenberg had set out to construct, in a matter of weeks, a new ministry which would, alone, seek to administer the vast reaches of the Soviet empire which Hitler's armies would conquer for him. The very idea of such a poor administrator suddenly assuming the job which, for the Central Committee of the Communist Party of Russia itself, had proved gargantuan, came as a shock to even such an amateur as Ribbentrop.[30] Rosenberg drew upon the personnel resources of other Reich ministries to staff his own mammoth organization. But, as one of his associates has recalled, most important posts were filled either with mediocre discards from other hard-pressed ministries, or else with "big guns," whose real ambitions were to seize power for their own agencies over specific divisions in Rosenberg's ministry.[31] Some Foreign Office men, it is true, were given leave and were detailed to Rosenberg's staff. But there were not to be any Foreign Office advisory representatives with the *Ostministerium*. Over Rosenberg's strong protests to the Führer, such representatives did march with the army groups on June 22, and did report back to the Wilhelmstrasse, but they went chiefly as observers, with no authority over substantive aspects of civil occupation policy.[32]

The swift movement of events after June 22, 1941, now
threatened both Ribbentrop and the Foreign Office with the
prospect of cumulative isolation from the arena of "broad"
policy-making which was becoming increasingly occupied by
other Reich agencies and personalities. The foreign minister
was not long in sensing this new state of affairs. In the decisive
Führer conference of July 16 (attended by Rosenberg, Keitel,
and Göring), which laid down the initial basic lines of German occupation policy and the character of Rosenberg's civil
administration in the East, the foreign minister had been conspicuously absent.[33] Delicate tasks of diplomacy, of course,
still remained to absorb his dynamic attention; the most important now was to maneuver Japan into the war against
Russia. But additional lightning German military successes,
and the achievement of the "final goal" of world domination,
were no longer such welcome prospects for the foreign minister. As he at that time confided to his one career-service intimate, Friedrich Gaus, the logical corollary of such a German
victory would be that Hitler would no longer have need of a
foreign policy "in the old sense," nor of a foreign minister
either, for that matter.[34] His customary zeal and outward op-
timism remained unabated. "It is characteristic of our rattle-
brained political leaders," wrote Hassell on August 22, "that
on June 28 Ribbentrop told him [Werner von Hentig] that . . .
in two weeks one would shake hands with the Japanese in
Novorossisk (he meant Novosibirsk)!"[35] But his complaints
of losing jurisdictional competence grew in volume, culminating (late in July 1941) in a tempestuous scene with the
Führer—a scene of extraordinary bitterness. As he told an
American official after the war:

I had a great deal of difficulty, and I asked to resign, and the Führer
had accepted my resignation, but then after he had—he was not well—
and so I asked him personally to take back the resignation. . . .
Q. What do you mean, "he was not well?"
A. He asked me then—he was not very well with his head. He had

something—he asked me whether I wanted to—I was his most difficult
subordinate . . . and that I hurt his health, and so on; and so I was
very much moved, and I asked him personally to take back the resignation, and so I stayed in office.[36]

G. M. Gilbert, the Nürnberg prison psychiatrist, discovered
that the mention of the year 1941 to the former foreign minister elicited the most powerful emotional reactions. "[we]
must . . . recall," he wrote, "that 1941 was the year in which
Ribbentrop's father died, as well as the year in which the
violent scene with Hitler occurred. Panicked at the threat of
losing favor, or of causing the mighty Führer's collapse, Ribbentrop had given his word of honor never to question his
judgment again."[37] The Foreign Minister and the Führer were
evidently ill for some days after this trying scene. The offer
of resignation was never repeated.

VI

CHANGE
AND DECAY

On Thursday morning, May 20, 1942, two special trains pulled into the Frankfurt am Main railroad station. On them were the first 400 German diplomats and their families to be repatriated from the western hemisphere. The Americas were now at war with Nazi Germany; for more than four months these diplomats had been interned, and then were transported to Lisbon on the Swedish liner *Drottningholm*. From there trains had carried them on the last lap of their journey home to the Third Reich. Other trains bringing 200 more were still en route.

The Frankfurt railroad station had been gaily decorated for this occasion. Banners of the Reich hung from pylons and steel girders, surrounded by freshly-cut evergreen boughs. Down the platform, and out to the station gates, honor guards of the *SA* formed human chains to restrain the throngs of onlookers who pressed inward to see the homecomers.

These were the diplomatic veterans of the war in the West. "All of them," wrote the *Völkischer Beobachter*, "mission chiefs, military attachés, officials and employees, secretaries and assistants, have returned home . . . after a bitter quiet war against the war-criminal policy of Roosevelt and his Jews."[1] There were important men in the group—the former Washington Chargé d'Affaires Dr. Hans Thomsen; the Washington Military Attaché, General of the Artillery von Bötticher; Ministers Reinebeck and Dittler, from their South American posts. State Secretary Ernst von Weizsäcker was on hand to greet them and, in the *Bürgersaal des Römers*, later in the day, he had words to say to them of their homeland, and of its virtues which contrasted so strikingly with the vices of the Western democratic world they had left:

You have survived the storm. With uplifted heads you have done your work, untroubled by death and the devil, inwardly serene in your faith in Germany and its leader. If, across the ocean and under the barrage of hostile propaganda and lies, you have survived; if you have observed our enemies conducting their war of words, you will discover that here in Germany there prevails a war of deeds. Here you see no "American way of life"; here is the good German way of doing things. Here you see no deliberations in committees; here is leadership. Here you will hear no "fireside chats" [*Plaudereien am Kamin*]; here are initiative, decisions, commands, aggressiveness, and blows at the enemy. . . . We disregard everything but our Führer; his will is ours, his confidence in victory is our faith in victory.[2]

These Ribbentropian comments, dutifully expressed by Weizsäcker, were not in the state secretary's usual style, nor were they sober reflections. But they contained elements of truth. Had he been less discreet, he might have been more explicit about the actual effects of the Führer principle in the Foreign Office itself. "Initiative, decisions, commands, aggressiveness" were, it is true, the order of the day for German diplomacy. There were "committees" in the Foreign Office; but their "deliberations," except in a tactical sense, were of little importance—the more so because of the deep and widening rift between the foreign minister and his huge official apparatus in Berlin.

Actually, eleven interdepartmental "country committees" were established in the Foreign Office during the war years.[3] But beyond providing a wartime haven for otherwise idle repatriated ambassadors and ministers, they were concerned chiefly with propaganda matters. In 1943 and 1944, for example, the America Committee (*Amerika Ausschuss*), under instructions from Ribbentrop, busied itself with a discussion of means to campaign, via radio, against Roosevelt in the then imminent presidential election.[4] As for the Russia Committee, headed by Graf von der Schulenburg, the following colloquy between one of its members and an American interrogator after the war, is of interest:

Q. Did you not form some kind of a so-called Russian Committee?

A. There was a Russia Committee, over which Schulenburg presided. [It] very seldom had a session, and had little influence, in fact almost none.

Q. So the work was done in the various divisions without the Committee?

A. But there was no Russian policy.

Q. But did not the Foreign Office work out plans as to what to do with Russia after the war?

A. I can't remember having taken part in this planning.[5]

Later, in April, 1943, the foreign minister was to create a Europe Committee which, under his supervision, was to "collect and prepare data to be used for the future settlement of the European New Order."[6] Teams, working under the direction of Professor Friedrich Berber, a special adviser to Ribbentrop, Ambassador Emil von Rintelen and Ambassador Paul Karl Schmidt (of the Press Division) were established to begin preparatory work, investigating such problems as the nature of a "legal settlement in the future realization of the European New Order." But, as in the Russia Committee, the career diplomats had little authority to do anything; indeed, the foreign minister's decree establishing it made this clear from the beginning: "For the time being, there will be no elaboration on definite plans for the reshaping of Europe as a whole."[7] The Committee's work "would proceed from the viewpoint that in the future Greater Germany's relations with individual European countries will be either of a close or of a loose nature." Concerning the future New Order, Ribbentrop had even less to say: "To make more detailed reference to the political structure of the future Europe is as yet out of the question." The Committee's chief purpose was to be that of emphasizing "general formulations," and to foster a "commonly shared fear" of a "Bolshevik" victory—a fear which might "prove an effective asset in preparing the European nations for the necessity of a future New Order."[8] Like the Russia Committee, the Europe Committee floundered in a never-never land of directionless speculation, seldom meeting as a group; the burden of long-range "postwar" planning remained in the hands of the Führer.

The paralysis of the Berlin headquarters, a consequence of the physical split between Ribbentrop and the Wilhelmstrasse, became evident in day-to-day foreign-policy planning. Daily ministerial conferences became largely absorbed with propaganda questions. A pervasive fear of decision-making permeated the office. As an Italian diplomat in Berlin petulantly wrote to Mussolini in May, 1943:

A large part of our justified complaints is due also to the fact that the Foreign Office works so slowly and with so much fuss: a direct consequence of the set-up of that Ministry. [Its] main office in Berlin which, according to the wishes of the Minister, extends its sphere of competence more and more to comprise all fields, is like the upper part of a funnel which becomes larger and larger. However—and here is the drawback—the tube of the funnel always remains the same size. All the work must go through this narrow opening, and Ribbentrop—who is always at headquarters far away from Berlin—wants to control it personally, with the aid of a very few trusted co-workers. Since nobody at the Foreign Office in Berlin dares to make any decisions, problems are solved with great delay, and the execution of orders is insufficiently controlled.[9]

The Foreign Office's wartime tasks, after 1942, had become almost wholly ancillary to those of other agencies of the Third Reich. The extermination of the European Jews;[10] the forcible importation of slave labor from France, Eastern Europe, and the Soviet Union; the recruitment of *Waffen-SS* units—albeit less "Nordic" than would have been desirable—to fight in the "common battle" against Bolshevism in satellite or occupied countries; the extradition of political prisoners from satellite countries to German occupation camps—tasks such as these occupied the attention of the Foreign Office when their accomplishment entailed negotiations with other governments, or when their implementation was deemed likely to have serious "foreign policy consequences."[11]

Since the foreign minister was, from all evidences, a broad constructionist in his conception of the domain affected by foreign-policy considerations, much of the Foreign Office's activities were devoted to jurisdictional disputes, the purpose of which was to enlarge this domain. As Walter Hewel once remarked to one Foreign Office colleague, Hitler had observed on one occasion that, if Ribbentrop had his way, the German railroads, too, should come under the Wilhelmstrasse's jurisdiction because they, after all, sold tickets valid outside the Reich.[12] Joseph Goebbels wrote in his diary on November 14, 1943:

I had a heavy set-to with Ribbentrop today about our propaganda section in France. Ribbentrop claims that France must be regarded as a foreign country and not as a defeated state because it has a chief of state and a prime minister. Consequently, only the Foreign Office has a right to political activity there.... It is amazing with what fanaticism the Foreign Office and especially Ribbentrop deal with questions of such subsidiary importance, whereas they simply push aside questions of great moment.[13]

Baron Steengracht, later Ribbentrop's state secretary, observed after the war that "at least 60 per cent" of the foreign minister's time during the war was used for quarrels of this character.[14]

For the most part these struggles were not so much over the substance of policy as over the procedural issue of who was to implement already-established policies. In broad measure, Ribbentrop accepted the avowed policy of Hitler and Himmler to exterminate the Jews, delegating to his most vigorous and competent subordinates the task of facilitating the "final settlement" of this question.

A macabre memorandum prepared by Undersecretary Woermann on March 1, 1941, indicates the kind of considerations which prompted the Foreign Office occasionally to make "realistic" distinctions in the implementation of anti-Jewish measures. Reviewing the Wilhelmstrasse's attitude toward domestic action against foreign Jews resident in Germany, Woermann noted that such measures could only be taken by internal Reich authorities after previous agreement with the Foreign Office "in each individual case." The Foreign Office, wrote Woermann, objected to such action against American Jews at that time since there were few of them resident in Germany and since such action would only give the United States government a pretext for intervention. "However," wrote Woermann, "it can be stated in advance that no objection for political reasons exists as far as measures against Hungarian Jews or Jews from the Balkan countries are concerned." Ribbentrop's own role in the extermination of Eastern European Jews requires little documentation, but is evident from the following memorandum of Undersecretary Luther, September 28, 1942: "The Foreign Minister directed me today by telephone to expedite, as far as possible, the evacuation of Jews from the various European countries since it is a proven fact that the Jews are indulging everywhere in anti-German propaganda and are responsible for acts of sabotage and attempted outrages. After speaking briefly on the present evacuation of Jews from Slovakia, Croatia, Rumania and the occupied territories, the Foreign Minister ordered that the Bulgarian, Hungarian and Danish governments be approached in order to start the evacuation of Jews from these countries."[15]

These undertakings prompted increasingly close collaboration with the *Reichssicherheitshauptamt*, the central administrative agency of Himmler's vast *SS* apparatus, which was initially under the direction of Reinhard Heydrich and later, Ernst Kaltenbrunner. Moreover, as the war progressed, in German embassies, legations, and consulates abroad, agents of the *RSHA*, disguised variously as trade attachés and scientific experts, began to make their appearance—"police attachés," whose functions were chiefly those of violent men: intelligence, subversion, and sabotage. By October, 1943, more than 70 such police attachés, disguised in various habiliments, were detailed to German missions in neutral or cobelligerent countries. In October, 1944, an incomplete listing of *RSHA* counterintelligence officials in neutral countries alone accounted for an additional 26.[16]

The greater part of routine Foreign Office work in matters requiring liaison with Himmler's *RSHA* was cleared through Undersecretary Luther's *Abteilung Deutschland* on Rauchstrasse. Luther, from 1941 until early 1943, normally represented the Foreign Office in high-level interministerial conferences in Berlin with *RSHA* officials (although, occasionally, Weizsäcker or his successor, Steengracht, attended).[17] While Luther played a decisive role in facilitating negotiations with the Bulgarian, Hungarian, Rumanian, and Slovakian governments during 1942, which led to mass deportations of Jews from these countries, his *Abteilung Deutschland* kept other interested divisions regularly informed of these activities. Instructions from the Wilhelmstrasse to its missions in Sofia, Budapest, Bucharest, and Bratislava concerning these negotiations were prepared in Luther's office.

Familiarity between the *SS* and Ribbentrop's ministry did not, however, breed mutual esteem. Before the war, relations between these two agencies, while hardly intimate, had in some ways proved mutually profitable. The foreign minister and the *Reichsführer-SS* had been on close personal terms. On occasion, the Wilhelmstrasse had financed various foreign-espionage projects of Himmler's Gestapo and Security Police, receiving, in turn, valuable intelligence reports.[18] Activities in SS-run concentration camps not infrequently evoked protests from foreign governments, causing some embarrassment to Wilhelmstrasse officials.[19] Some prewar Himmler projects, such as abetting the Japanese Colonel Oshima's fruitless schemes to assassinate Stalin,[20] had doubtless been discreetly kept from the attention of the diplomats. On occasion, career foreign-service officials had been subjected to close scrutiny by Gestapo agents, and some were actually arrested.[21] But Himmler's interest in amateur diplomacy was never so acute, before the war, as to cause the foreign minister to consider him seriously as a rival.

Such had been the foreign minister's desire to ingratiate himself and his ministry with Party circles that occasionally he had pleaded with his SS colleagues to make available younger SS men for minor Foreign Office posts. In a letter dated June 6, 1942, Ribbentrop had been explicit on this point. Yet Ribbentrop, despite the cordiality of his relations with the *Reichsführer-SS*, judiciously had refrained, throughout his tenure of office, from appointing any prominent SS personality to any Foreign Office post. After 1941, when the foreign minister, presumably under pressure from Hitler to "activize" his ministry, had filled all his important Balkan diplomatic posts with old Party (but not SS!) wheelhorses, this oversight became most apparent. By 1943, German legations in Bucharest, Budapest, Bratislava, Zagreb, and Sofia had been placed in the hands of old SA brownshirts turned diplomats—Killinger, Jagow, Ludin, Kasche, and Beckerle.[22]

As SS power and influence spread, it, too, came to impinge closely upon Ribbentrop's self-delineated sphere of foreign-

diplomatic activity. Much of the trouble was an inevitable
consequence of the war, which had led to the burgeoning of *SS*
intelligence networks to supplement the none-too-reliable military espionage establishment of Admiral Canaris, the *OKW-
Abwehr*.[23] In October, 1939, Ribbentrop had granted Himmler's *RSHA* the right to attach agents of its own intelligence
service directly to German diplomatic missions abroad. But
like the pact between the Arab and his camel, the original
interagency agreement had been a vague one, and caused
some serious misunderstandings. Security Service (*Sicherheitsdienst*, known as *SD*) agents working abroad were to be "solely
devoted to serving the interests of the Reich." The scope of
their work was virtually unlimited, covering "every field of
public affairs other than military matters and the diplomatic
missions," unless, as the agreement noted, "some case of high
treason makes intervention a legal duty."[24] Police attachés,
nominally subordinated to diplomatic chiefs of mission, were
to be appointed by the *RSHA*, and their reports, sent from
abroad to headquarters in Berlin, were to be transported *only
when necessary* by Foreign Office couriers.

The *RSHA*, agreeing to this arrangement, had "assured
the . . . Foreign Office that the *SD* is not engaged in any activities connected with foreign policy and does not aspire to do
so; but, by means of its forces abroad, merely maintains a
secret service . . . to be used exclusively by the Foreign Minister and the Foreign Office."[25] A flood of police attachés
poured into diplomatic missions abroad.[26]

Nominally, all *RSHA* agents abroad came under supervision of these police attachés after 1941. After difficulties of
supervising the latters' activities had developed, a special
Himmler-Ribbentrop agreement of August 9, 1941, explicitly
forbade them to "intervene in the internal politics of the state
in which they operate" unless "permitted to do so by previous
agreement of the foreign minister and the *Reichsführer-SS*.[27]
Himmler agents were thenceforth obligated to keep mission

chiefs currently informed of their activities which impinged on "foreign policy." All correspondence between them and the *RSHA* in Berlin was to be sent through the mission chief, who was entitled to scrutinize it. Correspondence concerning "illegal" activities was to be transmitted in green, sealed envelopes, without inspection by the mission chief, thus to absolve him of all responsibility for their contents.[28]

But such minute "treaty" regulations did little to check the rapacious growth of Himmler's foreign activities. Efforts of Himmler's *Volksdeutsche Mittelstelle,* known as *VOMI,* to establish illegal Nazi organizations in "friendly" countries aroused censure from the foreign minister.[29] Disregarding the Foreign Office, *VOMI* intervened in the internal affairs of Rumania and Croatia in 1942. It negotiated its own agreements with Near Eastern minority groups, even promising territorial concessions in return for assistance to Germany. Without Wilhelmstrasse knowledge it arranged official *SS* trips abroad, and brought foreign dignitaries on visits to the Reich.[30] Himmler personally carried on negotiations with the Mufti of Jerusalem and undertook to ensconce this Arab leader in an "office . . . in the neighborhood or even in the building of the *SS-Hauptamt* itself," to facilitate his work of recruiting Moslem *Waffen-SS* units in Yugoslavia.[31] Himmler agents took to denouncing Ribbentrop's diplomatic representatives[32] and, on occasion, foreign diplomats in Berlin directly negotiated with *RSHA,* by-passing the Wilhelmstrasse and once more arousing bitter protests from the offended foreign minister.[33]

"My Office," Ribbentrop declared after the war, "was called the House of Difficulties."[34] His persistent skirmishes with Himmler's secret service he described as "perhaps one of the worst, one of the most unpleasant aspects" of his job. "I . . . never really had at my disposal all the extensive news which was coming from abroad."[35] Frequent decisions of the

Führer were made upon the basis of intelligence reports which he, Ribbentrop, had not seen in advance. But this was only a half truth. Even on such occasions when Kaltenbrunner or Schellenberg did divulge valuable espionage data to the foreign minister, the latter, chagrined at new evidence of his competitors' skill, was moved to lavish even greater invective upon them. One such *RSHA* feat, Operation *Cicero*, which involved capture of top-secret British documents in Ankara, was ostentatiously belittled by Ribbentrop, who used it as pretext for additional remonstrances to Kaltenbrunner against intervention in "political affairs." On the same day that Police Attaché Moyzisch was en route from Turkey to Berlin bearing his famous documents, pilfered from the British ambassador's safe, he was swept into the maelstrom of this dispute. Ribbentrop's state secretary, in conference with Kaltenbrunner, insisted on "the absolute necessity of having political information submitted to the Führer by the Reich Foreign Minister." "The Foreign Minister," Steengracht told Kaltenbrunner, "submits to the Führer in the original such *SD* reports of whose accuracy and importance he is convinced . . . Kaltenbrunner agreed to this with the remark that there were also cases in which the Führer demanded a direct and immediate report."[36]

The Himmler-Ribbentrop agreement of August, 1941, explicitly had provided for transmittal, via the Foreign Office, of intelligence reports, but on condition that they be subjected to prior Foreign Office scrutiny. In Moyzisch's case, however, Ribbentrop attempted to prevent such reports from getting into *RSHA* hands even though he had seen them in advance.[37] Moyzisch, in his Operation *Cicero*, notes that Ribbentrop summoned him to Berlin early in November, for consultation. But when his plane stopped in Sofia, a special plane commandeered by Kaltenbrunner, was at the airport; it snatched him up and took him to Berlin. He was taken immediately to Kaltenbrunner's office with his documents. The *SS* general was

outraged when he learned that Ribbentrop had been conceal-
ing Moyzisch's reports from him.[37] Moyzisch, who single-
handedly had scored one of the war's greatest espionage feats,
was given a drubbing for submitting his captured documents,
including minutes of the Teheran Conference, to his chief
through proper channels. On June 17, 1944, Ribbentrop sent
the following telegram to Papen in Ankara:

In Telegram No. 955 of 13 June you forward a political report of
Herr Moyzisch to *SS-Oberführer* Schellenberg. This action is totally
objectionable and intolerable. Herr Moyzisch must present to you all
information of a political nature which comes to his attention. You
shall decide, according to your own judgment, if such reports are
properly yours. If occasion arises, it is your job to forward such
foreign policy reports to the Foreign Office. Herr Moyzisch under no
circumstances may forward such a political report as his own, to the
Reichssicherheitshauptamt. . . . I request that you forthwith lecture
Herr Moyzisch about the intolerable nature of his action, and that he
be told strictly to conform to his duties in the future.[38]

AN UNREFORMED LUTHER

As Heinrich Himmler's star rose, so did the still errant Martin
Luther, undersecretary in the Foreign Office, gravitate toward
it, breaking away from the orbit of Ribbentrop. State papers
seldom tell much in themselves of the growing estrangement
between men of political power and their subordinates. It is
difficult for us to assess the multifarious causes of Luther's
estrangement from Foreign Minister Ribbentrop. Yet this ex-
plosive affair, coming in the winter months of 1942–1943 may
serve as a kind of minuscule historical watershed, because the
German Foreign Office was never quite the same afterward.
    Luther was an ambitious, dishonorable, dishonest man.
There is honor among thieves, and even in the hierarchy of

the Third Reich his reputation never could have been of the
highest order. True, he of all Foreign Office officials most
zealously had served Hitler's cause of exterminating the Jews,
but it was he also who had absconded with treasury funds from
his local Party chest in Zehlendorf.

This reputation for laxity in financial matters was not un-
noticed by Luther's new associates. On December 12, 1942,
Ambassador Curt Prüfer, formerly chief of the Personnel
Division, was ordered by superiors[39] to check the financial and
organizational state of the Foreign Office's intelligence bureau
(*Informationsstelle*) which Luther had established and still
controlled. The bureau, under suspicion of having squandered
official funds in fraudulent enterprises, was subjected to
Prüfer's close scrutiny during the next few months, despite
Luther's protestations, threats, and obstructions. But the ambassador's searchings, thorough as they might have been, and
although they unearthed a "most unpleasant picture of internal conditions," were not destined to be completed.[40]

It is not likely that such an investigation could have been
undertaken without the approval of Ribbentrop. Nor could it
have been the only element of friction between the two men.
The insolence visited upon other higher Foreign Office dignitaries in Berlin by the foreign minister could not have been
spared Luther. His office, the channel of those interminable
and bootless squabbles between Ribbentrop and Himmler's
agencies, would have been most unique had it not been subjected to a measure of this invective. But unlike his colleagues
from the career service, Luther was not a temperate man, and
knew how to fight back. It could easily have occurred to him
that, were Ribbentrop to be removed, few were better suited
than himself carry on the liaison diplomacy of terror which
now was so important in the Wilhelmstrasse's work.

In any event, the director of *Abteilung Deutschland* came
to be convinced of the necessity to remove his chief. His own
influence in higher circles limited, Luther resorted to con-

spiracy with those whom he knew best in Himmler's camp. Sometime in the early days of 1943, he prepared a lengthy memorandum, dwelling in detail upon the mental infirmities of his foreign minister. This done, he dispatched it to Walter Schellenberg of the *RSHA*, for presentation to Himmler as evidence of Ribbentrop's incapacity for office.[41] But Luther, in doing this, overstepped his bounds. Even to the *Reichsführer-SS* such flagrant disloyalty to a minister was a serious breach of the leadership principle. The report was brought to Ribbentrop's attention in February, 1943: reprisals were swift and terrible. Luther was hastily summoned to Ribbentrop's headquarters at the front and arrested by Himmler's police—having time only to telephone his principal colleague in Berlin: "It is all over for us; order two wreaths at Grieneisen's!" (the chief Berlin undertaker's establishment)[42]—and subsequently thrown into one of Himmler's concentration camps which he, himself, had once done so much to fill. There he languished until the last days of the war.[43]

Not content with this one measure of reprisal, the harrassed foreign minister used it as pretext for a shake-up in his entire ministry. A purge of division chiefs and their subordinates followed soon after, as his scythe swung in all directions. Luther's *Abteilung Deutschland* was dissolved, as were its appendages, the Information Division and the *Propagandaleitstelle*. Their various functions were shifted to other existing bureaus or to hastily improvised ones. Ernst von Weizsäcker, the state secretary, although in no way implicated in the plot, found himself exiled to the Vatican as ambassador; Ernst Woermann, Ribbentrop's malleable Political Division chief, met a more singular fate, being ordered to proceed via submarine on a perilous 8,000-mile journey to Malaya and thence to China as ambassador to the Japanese puppet regime in Nanking. Even Friedrich Gaus, chief of the Legal Division, was removed.[44] To fill the positions of these departed captains,

Ribbentrop now turned to his meagre stockpile of trusted but
insignificant subalterns. As Weizsäcker's successor, he selected
Baron Steengracht, the mediocre adjutant from his personal
staff—a diplomat who, by his own later admission, had never
before that time "presented a political report to him [Ribben-
trop],"[45] whom Goebbels described as "at best only a high-
grade secretary,"[46] and for whom Martin Bormann, of the
Führer's Chancellery, had so little respect that he refused to
receive the new state secretary's courtesy call.[47]

Upon the ashes of Luther's *Abteilung Deutschland* arose its
successor, *Inland,* an agency (but not a division) which inherited the task of liaison with Himmler's empire. This time
the foreign minister judiciously entrusted these activities to a
minor and less colorful official than Luther—one Horst Wagner. His work, by explicit administrative order, was directly
subordinated to the foreign minister himself. A former per-
ennial youth leader and sports instructor, Wagner had come
to Ribbentrop's attention during the Berlin Olympic Games of
1936, and had entered the Foreign Office via the usual route,
Ribbentrop's *Dienststelle.*[48]

In brief, the foreign minister had taken in his reins on the
Berlin office more tightly than before. Henceforth, he decreed
on March 25, "the direction of foreign propaganda is reserved
exclusively for the foreign minister."[49] *Inland's* work on racial
policy, Jewish and Freemason problems, and conscription of
foreign "volunteers" for Germany's armies, were "directly
subordinated" to him.[50] New encyclicals emanated from his
Büro RAM warning officials against future misbehavior: "The
Foreign Minister, as he has repeatedly asserted, expects the
greatest reserve from members of the Foreign Office, and will
punish every case of defeatist utterances, holding transgressors
strictly accountable."[51]

The Luther episode was the first open fissure to appear in
the Foreign Office's façade. The diplomats' loyalty to Ribben-

trop now had openly been questioned. If Martin Luther could not be depended upon, who could be? Certainly the foreign minister's reputation among his colleagues, never high, had reached its lowest ebb at the time of this humiliation. Part of this picture has been preserved for us by the malicious pen of Dr. Goebbels, who zealously recorded in his diary such criticisms of Ribbentrop as came to his attention. Visiting Göring's Obersalzberg retreat on March 2, a house "high up on the mountain in an almost wintry quiet," the propaganda minister had been received by the *Reichsmarschall* (dressed, as Goebbels noted, in "somewhat baroque fashion"). The two leaders had spent the day discussing the foibles of their various associates. Goebbels wrote:

Goering also doesn't think much of Ribbentrop. He referred very critically to the complete and obvious lack of an active foreign policy. He especially blames Ribbentrop for not succeeding in drawing Spain over to our side.... Ribbentrop also lacks the elegant touch in the handling of people.... Goering consistently claims that this war is Ribbentrop's war, and that he never made any earnest attempt to achieve a *modus vivendi* with England, simply because he has an inferiority complex.[52]

The Führer also, his temper strained, was giving vent to his feelings about the foreign minister. At dinner with Speer and Goebbels on March 9, he dwelt sarcastically upon the "disgraceful" behavior of Ribbentrop during the last air raid on Berlin.[53] The Führer's chancellery secretaries, Bormann, Meissner and Lammers, also reflected in their dinner table conversation the foreign minister's fall from grace. To Bormann, the man was "too rigid to be able to spin his web in this difficult war situation";[54] Meissner considered him a "frivolous fellow," "physically and mentally worn out," not likely to survive the war.[55] Even the cautious Himmler spoke of his "completely inflexible views."[56]

The comments went not too far from their mark. For the climate of national disintegration and the strains of his work had taken liberal toll of the foreign minister's faculties. It is doubtful whether Luther's libelous memorandum had unduly embellished the facts. Weakened by a severe attack of pneumonia in the summer of 1943,[57] Ribbentrop gave increasingly serious signs of personal disrepair. He was beset chronically by severe headaches, nervous tension, neuralgia, and insomnia; he resorted increasingly to sedatives.[58] To those who saw him, the foreign minister now appeared a much older man than he really was.

"Ribbentrop," wrote Hassell on April 20, 1943, "now has become completely rabid. He hates the entire old Foreign Office (in which I, too, found much to criticize, but for other reasons than Ribbentrop)." The removal of Weizsäcker, Woermann, and Gaus appeared to Hassell the conspirator as a "blow to the old officialdom."[59] The foreign minister now was making rumblings of a more ominous sort. From a confidante, Hassell heard rumors that Ribbentrop "wanted forty SS men, forty SA men, and forty Hitler Youth leaders" with whom he could replace the older members of his ministry.[60] A few months before, in the presence of a subordinate, he had shouted his deep regret "that the Foreign Office together with its entire staff had not burned down years ago."[61] Now the long-postponed conflagration appeared about to begin.

But Ribbentrop was not prepared to translate his threat into deeds. The young Himmler stalwarts failed to appear. A new regime was to begin, markedly different from the old. At a special meeting of the higher Foreign Office officials, Ribbentrop introduced his new protegé state secretary, and gave as reason for the latter's appointment that he enjoyed the foreign minister's "complete confidence." The same day, in talks with Wilhelmstrasse division chiefs, Steengracht made it clear that he "intended to carry out his new task in a fundamentally different way" from that of his predecessor, Weizsäcker. The latter, said Steengracht, had stayed in Berlin, and thus had lost touch with Ribbentrop. This had only produced conflict and misunderstandings. He, Steengracht, would behave differently. He would spend half of his time with the foreign minister, the other half on the Wilhelmstrasse. Good will and "other-directedness," apparently, would conquer all, for, as Steengracht observed to the Legal Division's new chief, the one way for the Foreign Office once more to "influence governmental policy" would be by "constantly improving personal relationships with leading personalities, especially [those in] SS and Party circles, so that one would be constantly informed about their views and intentions."[62] The new state secretary was by no means an indomitable man;[63] the unexpected honor of his new job weighed heavily upon his shoulders. He had taken it with the most serious of misgivings, and few expected him to demonstrate, in it, much independence of mind.[64]

Several other noncareer officials were appointed to Foreign Office posts at this time. Dr. Franz Alfred Six of Himmler's *RSHA* succeeded Twardowski as chief of the Cultural Division;[65] Karl Megerle, a Ribbentrop favorite and diplomatic correspondent of the *Berliner Börsenzeitung*, became the foreign minister's permanent deputy for propaganda questions.[66] Gerhard Rühle, a Party jack-of-all-trades and former deputy to Twardowski, was appointed head of the ministry's new Radio Division.[67]

Thus five of the Foreign Office's units—*Inland*, Radio, Press, Cultural Affairs, and Personnel—were in the hands of imported Ribbentrop protegés. These were now his "activist" divisions, concerned chiefly with the manipulation of opinion and the extermination and deportation of men. Subordinated *de facto* directly to the foreign minister, their tasks were to search out new means of "winning the war." Were they doing their job adequately? State Secretary Steengracht did not think so. In July, 1944, in a long memorandum to Ribbentrop, he expounded his views about the Foreign Office's future role in the war. A new "operational division" now was called for, he wrote. It would "coördinate men, ideas, and actions for the purpose of utilizing all possibilities for winning the war by [means of] a clever foreign policy."[68] Martin Luther, he wrote, had "clearly realized that this was a weak spot in our organization," but, unfortunately, *Abteilung Deutschland* had failed "because of the character of its chief" and "because the clear aim of winning the war was not emphasized."

"The present vacuum," Steengracht continued, "is dangerous." "The more tense the war situation becomes, the more marked the tendency to find some official scapegoat." His proposed new division—a frantic affair—would leave no stone unturned; it would be charged with a "fanatical" search for projects which might "save the life of even one German soldier." It would "collaborate" with German missions abroad, "or the *SS, SD*, et cetera," "even with German minorities," in efforts to find projects. It would, finally, so act as to "inspire the entire staff of the Foreign Office" and to "eliminate unreliable and weakening individuals."[69]

"Such an agency," he concluded, "must express the fanatical and dogged determination of the [Foreign] Office to make a decisive contribution to victory." Contributions, he suggested, might include "the staging of a spectacular trial of American bomber airmen [in France]," "the trial and execution of sentences to be left to the French"; employing "minority group leaders in Rumania and Hungary" to "still better use"; and inspiring local non-German populations in Europe— the excitable Italians particularly—with the horror of possible Communist lootings which inevitably would follow a German evacuation.[70]

It is not known how the foreign minister took to Steengracht's bold new program; the division never materialized, however. It did not matter; tasks which Steengracht might have assigned to it were carried out by existing agencies. *Abteilung Deutschland*'s unfinished diplomatic project of exterminating the East European Jews was carried forward vigorously by Wagner's *Inland* section.[71] In April, 1944, an anti-Jewish propaganda agency (*Antijüdische Aktionsstelle*) was set up, under Minister Rudolf Schleier, a former Nazi agent provocateur,[72] to "strengthen and intensify anti-Jewish information work abroad through the coördination of all departmental specialists concerned with anti-Jewish information, and by intensifying Foreign Office collaboration with anti-Jewish agencies outside the Foreign Office."[73] All missions abroad were instructed to appoint one of their members—if possible, the cultural attaché—as "Jewish specialist." The anti-Jewish agency's officials edited anti-Semitic newspapers, organized conferences of "Jewish specialists," and used their office as clearing house for information on Jewish personalities abroad. The Foreign Office, particularly *Inland*, continued to advise Himmler's *RSHA* on tactics governing Jewish deportations in the East.[74]

With these changes, any pretense of rationality in the Foreign Office's structure had disappeared. The center of gravity which once had been in the state secretary's office and in the "core" of traditional divisions—Political, Legal, and Economic Affairs—now was gone. Around this core had grown a vast and loose undergrowth of new divisions, agencies, and *Sonderreferate*, carrying out divers tasks, many of which could hardly have been considered to have much to do with diplomacy in its usual sense. The chain of command, emanating from the foreign minister, which until 1940 had stretched through State Secretary Weizsäcker's office and thence to the division level, now had rusted and virtually disappeared. Ribbentrop now had arrogated to himself direct control over much of the day-to-day division work; he had few illusions about the competence of his new state secretary, even denying him the power of deputizing for him if the occasion should arise.[75] Now one could, at best, speak merely of threads

of command, interweaving in all directions through a con-
fusing maze of bureaus. Top-heavy with special ministers,
ambassadors-at-large, personal *Referenten*, and liaison officers
(all of whom were directly responsible to the foreign minister), the Wilhelmstrasse in some ways was an "office" only
in a figurative sense.[76] For some older diplomats, and a few
younger ones, a focus of sentimental unity had persisted until
April, 1943, by virtue of Weizsäcker's presence—a reminder
of olden times. But now he, too, was gone; Steengracht, his
colorless successor, was hardly capable of symbolizing anything, least of all the traditions of the Foreign Office. His daily
directors' conferences became immersed in propaganda questions;[77] and while perhaps he tolerated in them more frank
criticism of Ribbentrop's policies than had his predecessor,[78] it
was a toleration arising out of his own weakness of character.

It would be difficult, however, to agree with Hassell that
Ribbentrop's personnel changes early in 1943 had been much
of a "blow" to the "old officialdom." Ribbentrop's young men
now controlled all new divisions. But the traditional three
"core" divisions continued to be the exclusive resort of the
older career diplomats. Woermann and Gaus had been removed, but their places had been taken by Andor Hencke and
Erich Albrecht, both of whom were experienced career service
officers of Weimar days. Division Chief Wiehl of the Economic Affairs Division continued in his post—an indispensable technician. The three divisions were exclusively manned
by pre-Ribbentrop officials.[79]

As this minor Foreign Office "purge" proceeded, the tide of
battle was turning decisively against the Axis powers. On
February 3, 1943, the encircled Sixth German Army of General von Paulus capitulated at Stalingrad. On May 7, German
and Italian troops surrendered in Tunis. The way now was
open for an Allied invasion of Italy, and American troops
landed in Sicily on July 10. Two months later they had pene-

trated Axis defenses in southern Italy. On September 8, Mussolini overthrown, a new Italian government under Badoglio capitulated to Allied forces.

The Thousand-Year Reich was now disintegrating and so, in microcosm, was its Foreign Office. Beginning on November 22, 1943 (during the Teheran Conference), a series of gigantic Allied night air attacks struck Berlin with unprecedented force. The first of these was aimed at the heart of the German capital; it struck the ministerial quarter in a vast arc extending from Potsdamerplatz on the south, to the Zoo and Tiergarten in the north. With strange fortune, the Führer's Chancellery on the Wilhelmstrasse escaped great damage, as did Goebbels's Ministry of Propaganda nearby, and Rosenberg's *Ostministerium*. "The devil, who seems to be ruling the world, protected them," Hassell wrote in his diary.[80]

But divine instrumentalities did not spare the Foreign Office, nor many of the embassies and legations which lay about it. Wilhelmstrasse No. 74 was demolished to its first storey; the foreign minister's own official residence, the former palace of the Reich president, likewise was burned. For many hours fire lines barricaded the street; all but high Party and ministerial officials were barred from access to the street next morning, as the fires continued to rage. More raids followed, through December.

One by one, the ancient Foreign Office buildings were ground to rubble. Deep in reinforced concrete bunkers below them, and in special quarters underneath the nearby Adlon Hotel, the top officials of Ribbentrop's ministry carried on their work. Paul Otto Schmidt, once Hitler's interpreter and now chief of Ribbentrop's *Büro RAM*, has recalled that terrible winter, when, during respites from air attack, work could be carried on above ground: "The majestic crystal chandeliers were turned into fountains when it rained or snowed; pools of water lay on the thick carpets; the cold penetrated the hastily repaired windows. We worked in our hats and coats."[81]

The evacuation of the diplomats began. In the autumn of 1943, peripheral offices of the Wilhelmstrasse, together with their files, were moved out of the capital to somewhat safer havens. After that winter, only a skeleton staff remained in Berlin. Much of the Foreign Office emigrated southeast, to Krummhübel, a Silesian mountain resort near the old Czech border. Some offices were moved as far to the southwest as Lake Constance, near the Swiss border, and Bavaria and Thuringia.[82]

But the end was not yet. Few Foreign Office officials took the course chosen by Legation Counselor Eduard von Selzam who, in his own words, "disgusted with the atmosphere of the Office," voluntarily resigned in October, 1943. He told an American official later:

> The employees of the Foreign Office were subdued by the terror of National Socialism, and only a very few had enough strength of character and were in a position to commit sabotage without endangering themselves or their families. . . . In addition to the terror, the thought that the regime and its acts would probably soon collapse through a military revolt might have been considered important by some. Finally, there might have been some of them who were capable of compromising with their conscience for opportunistic reasons; a few might have had no conscience at all.[83]

Some did have that "strength of character" of which Selzam spoke. But, as he noted, it was a very few. Since the beginning of the war, a group of younger foreign-service officials, notably Adam von Trott zu Solz, Hans Bernd von Häften, Gottfried von Nostitz, Albrecht von Kessel, Herbert Blankenhorn, and Theo Kordt, had secretly joined with the Army-dominated conspiracy against Hitler. Along with Werner von der Schulenburg, the former ambassador to Moscow, and Ulrich von Hassell, they comprised the Foreign Office's contribution to this ill-starred venture.[84]

Weizsäcker, the state secretary, was not closely associated with this conspiracy. As he later noted, somewhat pretentiously, in his memoirs, "I was not an initiate of such a group. My constant work lay in foreign policy obstruction."[85] By means of his personnel policy, however, he had afforded comfort to some of these men, transferring them to strategic posts in neutral countries after the war had broken out. Theo Kordt, the former embassy counselor in London under Dirksen, was sent to Berne as legation counselor. With him in the Swiss capital were Blankenhorn and Selzam himself. In Geneva, for the greater part of the war, were Consul General Krauel, Nostitz, and Kessel. Others were scattered through various missions in other neutral capitals. Trott (a former Rhodes scholar and member of the *Kreisauer Kreis*, an important circle of the conspirators), Hassell, and Schulenburg were the only significant Foreign Office conspirators who spent the greater part of the war, after 1941, in Germany. They alone played at all a major role in the plot. Yet through the Berne legation and through occasional trips by Gisevius and Trott to Switzerland, Western espionage circles were kept aware both of the conspiracy's existence and of its members' activities.[86]

When measured against the German army's contribution to the plot, however, that of the Foreign Office was modest indeed. After 1941, when Erich Kordt departed for Japan, no active higher Foreign Office official in Berlin had been directly involved. Hassell, of course, had been on inactive reserve and in virtual retirement since 1938. Schulenburg, outside of his chairmanship of the abortive Foreign Office Russia Committee, held no policy-making position after 1941. Trott, possibly the most active, was also the youngest, and held only minor posts in the Foreign Office (serving as specialist on American and Far Eastern affairs in the Information Division and, later, as expert on prisoner-of-war affairs).[87]

But when the conspiracy finally came to its tragic climax on July 20, 1944, immediate reprisals were visited upon the Foreign Office as a whole. Hassell, Schulenburg, Häften, and

Brücklmeier, a disenchanted Ribbentrop protegé, were arrested by the Gestapo, tortured, summarily tried, and executed. During his trial, when asked by the Nazi Judge Freisler to describe the Foreign Office's attitude toward the Nazi regime, Trott replied that it would have been an easier task to count the "reliable" than the "unreliable" elements in it; 60 per cent of the Foreign Office was unreliable.[88]

Trott exaggerated the case, but his testimony before Judge Freisler did not escape Hitler's attention. The full fury of reprisals for the July 20 plot turned primarily against the "reactionary generals"; but the diplomats, too, were not entirely to escape. The Foreign Office never had enjoyed the Führer's full confidence; now it stood charged with high treason, in the image of the handful of diplomats so summarily slain by Hitler's Peoples Court and police.

Had twelve years of Nazification failed, in this "world historical crisis," to imbue the Führer's diplomats with that passionate loyalty which had been so lacking in them before 1933? Gauleiter Bohle, at least, thought so. And in September, 1944, he dutifully undertook to inform Himmler of this. Of 690 higher officials in the foreign service, he wrote, more than 600 still stubbornly espoused creeds alien to the true Germanic faith—506 confessed to the Protestant Church, 119 to the Roman Catholic. Only 64 professod to being *gottgläubig*—to being of that atheistic cult which could admit of belief in the ancient Valhalla gods whom Wagner had resurrected and whom Himmler, in his Nordic piety, worshipped. Bohle wrote ingratiatingly:

As for the *Gottgläubig*, they are for the most part those young officials who have come from the Party or the Hitler Youth, and who have been admitted only during the last few years. The confessional connections of our diplomatic and consular officials, as I see it, have contributed ... to an inner rejection of National Socialism. It is undeniable that these religious affiliations among our diplomats contribute in considerable measure to a weakening of their ability to perform in times of crisis.[89]

If, as Trott had testified, 60 per cent of the Foreign Office personnel were "unreliable," Bohle's estimates were far higher. In the fall of 1944, all diplomats with foreign wives were ordered pensioned.[90] Still more drastic cuts followed. In December, 150 higher Foreign Office officials were ordered discharged. Lammers conveyed these unhappy tidings from the Führer to Ribbentrop. According to a memorandum Lammers prepared on December 13 for a conversation with the foreign minister, all officials with "international ties" were to be purged, as were all those related to "Jewish half-Aryans." Civil-service regulations providing for an interim period of service before pensioning were to be suspended.[91]

The implications of this purge of his Foreign Office were not lost upon Ribbentrop. As he later told an American interrogator, Hitler "now wanted the Office to be quite small, and me at the head of it only as a sort of body which was to advise him or to be ready for diplomatic missions." "That," he complained, "was the whole conception of the Führer of my Foreign Office."[92] Out of favor at Hitler's court and despised by his colleagues, the foreign minister now was witnessing the impending dissolution of his entire apparatus. In September, a subordinate, Emil von Rintelen, was commissioned to prepare a lengthy eulogistic memorandum testifying to the indispensability of the entire Foreign Office which Ribbentrop himself so detested, but whose continuation was so necessary to the conservation of his own rapidly dwindling power. In a preface to this report, Rintelen wrote:

> The Foreign Office, both in its structure and its organization, is so arranged that it stands at the Foreign Minister's disposal as a compact, unified instrument, making possible for him the fulfillment of the following duties incumbent upon him: *first*, that of keeping himself constantly informed—as swiftly as conditions permit—of all important political developments abroad, in order that he may convey to the Führer at all times a reliable picture of the diplomatic situation; *second*, that of administering an apparatus which can guarantee the speedy realization of all the Führer's political schemes and decisions.[93]

The removal of any part of this machine, Rintelen concluded, would irreparably damage the whole, and impair "the responsible conduct of Reich foreign policy."[94] From Ribbentrop's aide, these were indeed belated eulogies to the efficiency of his Foreign Office. But they had no deterrent effect upon the Führer's determination to smash the administrative apparatus which he believed had betrayed him.

There are few published materials available today from which we may piece together a coherent picture of the last days of the Nazi Foreign Office. In all likelihood such a task would not prove a rewarding one. Its buildings ravaged, its ranks depleted by war, treason, and administrative curtailments, its remaining offices scattered across the length and breadth of what remained of the Third Reich, the Wilhelmstrasse now persisted only in a figurative sense.

From known facts we may surmise certain others. As was his wont, Ribbentrop seems to have remained with Hitler's entourage through most of this last winter of discontent. The foreign minister had been with the Führer at Rastenburg in East Prussia during the attempted July 20 assassination. Observers at the Führer's quarters on that frantic day recalled Ribbentrop's humiliation in the agitated tea party which followed the attack on Hitler's life. When Göring attempted to strike him with his field marshal's baton and reportedly addressed him, with vituperation, without using the full luster of the foreign minister's name, Ribbentrop had dodged and cried, "I am *still* Foreign Minister and my name is *von* Ribbentrop!"[95] Here, on the eastern front, the "court" had remained until late autumn. Then, on November 20, he briefly had returned to Berlin, staying in the capital only until December 10. Then, Hitler for the last time had gone west, to Bad Nauheim, to direct his final gesture of military defiance— the Rundstedt Offensive—in the Ardennes. Finally, this hope exhausted, he once more returned to Berlin on January 16, 1945, where he remained until the end.[96]

In all events, Ribbentrop was at his Wilhelmstrasse post in late February, for there Count Folke Bernadotte—on an errand of mercy—had found him, in his miraculously unscathed office, in seemingly "excellent form" and "filled with the consciousness of his own importance and dignity." For an hour and seven minutes (by Bernadotte's stop watch), the foreign minister tediously and in tones "suitable only to the tribune of a packed Kroll Opera House" had extolled the virtues of National Socialism, and dwelt upon the common threat of Bolshevism and upon his own willingness to see it prevail rather than to tolerate Germany's surrender.[97]

Few discerning foreign statesmen ever had been greatly impressed by Ribbentrop's stature. But now, divested of his conquests, the German foreign minister seemed rather trivial. "Sitting with him in his room in the Auswärtiges Amt and listening to his long-winded speech, which reminded me of a somewhat worn gramophone record," wrote the Count, "I reflected that here was a man of very small mental stature and, moreover, rather ridiculous."[98]

Little remained behind the outer pretense of conceit and arrogance observed by Bernadotte. The captains and kings of Hitler's tributary states had departed, and Ribbentrop's willingness to squander such time and oratory upon this (then) obscure Swedish Red Cross official was in itself a measure of his downfall. The foreign minister now took no part in those strange palace intrigues with which Hitler's chief colleagues had diverted themselves in the last days; and with good reason, for, as Trevor-Roper has written, "Ribbentrop had now no party, no supporters, with whom to combine in the incalculable politics of the court. All the others, bitter rivals in all else, were agreed upon one thing: Ribbentrop must go."[99] Only Hitler, still loyal to his "second Bismarck," persisted in avowing his indispensability.

Yet Ribbentrop did go. As Russian forces neared the city, he ordered his *Büro RAM* chief, Paul Otto Schmidt, to evacuate the *Büro* from Berlin. On April 14, Schmidt departed southward for Garmisch, the new "seat of government"; Ribbentrop himself disappeared westward, into oblivion, declining the opportunity to join the Führer's *Götterdämmerung* in the Chancellery ruins.[100] Hitler, in his last hours, did not overlook this act of desertion. Naming Dönitz his own successor, he appointed Schwerin von Krosigk foreign minister.

On June 16, Ribbentrop was found living with a divorcee in a Hamburg flat, and was arrested by British soldiers.[101] But by then, both his job and the Third Reich no longer existed. The task of managing German foreign policy had devolved upon other—non-Reich—agencies. The German Foreign Office had ceased to exist.

VII

THE
VANISHING
DIPLOMATIST

Throughout the memoirs of German Foreign Office officials there runs a sense of frustration, of outraged sensibilities, of opportunities missed and but few occasions of petty triumphs. The literary expression of such sentiments, after the deed, is not uncommonly the consolation of embittered ex-statesmen, and is, of course, not unique to German diplomats alone. They, like other men, are mortal and cannot be denied their defense before the bar of history.

One might be inclined, however, to ponder the importance of these reminiscences, published in such great numbers after World War II. Admittedly, they are grist for the historian's mill and as such have some utility. But does their very volume accord with the importance of their authors? In a way, it does. As voices of "loyal" technicians, stilled throughout the long period of their service to the Nazi state and become vocal in the hour of defeat, what they have to say bears powerful testimony to the role of the technician in the modern police state. Yet, also, these are testimonials of failure—failure to perceive, failure to act in time, and, above all, failure of moral courage. Measured by any criterion save that of sheer survival, the records of these men do not appear to be ones upon which history will accord great attention, much less praise. In all likelihood it will not be said of them, as once was said of the Byzantine general, Belisarius, by the historian Gibbon, that their "imperfections flowed from the contagion of the times," but their "virtues" were their own. For the "contagion" of the Hitlerian era was, in no little part, of their own making, and their "virtues" had been placed at its disposal.

This is the record of German professional diplomacy in the Nazi interlude of our time, and it is not the record of much enduring substance. But our picture would not be complete were we to view it only in an isolated fashion. For, the reader might inquire, was the demise of German professional diplomacy really unique? Was the record of the German Foreign Office without parallel in other countries? Was it merely a phenomenon which owed its "causes" to phenomena unique to the Nazi state and to German society, or was it also one aspect of a larger picture? In short, did the period of European history with which we deal show evidences elsewhere of the demise of professional diplomacy?

All these questions must be faced. There have been writers sensitive to the travails of the European diplomatic profession, observant since the end of World War I of the diminishing role of the European diplomat both in the shaping of foreign policy and in its execution. They have drawn attention to the fatal loss of prestige of the career diplomats in their own countries; to the tendency of political chiefs to ignore the diplomats' words of advice and warning; and to the exclusion of their "technical" advice from the great decisions of state.

Reading through their works, one would conclude that, in certain senses, the professional diplomat (or, as Harold Nicolson would have us say, "diplomatist"), was a belated casualty of World War I, of a technological revolution which rendered him in many respects obsolete, and of a social and political upheaval which left him all too frequently politically isolated from decisively important centers of political power in his own homeland.

"Who, then, makes war?" rhetorically inquired the London *Times* on November 23, 1912, two years before the outbreak of World War I. The editorialist continued:

> The answer is to be found in the Chancelleries of Europe, among the men who have too long played with human lives as pawns in the game of chess, who have become so enmeshed in formulas and the jargon of diplomacy that they have ceased to be conscious of the poignant realities with which they trifle. And thus war will continue to be made until the great masses who are the sport of professional schemers say the word which shall bring, not eternal peace, for that is impossible, but a determination that war shall be fought only in a just and righteous cause.[2]

To many who, after the November, 1918, armistice, hastily had sought an explanation of the causes of World War I, not by means of laborious research into the nature of European imperialism but by a simpler means, the war had been the fruit of "secret diplomacy," of the arid schemings of closeted statesmen and their professional advisers. "Secret diplomacy" had been the preserve of the prewar diplomat, and this method of international intercourse would, or should, be done away with. Harold Nicolson (who himself wisely refrained from passing too summary justice upon the diplomats) observed, in 1934, that "No system should ever again be tolerated which can commit men and women, without their knowledge and consent, to obligations which will entail upon them either a breach of national good faith or the sacrifice of their property and lives."[3] Woodrow Wilson had demanded, as a price of peace, that the principle of "open covenants, openly arrived at" should be accepted as the foundation stone for postwar diplomacy. And to the degree that this demand was espoused by influential postwar European public opinion, it reflected widespread distrust of traditional diplomacy, and a desire for reforming not only the European diplomatic services but the entire machinery of national foreign-policy formation. Because of its traditional working methods (which only rarely had permitted immediate and candid publicity), it was urged that European diplomacy had to be reformed. It should become the vehicle of "democratic" aspirations, and it should be manned by personnel whose devotion to democratic principles was unquestioned. It could not longer persist, unaltered, into the new era of the "world made safe for democracy."

In all major Western democratic powers, such measures of reform were undertaken in varying degrees. We have noted, however, in Chapter I, the failure of the Weimar Republic to "socially democratize" its foreign service. In Britain, also, postwar civil-service reforms did not measurably alter the social and educational backgrounds of British diplomats of the 'twenties from what they had been in prewar days.[4] In France, similarly, the postwar foreign service of the Third Republic continued to recruit its officials through politically reactionary educational training centers of French society.[5] In the United States, while the Rogers Act (like similar European legislation) unified the diplomatic and consular services and strengthened the "merit system" of selecting career diplomats, this reform did not alter the fact that the American foreign service, until the great expansion occasioned by World War II and its aftermath, selected its officials preponderantly from "upper income groups" of American society. Indeed, in 1942, the majority of the leading State Department officials were launched into their professional careers from only six out of a possible 700 institutions of higher learning in the

United States: Harvard, Georgetown, Yale, Princeton, Annapolis, and West Point.[6] The curious resilience of the diplomatic guild to incursions by "outsiders" was observable in all Western countries where such reforms were attempted. As Robert Bendiner wrote, of the United States Department of State in 1942: "To some extent the traditions of an institution like the Department of State mould the minds of its personnel regardless of their original predilections, but to a far greater extent the institution tends to attract—and select—men who, to begin with, might be expected to respond to those traditions."[7]

The prewar institutions of European diplomacy survived the ravages of World War I and the reforms of the peace which followed it. But the new diplomatic world of the interwar period proved vastly different from that of prewar conditions in the once secluded and insulated chancelleries, legations, and embassies. "Open diplomacy" on the rostrum of the League of Nations palace in Geneva, "diplomacy by conference," "multilateral diplomacy," the open press conference, and the radio address, were devices and methods new and far less familiar to the professional diplomats than the conventional practices in which they had been trained—the private and discreet conversation in the chancellery or foreign office; the cabled instructions, the carefully composed "situation report," the carefully worded verbal note, and the direct chain of command. Then, too, the metronomic tempo of diplomacy had been quickened by radio and airplane, those novel frontier- and ocean-spanning devices which the late war had done so much to improve. A foreign minister now could be in London at noon and in Rome by 4 P.M. The possibility of personal contacts between chiefs of state multiplied. The volume of intergovernmental business greatly increased as well. Gone were the days when it could have been said of British "diplomatists," for example, that they were "like the fountains of Trafalgar Square—they played from 10 to 4, with an interval for lunch."[8] The practices of diplomacy, too, had quickly become far more complicated than they had been in 1914. As Anthony Eden remarked, in 1943, of British diplomacy:

> The conditions which the Diplomatic Service originally grew up to meet no longer exist unchanged in modern international affairs. Economics and finance have become inextricably interwoven with politics; an understanding of social problems and labour movements is indispensable in forming a properly balanced judgment of world events. The modern diplomat should have a more intimate understanding of these special problems, and greater opportunities to study them than he has usually possessed in the past.[9]

The trouble was, however, that many professional diplomats of the 'twenties knew little of such "special problems." And since they did not, nondiplomatic "experts" made their appearances at international conferences and in diplomatic missions to fill this gap of understanding.[10] Commercial, agricultural, cultural, and labor attachés, drawn chiefly from internal ministries, were appointed to missions abroad to do what the diplomats were either untrained or unqualified to do.

But along with these developments, a new kind of diplomat—like the expert not drawn from the ranks of the older "professionals"—began to make his appearance on the international stage. He was, at least among the professional diplomats, known as the "politician-diplomat," or, under other circumstances, as the "amateur" diplomat. His habit, decorum, accoutrements, and behavior set him apart from the career diplomat. Instead of the traditional cutaway, the striped pants, and elaborately beribboned uniform, the garb of these new diplomats, in the words of Gordon Craig, consisted of "scots brogues, shaggy coiffures, white linen neckties, underslung pipes and various kinds of unbrellas."[11] These were, of course, such men as Lloyd George, Aristide Briand, Stanley

Baldwin, and Gustav Stresemann, cabinet ministers, party officials, frequently with no previous experience with the arts of diplomacy—unapprenticed "newcomers" to this ancient craft. The "new diplomacy" which they carried out at various places—Geneva, Lausanne, Thoiry, the banks of the Washington Potomac, in modern conference chambers, and on park benches—on many occasions proved disturbing and unwelcome to the career diplomats. In the latters' estimation, these men were still but politicians turned diplomat. Admittedly, their public offices accorded them the constitutional right and the power to speak authoritatively for their governments; the diplomats, after all, had never been but the servants of these men. But their working methods were of a far different order. In the eyes of the practiced professionals, who took pride in their gifts as negotiators, the "politicians" appeared far less patient than were their technical subordinates with the slow, meticulous, and elaborate procedures of diplomatic negotiations and more inclined to pluck the fruits of negotiation while still unripe. More sensitive to the applause of their domestic constituencies and legislators, the politicians appeared more demanding of immediate diplomatic triumphs than of the need for substantial and enduring results. Not infrequently they proved suspicious and impatient with their professional advisers. Not infrequently, also, this antipathy to "professional advice" could be attributed to a not easily bridged gap between them and what was a professional aristocracy. In part, this gap was a psychological one, arising from different habits of mind. "There is something restricted and restricting," wrote Lord Vansittart, "about an expert, which makes him look narrow to the wide-eyed; and . . . he is sometimes compelled, if he has any guts, to adopt the governess touch, which is unfair to him."[12] But there frequently were social considerations, too. The sympathetic understanding between minister and professional diplomatic adviser, built upon similar social origins, educational background, and political views, was breaking down. Harold Nicolson wrote of Lord Curzon that he was the "last of that unbroken line of Foreign Secretaries . . . born with the privileges of a territorial aristocracy and nurtured on the traditions of a governing class." These statesmen, Nicolson believed, had been "calm, confident and unassuming men. They had always known each other; they had always understood each other; they had always, from generation to generation, handed down the same standards of personal conduct and of public duty."[13] But, as Nicolson sadly demonstrated, no such sentimental ties bound Lloyd George, the Celtic mystic, to the postgraduates of the playing grounds of Eton. Nor, particularly, to the professional diplomats with whom he worked as prime minister. "Diplomats," he once observed, "were invented simply to waste time."[14] Like so many statesmen who followed him, Lloyd George did not always trouble himself with the routines of the Foreign Office, nor its advice. It could not critically be said of him, as once was said of Sir Edward Grey, that his diplomatic deficiency lay in a congenital unwillingness to go abroad, but rather that he went abroad too much, and that what he did there was done quite frequently without the advice, consent, or knowledge of his professional advisers at the time.[15] "It was not only a privacy of method," Curzon's biographer observed of Lloyd George, "it was a privacy of aim."[16]

Previous chapters have described the suspicion and mistrust which such Nazi leaders as Hitler and Ribbentrop visited upon their professional advisers. Yet democratic statesmen, too, did not credit their subordinates with the respect and attention of their predecessors. Chamberlain, like Lloyd George, surrounded himself, when prime minister, with powerful advisers from outside the Foreign Office in the critical days of 1937–1938. Lord Vansittart recently confessed that as "Chief Diplomatic Adviser [at that time] I saw Neville Chamberlain only thrice in three years, and never once alone."[17] French diplomats, too, had their troubles with their politicians. What, exactly, had the French Foreign Minister Briand promised to Stresemann at Thoiry in 1926? No French diplomat at that time could have said, for none was present, and Briand told none of them the whole story later—not even the permanent secretary of the Quai d'Orsay. Likewise, what did Laval promise Mussolini in January, 1935? The same held true.[18] Sumner Welles, former American undersecretary of state, wrote, of President Roosevelt, that one of his more serious "idiosyncracies" was a "deep-rooted prejudice against members of the American Foreign Service and against the permanent officials of the Department of State."[19] All too frequently did the president fail to invite to White House foreign-policy conferences any of the State Department's regional specialists. In the Cairo conference with Chiang Kai-shek in 1943, no American Far Eastern specialist sat beside, or behind, the president. It is also well to recall the famous account of James Byrnes of the president's trip on a warship to the Yalta conference early in 1945: "Not until the day before we landed at Malta did I learn that we had on board a very complete file of studies and recommendations prepared by the Department of State."[20] The president's suspicion of the State Department sprang from his own judgment of its questionable loyalty to him.[21] Another of his peculiarities, wrote Welles, was his "almost invariable unwillingness to dictate any memoranda of his conversations with foreign statesmen or . . . diplomatic representatives in Washington as a record to inform and guide those who were running the Department of State." The examples of these "idiosyncracies" among statesmen of the Western democracies are too abundant to be dismissed as merely a peculiar characteristic of totalitarian diplomacy under Hitler.

The truth of the matter was, of course, that the "diplomatist," in the traditional sense of the word, was obsolescent, technologically and politically superseded. Thanks to "modern devices" many of his traditional functions could be performed, if not with comparable effectiveness, by less experienced substitutes. Diplomatic "situation reports," once so meticulously composed by ambassadors, embassy counselors, and secretaries, now had to compete against the telephone conversation and the curt cabled telegram, for the attention of distracted and harrassed superiors at home; in many instances they proved far too rich a literary fare for foreign secretaries to digest.

"Modern" means of speedy transportation and communication coupled with the development and proliferation of international organizations, made possible—and even necessary— the direct, routine assembling of foreign ministers and other government chiefs.[22] Meetings of the League Council and Assembly at Geneva made possible the most intimate working contacts among such men, and developed readily among them the habit of personal conversations. The sphere of diplomatic negotiations, once normally that of the diplomat, was taken over by his political superior. These same technical, administrative developments also made it possible for roving personal emissaries—the Harry Hopkinses, Norman Davises, and Ribbentrops—to gain speedy and frequent access to the "king's ear" at foreign capitals, and frequently to speak with far greater and more informed authority for their chiefs than could the regularly accredited diplomatic representatives. Then there were the "ministerial traveling circuses" (as Sir Victor Wellesley called them)—packaged groups of experts selected from internal ministries and from private life to represent their countries at international conferences. The ambassador and his staff retained their ceremonial and representational functions unimpaired, and, not infrequently, continued to exercise a powerful role in policy making. But no longer could they be assured that they would be, or would remain, the sole, primary accredited negotiators of their governments at their posts. Frequently the ambassador could be retained at his post long after his diplomatic usefulness had completely disappeared. Thus did Joseph Kennedy, the Irish Bostonian isolationist at the Court of St. James, remain in London in 1940, long after he had overtly broken with the views of the Roosevelt administration over the issue of U.S. intervention and all-out aid to Britain. The president of the United States by then had other adequate and more direct means of access to the British government and its prime minister, and could afford to put up with him.[23]

Moreover, the diplomat was no longer held in high esteem in his own country. The advent of "democratic control of foreign policy" had exposed the diplomatic profession to much wider public scrutiny than had been the case before World War I; and the diplomat, often enough, did not live up to the "popular" impression of what he should be, how he should act, and what he should think. "What really distinguishes the diplomatist from the common herd," the French diplomat Jules Cambon wrote in 1926, "is his apparent indifference to its emotions." For its part, the "public" responded with its own measure of contempt for the diplomat. Again, in Cambon's words, the "public in general looks upon diplomacy as mere intrigue, and fancy that, apart from the time when he is thus engaged, an ambassador is a mere idler whose life is one long round of junketings and feastings."[24]

This professional self-analysis was carried still further. Was the diplomat's temperament really suited to the new era of international politics which required of public officials the demonstration of powerful convictions and public decisiveness? "His whole training," Nicolson wrote, "has tended to convince him that good diplomacy is a slow and cautious business, and he looks with exaggerated suspicion upon all dynamic innovations." Reality, for him, had become relative, not absolute. "He believes," Nicolson continued, "in gradations, in gray zones; he is always impatient of those who think enthusiastically in terms of black and white. Lethargy of

judgment descends upon him, a slightly contemptuous dis-
belief in all forms of human certainty."[25]

While this generalization at best only approximated reality,
it could at least have been argued that the public ideological
struggles of the interwar period placed the career diplomat—
the "peacemaker"—in a troublesome political position. "The
past," Lord Vansittart nostalgically wrote, "put a premium
on courtesy. Wherever they went—mainly without let or hin-
drance—sane diplomatists tried to absorb as much as possible
for their real purpose—peace, which they much enjoyed."[26]
Diplomacy "was one of the many veils in which we sought to
soften the outlines of the real harshness of human nature and
existence."[27] But, in an age of hostile nationalist and totalitarian doctrines, that diplomat who neglected overtly to
espouse the prevailing ideological principles of his government—whether he did so out of contrary conviction or from
diplomatic tact—was frequently, because of this, the more
vulnerable to public attacks upon his character and his loyalty,
at home. The problem was the more serious, since, as has been
noted, European professional diplomats did not always share
prevailing public enthusiasm for the regime which they served.
Many of them, recruited from an aristocratic leisure class, and
moving in professional and social circles which placed a
premium on congeniality, too frequently found themselves
isolated from extremely important, articulate, and powerful
social and political forces. To many of them, doubtless, moral
"relativism" came to appear as an inevitable occupational
hazard. And for this they were attacked. Thus during World
War II one critic of the American State Department wrote of
American diplomacy, that it was a "code of elegant cynicism,
of tactical shrewdness that has small relevance beyond the
horizons of the chess board."[28]

By 1950, so great had public distrust of professional diplomacy become in the United States, that one prominent
American foreign-service officer was led to remark, when urg-

ing a "more effective use" of the principle of professionalism
in the conduct of foreign policy:

I am quite prepared to recognize that this runs counter to strong
prejudices and preconceptions in sections of our public mind, particularly in Congress and the press, and that for this reason we are
probably condemned to continue relying almost exclusively on what
might be called "diplomacy by dilletantism."[29]

THE CONTROL OF TOTALITARIAN DIPLOMACY

These problems having been shared by the Western diplomatic
profession as a whole, how far may we go in arguing that the
conditions which prevailed in the German Foreign Office were
unique, and, in fact, explainable chiefly in terms of the Nazi
state and German society, rather than in the diplomatic profession as a whole?

The decline of the German diplomatic service as a self-
sufficient bureaucracy doubtless was due in some measure to
these general professional considerations. But while similari-
ties existed between the domestic position of the German diplomat and his Western "colleagues," it would be inaccurate
and wholly misleading to emphasize them. It is the purpose of
these concluding passages to demonstrate that the conditions
we have observed in the Nazi Foreign Office were inherent in
the Nazi state itself—the disintegration of traditional administrative procedure, the intense jurisdictional wrangles, the
friction between the "new" and the "old" (pre-Hitler) officialdom, the struggle for bureaucratic self-preservation, and the
tenor of the system itself. The notion, shared by many old
career officials—that a self-sufficient professional diplomacy
could remain as a kind of "state within a state," managing
and manipulating its own machinery to its own purposes—

proved wholly incompatible with the totalitarian regime in which it existed.

The power of "experts" within the tightly knit bureaucracy of the autocratic state to influence and shape the policies of their superiors according to their own judgments did *not* prove true in Nazi Germany.

Autonomous bureaucratic power in a totalitarian state diminishes in direct ratio to the degree to which state leadership chooses to rely upon a variety of sources for advice, information, and active assistance in shaping policy. The diplomats of Nazi Germany failed to maintain a monopoly of the traditional instrumentalities of diplomacy. Their advice and reports were, after 1938, of minor importance in shaping high-level policy, but not merely because of the reasons mentioned above which affected Western diplomacy. Both Franz Neumann's *Behemoth* and Hannah Arendt's *Origins of Totalitarianism* draw attention to the peculiar "shapelessness" of the totalitarian government in the Third Reich. Miss Arendt writes:

All levels of the administrative machine in the Third Reich were subject to a curious duplication of offices. With fantastic thoroughness the Nazis made sure that every function of the state administration would be duplicated by some party organ.... None of the organs of power was ever deprived of its right to pretend that it embodied the will of the Leader. But not only was the will of the Leader so unstable that compared with it the whims of Oriental despots are a shining example of steadfastness; the constant and ever-changing division between real power, secret authority, and ostensible open representation made the actual seat of power a mystery by definition, and this to such an extent that the members of the ruling clique themselves could never be absolutely sure of their own position in the secret power hierarchy.[30]

In the German Foreign Office, as no doubt elsewhere, National Socialism did not destroy the academic career bureaucracy inherited from the Weimar Republic. This was unnecessary. Here, as in other sections of the German civil service, no resistance was made to the Nazi claim to power. By refraining from any drastic measures against the officialdom, by the gradual, piecemeal alteration of civil-service laws in 1933–1937, by the use of judicious pressure on civil servants to join the Party, by the infiltration of reliable Party members into important state administrative posts, by the preferment of Party members in civil-service advancement, and by the occasional elimination of "unreliable elements," the Nazis transformed the German Foreign Office into a pliable instrument of their policies.

After the enactment of the civil-service law of 1937, career diplomats could no longer claim to be nonpolitical, "neutral" servants of the state. Weizsäcker's protestations at Nürnberg in 1948 that "as a civil servant, one does not serve a constitution, but the Fatherland. One serves whichever government and constitution is given the country by the people," was most certainly the expression of a common traditional attitude in the German civil service. In the light of Nazi legal theory, however, it was preposterous.

By 1940 a great majority of higher Foreign Office officials were Party members. As was shown in Chapter III, all but a handful of these had been in the Foreign Office *before* they joined the Party. Thus, in quantitative terms, the "heathen" were not exterminated, they were converted. The process of Nazification was gradual and piecemeal, but, in the long run, thorough. We should do well to remember, also, that individual decision played a great part in it. Few were rejected for membership by the Party when they applied; and, similarly, few never applied for membership.

Certain factors spared the German Foreign Office from greater intrusions by Party favorites and fanatics, and caused it to remain, throughout the course of the Third Reich, an aristocratic anomaly in this *petit-bourgeois* state. First, of course, before the war, Hitler realized the value of retaining this respectable diplomatic shock absorber to cushion the outside world from the grim realities of Nazi power and purpose. Unquestionably, pressure from Party sources to acquire diplomatic posts as spoils of office was great. Yet Hitler retained Neurath as foreign minister until 1938; indeed, the entire group of German mission chiefs abroad in 1938 came from the career service. Even after Ribbentrop took over the Foreign Office in 1938, few important diplomatic plums went to deserving Party functionaries. Nor was this seemingly moderate policy a demonstrable liability to Hitler in achieving his ends. Beyond the minor intrigues of a few permanent career officials like Erich and Theo Kordt and, after 1939, of the handful of Foreign Office conspirators who actively worked with the German underground, there is no evidence that the permanent bureaucracy at any time undertook to sabotage Hitler's foreign policies. "My permanent task," wrote Weizsäcker after the war, "lay in the sphere of foreign policy obstruction." For Weizsäcker, this was not true after 1939. But even if it had been true, how significant would such opposition and obstruction have been? Hitler, in 1935, provided a clue to the answer. "Problems," he said, "which the formal bureaucracy proves unfit to solve, the German nation will assign to its *living* organization in order to fulfill the necessities of its life." Thus, in jobs where a Weizsäcker would not suffice, a Martin Luther was available; for tasks which the Foreign Office as a whole was "unfit to solve," there were available that willing plethora of Party agencies and personalities. The vast undergrowth—special agencies and *Dienststellen,* ambassadors at large, adjutants, and other hangers-on— which burgeoned about the Foreign Office was not merely explainable as a consequence of the expanded scope of "diplomacy" in the Third Reich. It was not explainable merely as the result of pressure upon the Party, upon Hitler or Ribbentrop to provide official haven for deserving Nazi job seekers. Beyond these partial explanations, it was also insurance that the implementation of the Nazi "diplomacy of terror" would be a privilege avidly sought by many ambitious men, and that this diplomacy would be handled by competent, if not always enthusiastic, men. The "traditional" Political Division of the Foreign Office, as we have seen, remained throughout the war in the hands of "moderate" men, few of them members of the Party. They were not shoved aside, for, in the sphere of their activity, "problems" still remained which the "formal" bureaucracy would "solve." A Weizsäcker or a Woermann, high in the official bureaucracy, brushing aside the inquiries, expostulations, or protests of foreign representatives, modulating the brutal language of their superiors to sensitive foreign representatives[31]—these were capable and circumspect men, and the tasks which they performed could have been but poorly done by boors like Martin Luther.

The utility of retaining such "moderates" as Weizsäcker, for these reasons, certainly diminished as the war spread, and as the character of National Socialism stood more fully revealed to the outside world. We know that, on various occasions after taking office, Ribbentrop expressed a wish to purge his foreign service thoroughly of the "old career diplomats." With this in mind, for example, he established his Foreign Office Training School for new diplomats. Yet the Ribbentrop purge never came about, and when Hitler himself undertook one of his own late in 1944, his action profoundly shocked and alarmed his foreign minister. In view of Ribbentrop's oft-repeated statements of intent, and—if we may take the word of his closest advisers—the passionate outbursts of fury and invective which he continuously vented upon his career subordinates, his actions seem paradoxical. Time and again, as with Weizsäcker in 1938, with Erich Kordt in 1940, with Rintelen in 1943, Ribbentrop let it be known that the days of the old, permanent officialdom were numbered. Yet these threats came to nought. Why?

That Ribbentrop was master in his own house was a principle upon which he continuously and belligerently dwelt. But the principle was never realized in practice. The house of German foreign policy had many mansions, and the foreign minister never managed successfully to obtain title to all of them. The proliferation of agencies—Rosenberg's *Aussenpolitisches Amt der NSDAP*; Bohle's *Auslandsorganisation*; Himmler's *Volksdeutsche Mittelstelle* and his *Reichssicherheitshauptamt* foreign intelligence units; Goebbels's *Propagandaministerium*—made it far from possible for Ribbentrop's monopoly of the administration of Nazi foreign policy to be achieved. A "Hoover Commission," pondering over these interweaving threads and chains of command, the overlapping jurisdictional spheres, the contradictory purposes all too frequently pursued by these many agencies, might well have diagnosed the system as hopelessly inefficient and even unworkable.

Ribbentrop's own "case history" could be used to document such a verdict. In the confusion, in the ceaseless intrigues and cabals of Hitler's court, the foreign minister's personal position never was secure. Without repute in Party circles, he was totally dependent upon the Führer's own continued grace. This may account in great part for the servility of the foreign minister's views, his constant deference to Hitler's judgment. These qualities were far more pronounced in him than in his colleagues.

For our purposes, this observation is of crucial importance. It is here submitted that Ribbentrop's interpretation of his role as foreign minister was largely responsible for the survival of the Foreign Office bureaucracy. Precisely because Ribbentrop's own position in the Nazi state was weak, insecure, and almost exclusively dependent upon the whims of Hitler, the Nazi foreign minister came to be, for the Foreign Office, a beneficient (albeit not benevolent) *deus ex machina*. Neither could long have existed without the other. In this manner, then, an insolvent and detested chief was bound to his contemptuous but subordinate officialdom in a tenuous but persistent coali-

tion of fear. That mutual resentment need not always lead to
open hostility, but may under certain circumstances generate
close collaboration, is a psychological phenomenon of profound importance within a modern police state.

Ribbentrop's paranoical battle to broaden (or at least to
defend) the jurisdictional sphere of the Foreign Office assured the latter of its institutional survival in a sea of competitors. Ribbentrop's fears of inroads by powerful Party
competitors into his bureaucracy was understandably shared
by his subordinates. His ruthless extirpation of intruders was
of recognized benefit to those bureaucrats who might have
resented him, but who were fully aware of the possible consequences of his replacement by an equally hated, but more
powerful figure.

Can we accurately, however, characterize as "inefficient"
Ribbentrop's administration of the Wilhelmstrasse? Certainly
from 1940 on we see a panorama of progressive administrative
deterioration. The "rational" structure of the Foreign Office
gradually collapsed; the metamorphosis was apparent on all
sides: the widening gulf between Ribbentrop and his personal
staff on the one hand, and the administrative central office in
Berlin on the other; the debasement of the state-secretary post
within the headquarters, which once had been the focal point
of the office's diplomatic work; the continuous interference of
Ribbentrop and his staff in the minutiae of administrative
work, and the direct subordination of the *Deutschland,* Protocol, Information, Press, and Radio divisions to the foreign
minister rather than to the state secretary; the increasing use
made of ambassadors at large—such roving ambassadors of
ill-will as Wilhelm Keppler, Rudolf Rahn, Edmund Veesenmayer, and others.

Yet how far may we take the word of those most thoroughly
engulfed in the labyrinth of Nazi Germany's foreign policy,
that this chaos was "inefficient"? Nothing undertaken in Nazi
Germany during the war apparently was less "useful" than

the extermination of the Jews; a large part was played in this program by the German Foreign Office, and despite the remarkable and even grotesque jurisdictional squabbles which arose in its diplomatic efforts to deport the Jews of Eastern Europe, the job was done, with vigor and ruthlessness. What deficiencies existed in administrative organization were amply compensated for by the intense pressure and incentive of the whole system itself.

What of the diplomats themselves? We have seen that Nazi totalitarianism demolished the philosophical bases of the authoritarian German civil service, and at the same time destroyed the reality of rational bureaucratic power. Yet neither of these facts seems to have been fully comprehended by leading officials of the Nazi foreign service. This may be attributed in no little part to the persistence of their formal institutional power and prerogatives long after the substance of their power had vanished. The administrative irrationality of the system was apparent to the perceptive eyes of men such as State Secretary Weizsäcker, and yet they seem not to have perceived its most crucial significance; for it was precisely this irrationality—the miltifarious proliferation of administrative machineries, the dual Party–State relationship, the quality of "charismatic" leadership exercised within their province—which served to shatter the institutional fabric of traditional state machinery and to increase the manipulative powers of the Nazi leadership.[32] We have observed that many of them, including Weizsäcker, argued that their continued presence in the Foreign Office was prompted by a fancied aim to "obstruct" or to mitigate the excesses of Hitlerian policy. And yet, as was inevitable, continued presence in office led them, step by step, to espouse, defend, and execute ever greater "lesser evils" in order that they might counter still grosser ones proposed elsewhere. The bureaucratic instinct to survive proved far more potent than the bureaucratic impulse to shape policy according to its own desires. The diplomats of whom we

have spoken remained in office long after the original rationalization for remaining had been demonstrated false. New considerations became more important than those of shaping
policy. With what vigor, for instance, Weizsäcker joined with
his foreign minister to fend off external encroachments upon
the Foreign Office: "If only he had been normal," Weizsäcker
wrote later of his chief, "if only he had proved successful in
his jurisdictional battles, the Foreign Office might once more
have been usefully meshed into the machinery of the State."
The remarks reveal his lack of comprehension of the system
in which he was involved. Not only, as the state secretary came
to know, was his foreign minister *not* "normal" (for who, in
that system, was?); but also, Ribbentrop could never have
been "successful" in his "jurisdictional battles"—for such
success would have contradicted the very nature of that totalitarian regime, the vitality of which sprang from its very
amorphousness, and from that ruthless interbureaucratic struggle to espouse Hitler's most radical policies merely to have the
power to carry them out. These frenzied struggles, these constant insecurities and torrents of abuse and censure, took their
toll of human stamina and spirit from men poorly endowed
with qualities of endurance and moral courage. War and
totalitarianism can flourish despite the waste of such resources,
and Nazi diplomacy was the diplomacy of war and totalitarianism.

The state secretary, however, erred in yet another sense.
For the Foreign Office, as its survivors could and did testify,
was "enmeshed" in the state machinery, even though not always in those fateful meetings at Godesberg, Berchtesgaden,
Hitler's *Wolfsschanze*, Schloss Fuschl, or Schloss Klessheim
which the interpreter Paul Otto Schmidt so elaborately and
nostalgically has described. For the most part, the diplomats
of Weizsäcker's stature remained at their desks in Berlin,
"enmeshed," not in the great decisions of state, but in that
gray area of policy work, so indispensable to the functioning

of the state, which lies between the level of high policy and that of the base, routine implementation of rigid directives.

Surely this was not congenial to them. After 1940, certainly their work might easily have been done by others, and it became less pleasant. Passively to await, among friends, the painful issue out of their discomfiture was not heroic. But these were neither heroic nor passionate men. There they remained; the price of their survival was impotence and compliance. Few men are given to heroism, to symbolic gestures of defiance, or to equally perilous courses of bureaucratic sabotage. In an atomized society pervaded by fear, the attention of men seems to focus upon concerns of more private importance—the protection of family, the advancement of career, the avoidance of personal humiliation and public ostracism, and, above all, the preservation of personal identity. If we resort to the yardstick of personal moral responsibility when assessing the tractable and compliant public servant of totalitarianism, we would do well not to overestimate the measure of resolution and the breadth of individual influence possessed by average men in a system of irresponsible power. If we would take it upon ourselves to urge that they might have behaved more nobly, we would do well to recognize that the phenomenon of totalitarianism is not unique to Germany; that similar moral choices confront other men of political responsibility in other circumstances; and that the problem of moral choice under political duress is one which comes to many men—including contemporary Americans—but is avoided by most.

NOTES

KEY TO ABBREVIATIONS OF DOCUMENTARY SOURCES

Documents on German Foreign Policy, 1918–1945	DGFP
Documents on British Foreign Policy, 1919–1939	DBFP
International Military Tribunal Proceedings	IMTP
Nazi Conspiracy and Aggression	NCA
Reichsgesetzblatt	RGB
Verhandlungen der deutschen Nationalversammlung	VDN
Verhandlungen des Reichstags	VDR

PREFACE

[1] Some important postwar works on German foreign policy under the Nazi regime are: L. B. Namier, *Diplomatic Prelude, 1938–1939*; Elizabeth Wiskemann, *The Rome-Berlin Axis*; Erich Kordt, *Wahn und Wirklichkeit*; John Wheeler-Bennett, *Munich: Prologue to Tragedy*; and the interesting article by DeWitt C. Poole, "New Light on Nazi Foreign Policy," *Foreign Affairs*, October, 1946.

NOTES

² The following are some standard works on European and American foreign offices: Graham Stuart, *American Diplomatic and Consular Practise* (New York: Appleton-Century, 1936); Graham Stuart, *The Department of State* (New York: Macmillan, 1949); Sir John Tilley and Stephen Gaselee, *The Foreign Office* (London: Putnam, 1933); Frederick L. Schuman, *War and Diplomacy in the French Republic* (New York: McGraw-Hill, 1931). Critiques of personnel practises employed by the British and American foreign services may be found in Robert Nightingale, *The Personnel of the British Foreign Office, 1851–1929* (London: The Fabian Society, 1930), and Robert Bendiner, *The Riddle of the State Department* (New York: Farrar and Rinehart, 1942).

³ Hans Gerth and C. Wright Mills, *From Max Weber: Essays in Sociology*, pp. 196–244.

⁴ See, in this regard, Robert Merton's "The Role of the Intellectual in Public Bureaucracy," *Social Forces*, XXIII (May, 1945), 405–415; also Reinhard Bendix's critique of Weber in his introduction to *Higher Civil Servants in American Society* (Boulder: University of Colorado Press, 1949). One of the most penetrating, pioneering studies of the ideological transformation of a bureaucracy under the impact of social and economic forces is Eckardt Kehr, "Das soziale System der Reaktion in Preussen unter dem Ministerium Puttkamer," in the Socialist periodical *Die Gesellschaft*, 1929 (II), 253–274.

⁵ For discussion of this problem in the context of American politics, see J. Roland Pennock, *Administration and the Rule of Law* (New York: Farrar and Rinehart, 1941).

⁶ See, for example, the letter to the New York *Times*, of January 14, 1954, by five former American diplomatic officials, drawing attention to the demoralization of the American foreign service resulting from persistent "attacks from outside sources" questioning the "loyalty and moral standards" of its members.

⁷ H. R. Trevor-Roper, *The Last Days of Hitler*, p. 233.

CHAPTER I

¹ For a more detailed description of the Foreign Office's growth, see Herbert von Hindenburg, *Das Auswärtige Amt im Wandel der Zeiten*, pp. 3–7.

² *Baedeker Guide to Berlin*, 1912 ed., p. 122.

³ Walter Zechlin, *Diplomatie und Diplomaten*, p. 74. The original text reads "...neben dem Gehirn auch die beiden anderen G's (Geburt und Geld) in der Diplomatie stets eine wichtige Rolle gespielt haben."

⁴ Robert Nightingale, *The Personnel of the British Foreign Office, 1815–1929*, p. 5.

⁵ Pierre Tissier, *I Worked with Laval* (London: Harrap, 1942), pp. 7–17.

⁶ Robert Bendiner, *The Riddle of the State Department*, pp. 110–111.

⁷ François de Callières, *On the Manner of Negotiating with Princes*, p. 39.

⁸ L. W. Muncy, *The Junker in the Prussian Administration under Wilhelm II, 1888–1914*, p. 47. The preponderance of non-Prussian noblemen in Imperial Germany's foreign service, writes Miss Muncy, was partly a consequence of the Junkers' reluctance to enter this branch of official activity. "Because of their small incomes, their narrow, rural environment, and their blunt, forthright na-

tures they generally did not find the smooth, sophisticated ways of diplomats congenial nor did they make such good material for the delicate, complicated and socially exacting missions of the German Foreign Office as did the somewhat more cosmopolitan higher nobility or the more versatile aristocrats of south and west Germany."

[9] British Foreign Office, *Return Showing Conditions of Entry into the Austro-Hungarian, German and Other Diplomatic and Foreign Offices.*

[10] Philipp Zorn, "Deutsches Gesandtschafts- und Konsularrecht," in *Handbuch des Völkerrechts,* III, 26–27.

[11] Erich Kordt, *Nicht aus den Akten,* p. 30.

[12] B. W. König, *Handbuch des deutschen Konsularwesens,* p. 132. According to the salary law of July 15, 1909, an ambassador received an annual salary of RM 20,000; a minister, RM 18,000; consuls-general and ministers-resident, RM 8,000–12,000, and first secretaries of embassy, RM 6,300.

[13] O. R. Schifferdecker, *Die Organisation des Auswärtigen Dienstes im Alten und Neuen Reich,* p. 45.

[14] Miss Muncy has noted that 43.9 per cent of Junker diplomats between 1870 and 1914 had belonged to university student corporations, and that, of these, 90 per cent were members of the three most "aristocratic" ones: *Hasso-Borussia, Saxo-Borussia,* and *Saxonia.* Muncy, *op. cit.,* pp. 105–106.

[15] Max Weber, *Gesammelte Politische Schriften,* p. 309. Before 1919, the German diplomatic and consular corps, like those of Britain and the United States, were separate services. But a unique and persistent characteristic of the personnel structure of the German Foreign Office both before and after World War I was its rigid distinction between the higher official service, and the middle and lower categories of civil servants. The latter two groups were considered exclusively as technical administrative and service staffs. Criteria for admission to them were far less rigorous, but their members were not permitted to transfer upward into the higher group unless they met all the detailed requirements mentioned above. This made the possibility of advancement from the lower categories to the higher service virtually impossible and led to a permanent hierarchical gap between them.

[16] For detailed treatment of the evolution of the Foreign Office before 1914, see Schifferdecker, *op. cit.,* and Herbert von Hindenburg, *op. cit.*

[17] For an English commentary on the Weimar constitution, see Heinrich Oppenheimer, *The Constitution of the German Republic.*

[18] Wipert von Blücher, *Deutschlands Weg nach Rapallo,* p. 38.

[19] *Ibid.,* p. 39.

[20] *Verhandlungen des Reichstags* (hereafter cited as *VDR*), Band 348, p. 3094.

[21] Remarks of Deputy Wels (*SPD*), *Verhandlungen der deutschen Nationalversammlung* (hereafter cited as *VDN*), Band 328, p. 1985.

[22] Schüler was formerly director of personnel for the consular service. He received, from Foreign Minister Brockdorff-Rantzau and his successor, Hermann Müller, a *carte blanche* for a broad reorganization of the Wilhelmstrasse. Both foreign ministers, deeply enmeshed in the Paris peace negotiations, had little time for long-range service plans.

[23] *VDN,* Band 327, p. 933.

[24] *Ibid.,* Band 330, p. 3355.

[25] *Ibid.,* Band 330, p. 3353. Remarks of Deputy Waldstein.

[26] Herbert von Dirksen, *Moskau-Tokio-London,* p. 29. The doorkeeper's re-

marks, rendered in Berlinese, were "*Ick wees nich—det deutsche Reich wird immer kleener, und det Auswärtige Amt wird immer jrösser!*"

[27] Britain and the United States likewise unified the two services after World War I. Persuasive arguments for amalgamation lay more on pragmatic than "moral" grounds. Many officials trained in consular work became more competent in dealing with complex commercial and economic aspects of foreign policy than their colleagues in the diplomatic services; yet the old system had served to exclude them from top-level posts. It is interesting to note that, in Germany, from 1921 to 1924 the post of deputy division chief in the Foreign Office Personnel Division (important in dealing with routine but substantive personnel questions) was held by a former consular career officer, Carl Richard Gneist. See his sketch in *Wer Ist's*, 1928 ed.

[28] Foreign Minister Curtius, in his memoirs, recalls, from his own observations, that the attaché examination (*Attachéprüfung*) was "entirely too difficult." "After one of the examinations," he writes, "I told the [examination board members] that I most certainly would have failed to pass." Julius Curtius, *Sechs Jahre Minister der deutschen Republik*, p. 148.

[29] Erich Kordt, a "fledgling diplomat" in the Weimar Republic, recalls that, of the "urbane" and "snobbish" applicants who took the first foreign-service examination with him, and whom he assumed would be selected, none survived to take the attaché examination. Kordt, *op. cit.*, p. 20.

[30] *VDN*, Band 330, p. 3353.

[31] *Ibid.*, Band 330, p. 3377.

[32] *VDR*, Band 355, p. 10538.

[33] Adolf Müller, pre-World War I editor of the *Münchener Post*, and a leading Social Democrat, was minister in Berne for almost 12 years. Other Social Democratic diplomats were Otto Landsberg, former *Volksbeauftragter*, minister to Belgium; and Ulrich Rauscher, minister to Poland. According to Dirksen, the German government in 1929 briefly considered sending Rauscher to Moscow, but the Soviet government rejected the proposal, letting it be known that it preferred the Brockdorff-Rantzau type, a "grand seigneur." *Poole Mission*, interrogation xi, of Herbert von Dirksen, October 10, 1945. Had the appointment gone through, Rauscher would have been the only Social Democratic ambassador to a great power during the 'twenties. The paucity of left-wing diplomats moved the Communist Deputy Stöcker ironically to remark in the Reichstag, in 1921: "Let us just take a look at the representatives the new German Republic has sent out into the world! Everywhere they are men from the worlds of finance and industry. From all the achievements of the Revolution there remain two whole Socialists [as diplomats]. And not even whole—no, two 'half-Socialists': Landsberg in Brussels and Müller in Berne. Even the Socialist Müller, when he was foreign minister, never dared—as the loyal servant of his masters—to send Social Democrats to such important centers of diplomacy as London, Paris, or Rome.... Only such paltry little posts as Berne or Brussels are fit for Socialists." *VDR*, Band 348, p. 3106. In justice to Müller, it should be said that conservative opposition to such "radical" appointments was not the only consideration which contributed to this situation; most prominent Social Democratic leaders were desperately needed at home.

[34] See *Handbuch für das deutsche Reich*, 1922 (Berlin: Carl Heymanns Verlag, 1922), pp. 58–60, for organizational chart of the Foreign Office. Three of the above officials had served in the prewar consular service: Gneist, Knipping, and

Köpke. The divisions were: I, Personnel and Administration; IIa, Western European Affairs; IIb, Balkan Affairs; III, Western Hemisphere, Britain and British Empire Affairs; IVa, Scandinavian, Baltic, and East European Affairs; IVb, Far Eastern Affairs; V, Legal Affairs; and VI, Germans Abroad and Cultural Affairs.

[35] *Wer Ist's*, 1928 and 1935 eds.

[36] Wirth held the portfolio of foreign minister on three occasions in 1921 and 1922, while serving as Reich chancellor. For information on these cabinet changes, see Edgar von Schmidt-Pauli, *Diplomaten in Berlin*, pp. 32–33.

[37] A reference for these and later cabinet changes may be found in Lindsay Rogers, *et al.*, "German Political Institutions," *Political Science Quarterly*, XLVII, 321–349.

[38] Dirksen, *Moskau-Tokio-London*, p. 54.

[39] *Wer Ist's*, 1928 ed.

[40] Of the six division chiefs mentioned, four were sons of civil servants. Two others—Haas and Schneider—were not listed in *Wer Ist's*. The six there mentioned were Koester, Gaus, Zechlin, Dirksen, Köpke, and Freytag. All six had doctorates.

[41] These posts were: Paris, London, Rome, Washington, Moscow, Vienna, The Hague, Stockholm, Berne, Madrid, Buenos Aires, Rio de Janeiro, Tokyo, Oslo, and Ankara.

[42] *Jahrbuch für Auswärtige Politik*. *Wer Ist's*, 1928 and 1935 eds.

[43] These functions were transferred to an official of the division-chief level. The move was motivated by considerations other than mere economizing, however. "We consider it correct," a spokesman of the Reichstag budget committee observed, ". . . that the position of the political state secretary be transformed into that of a permanent state secretary." *VDR*, Band 359, p. 10532. (The elimination of a coördinate economic official on the same level in the Foreign Office, was intended to erase doubts about the real locus of power in the Foreign Office. Schubert in 1924 became the first "permanent" secretary, and so remained until 1930.)

[44] *Ibid.*, p. 10538.

[45] See Bernstein's speech, March 17, 1921, *Ibid.*, Band 348, p. 3094.

[46] H. K. Norton, "Foreign Office Organization," *Annals of the American Academy of Political and Social Science*, Supplement, CXLIII (May, 1929), 42. The ratio of applicants to those admitted was far more favorable in the United States at the time.

[47] *VDR*, Band 445, p. 1628.

[48] *Ibid.*, p. 1629. At that time the total Foreign Office share of the Reich budget (1931–1932 fiscal year) was only RM 51,200,000. See *Statistisches Jahrbuch für das deutsche Reich*, Band 51, p. 435.

[49] *VDR*, Band 390, p. 6440.

[50] Franz L. Neumann, *Behemoth*, pp. 367–373.

[51] Ernst von Weizsäcker, *Erinnerungen*, p. 80.

[52] Blücher, *op. cit.*, p. 39.

[53] Weizsäcker, *op. cit*., pp. 102–103.

[54] Hajo Holborn, "Diplomats and Diplomacy in the Early Weimar Republic," in Craig and Gilbert, *The Diplomats*, pp. 123–171.

[55] *VDR*, Band 445, pp. 1631–1632.

[56] George Hallgarten, "General von Seeckt and Russia," *Journal of Modern History,* XXI (March, 1949), 28–34.

[57] Ruth Fischer, *Stalin and German Communism,* p. 265.

[58] Dirksen, *op. cit.,* pp. 103–110.

CHAPTER II

[1] Paul Schmidt, *Statist auf diplomatischer Bühne,* p. 311.

[2] See *Wer Ist's,* 1935 ed., for names and *NG 035,* for organization chart.

[3] See pp. 36–37.

[4] Kordt, *Nicht aus den Akten,* pp. 55–56; also New York *Times,* June 4, 14, 20, and 23, 1933, for accounts of Ley's trip. His remarks were made to the German press representatives in Geneva, but found their way into a Geneva newspaper, *Le Journal des Nations.* See New York *Times,* June 20, 1933.

[5] Schmidt, *op. cit.,* pp. 261–263.

[6] London *Times,* May 29, 1933, p. 14; *ibid.,* June 13, p. 14.

[7] "London Boos German Economic Delegation as von Neurath and Aides Leave for Home," New York *Times,* June 22, 1933.

[8] Sir Horace Rumbold to Sir John Simon, February 4, 1933. *Documents on British Foreign Policy, 1919–1939* (hereafter cited as *DBFP*), Second Series, IV, 406–408.

[9] André François-Poncet, *The Fateful Years,* pp. 29–30.

[10] Weizsäcker, *Erinnerungen,* p. 132.

[11] Dirksen, *Moskau-Tokio-London,* p. 184. When Dirksen returned to Berlin for consultation in 1936, he found that Neurath was absent on a hunting trip. When he inquired of Bülow when the foreign minister would return, the state secretary laconically replied, "As soon as he has shot his three deer." *Ibid.,* p. 184. Ambassador Dodd's diary, scattered with occasional references to Neurath's critical attitude towards Hitler's ideas, did not put much stock in the foreign minister's candor nor in his backbone. On July 14, 1937, Dodd wrote: "I am more inclined to accept the Chinaman's conversation as true than I am that of any high German official. Von Neurath is personally opposed to much that Hitler does, but he always surrenders." *Ambassador Dodd's Diary,* p. 424.

[12] Weizsäcker, *op. cit.,* p. 132.

[13] *Nazi Conspiracy and Aggression* (hereafter cited as *NCA*), PS 1759, affidavit of Raymond Geist, former U. S. consul in Berlin, August 28, 1945.

[14] Brüning affidavit, *Document Book Weizsäcker,* II, Doc. 1.

[15] Kordt, *Nicht aus den Akten,* pp. 51–52.

[16] Theodore von Laue, "G. V. Chicherin, Peoples Commissar for Foreign Affairs, 1918–1930," in Craig and Gilbert, *The Diplomats,* pp. 234–281.

[17] Kautsky, however, had beeen entrusted, in the early Ebert-Haase cabinet, with editing the "war guilt" documents from Foreign Office archives. See his biographical sketch in *Der grosse Brockhaus,* 15 ed.

[18] Dino Grandi, Mussolini's first Fascist foreign minister, had been tempered by his contact with permanent officials of the Italian Foreign Office; during his tenure of office, inroads of Fascist appointees had been checked by these officials. But Grandi's efforts to steer a "traditional" course for Italian foreign policy in 1933 found little favor with Mussolini, who considered him a "prisoner of the

League of Nations." In fact, Grandi had already been removed from office in 1932 and transferred to London as ambassador. See Stewart Hughes, "Ciano and his Ambassadors," in Craig and Gilbert, *op. cit.*, especially pp. 512–517.

[19] *Poole Mission*, interrogation xi, October 10, 1945.

[20] New York *Times*, April 12, 1933. Several days before his removal, Schwarz had entertained Professor Albert Einstein and wife at his New York home. Schwarz refused to return to Germany. Prittwitz's resignation was announced on March 14, 1933.

[21] *Ibid.*, April 25, 1933. The Foreign Office could not have been seriously affected by this early purge of Jewish civil servants. It is difficult to ascertain how many German diplomats in 1933 were of Jewish extraction. However, according to Raoul Hilberg's study, "The Role of the German Civil Service in the Destruction of the Jews," only about 2,000 Jews in all were employed in higher official positions in the central, provincial, and local administrations, and in the armed forces of the Reich early in 1933. See Hilberg, p. 32.

[22] New York *Times*, August 5, 1933.

[23] *Wer Ist's*, 1935 ed.

[24] Weizsäcker, *op. cit.*, p. 107; also Dirksen, *op. cit.*, pp. 120–121.

[25] Hermann Rauschning, *Hitler Speaks*, pp. 268–269.

[26] Henry Picker, *Hitlers Tischgespräche im Führerhauptquartier*, p. 106.

[27] *Ibid.*, p. 97.

[28] For a thorough account of the *Auslandsorganisation* see U.S. Department of State, *National Socialism: Basic Principles, Their Application by the Nazi Party's Foreign Organization, and the Use of Germans Abroad for Nazi Aims*, pp. 93–139.

[29] For details on Rosenberg's career, see Lang and Schenck, *Memoirs of Alfred Rosenberg*.

[30] *Völkischer Beobachter*, Munich ed., April 4, 1933.

[31] *Loc. cit.*

[32] *Ibid.*, April 5, 1933.

[33] *Loc. cit.*

[34] *Frankfurter Zeitung*, April 4, 1933.

[35] *PS 2319*, organization chart of the *APA*, prepared in 1937.

[36] Adolf Hitler, *Mein Kampf*, p. 183.

[37] See *Mein Kampf*, pp. 163–195, for Hitler's analysis of the "errors" of Imperial Germany's foreign policy.

[38] *Ibid.*, p. 900.

[39] London *Times*, May 9, 1933.

[40] *Ibid.*, May 10, 1933.

[41] *Ibid.*, May 15, 1933. This visit, far from being deplored by the Foreign Office, seems to have been eagerly facilitated to demonstrate to Hitler the consequences of employing Party boors in diplomatic work. See Paul Schwarz, *This Man Ribbentrop*, pp. 87–88.

[42] Considerations of relevance make it superfluous to describe at length the pompous and inept *APA* activities. For a full description see *NCA, PS 003*, a short activity report prepared by Rosenberg in October, 1935; *NCA, PS 007*, a comprehensive, undated report made by Rosenberg, covering the period 1933–1943; *NCA, PS 2319*, a survey of the office's structure in 1937. These querulous, occasionally fanciful documents, which dwell bitterly upon Foreign Office obstruction, reveal the highly amateur caliber of Rosenberg's diplomacy. To *APA*

initiative in 1935 were attributed, for example, the "orienting" of the Duke of Kent on National Socialism so that he might convey appropriate impressions to King George V—a feat which "has exerted a definite pressure for a change of cabinet ... in the direction of closer cordiality for Germany." Other "prominent" Englishmen "influenced" by *APA* agents at that time were one Captain McCaw, a "semi-official counsel of the English Ministry of War"; Archibald Boyle, a "truly enthusiastic adjutant of the Duke of Connaught." (Neither of these "influential men" appears in the contemporary [1935] *Who's Who*, nor in later editions.) Early *APA* efforts in Rumania, China, and the Near East, it would seem, were "sabotaged" by the Foreign Office. See *PS 003*. Actually, Rosenberg's area of work was circumscribed by Party agencies as well. Thus, *APA* was forbidden to engage in work in Austria, Italy, or Yugoslavia. The caliber of Rosenberg's chief "diplomatic attachés" may perhaps be measured by the following excerpts from a report prepared by his chief adviser, Thilo von Trotha, in 1934. This report, dealing with Germany's relations with Scandinavian countries, makes the following observations: "The situation in the North can be regarded as follows: All five countries (except Iceland) are in a rapid economic decline. Politically, Sweden and Denmark are governed by Reds; Norway is confronted by a similar decision. Finland and Iceland are governed by conversation.... So-called pure means of foreign policy are not suited to the North, which is little interested in pure foreign policy." *PS 036*, Thilo von Trotha to Rosenberg, January 31, 1934. In retrospect, *APA* proved of consequence only on one occasion. In the winter of 1939–1940, the Norwegian pro-Nazi, Quisling, was brought to Hitler's attention through Rosenberg's good offices. An interesting account of an *APA*–Foreign Office tangle in the Far East may be found in Ambassador Dirksen's memoirs, and in *PS 007*. In 1934, an abortive move by Göring, Keppler, and Göring's brother-in-law Riegele was undertaken to have a certain Heye appointed by Hitler as *Beauftragter für Manchukuo*, chiefly to facilitate certain private economic schemes of this group in Manchuria. The appointment would have amounted to virtual recognition by Germany of Japan's conquest of Manchuria. The measure was routed through Rosenberg's office in order to escape Foreign Office attention. But it was discovered in time and quashed. See Dirksen, *op. cit.*, pp. 159–160. "The Manchurian incident," Rosenberg wrote in 1935, "without question was sabotaged in the worst fashion by the Foreign Office." See *PS 003*.

[43] "We Germans," wrote Weizsäcker, "were not suited to Geneva. Our diplomats were unaccustomed to public addresses.... The German, moreover, does not cut a happy figure at congresses.... The chief beneficiaries of conferences, as far as I could see, were the representatives of dark-haired nations." Weizsäcker, *op. cit.*, p. 89. Neurath, at Nürnberg, later admitted that he had advised Hitler to break with the League, since no further results could be made in Geneva. *NCA*, Supplement B, p. 1504.

[44] The most comprehensive treatment of the attitudes of Foreign Office officials between 1933 and 1938 toward Hitler's foreign policy is "The German Foreign Office from Neurath to Ribbentrop," in Craig and Gilbert, *op. cit.*, pp. 406–436.

[45] See especially L. B. Namier, *In the Nazi Era*, pp. 13–33, 63–103, for a comparison of the attitudes of General Beck, State Secretary Weizsäcker, and Erich and Theo Kordt.

CHAPTER III

[1] This relationship, smacking of nepotism, once moved the French Ambassador François-Poncet to remark, when leaving the Wilhelmstrasse one day: "I have seen the Father, and the Son, but where is the Holy Ghost?" Weizsäcker, *Erinnerungen*, p. 133.

[2] Quoted in *Frankfurter Zeitung*, February 3, 1938.

[3] *Loc. cit.*

[4] *Frankfurter Zeitung*, February 4, 1938.

[5] *Ibid.*, February 5, 1938.

[6] In the words of Lammers, who also was a member, the Council "could only be summoned by the Führer himself. It had no right to call a meeting itself. The Führer never summoned it, and ... the Council never met." See *Case XI Transcript* (English version), p. 20033.

[7] Interrogation of Neurath by Major James J. Monigan, Jr., at Nürnberg, October 3, 1945. *NCA*, Supplement B, p. 1491.

[8] For an excellent treatment of the February 4 crisis, see Telford Taylor, *Sword and Swastika*, pp. 118–174. The Hossbach memorandum of Hitler's conference of November 5, 1937, may be found in *NCA, PS 386*. An account by a foreign diplomat in Berlin of these events is given in François-Poncet's *The Fateful Years*, pp. 225–235.

[9] Ribbentrop was awarded the *Ehrenkreuz* first class.

[10] While Ribbentrop doubtless was at the peace conference in some minor capacity, his name is nowhere mentioned in Victor Schiff's comprehensive study, *Germans at Versailles* (London: Williams and Norgate, 1930).

[11] Gertrud von Ribbentrop, although a distant relative, had been a close family friend and had lived with them for long periods during Ribbentrop's youth in Metz. See Schwarz, *op. cit.*, pp. 40–41. When entering the SS, Ribbentrop withheld details of this "adoption" from his genealogy chart, but was later requested by the SS *Sippenforschungsamt*, an SS genealogical office, to supply details. For Ribbentrop's reply, furnishing details, see *NCA, D 636*.

[12] Bülow-Schwante later became protocol chief in Neurath's Foreign Office. In 1925, he had married the widowed sister of Foreign Office State Secretary von Schubert. Paul Schwarz, *op. cit.*, pp. 74–77.

[13] *Ibid.*, p. 75.

[14] The visit, Ribbentrop later recalled, was made possible by Count Helldorf, later Nazi police chief in Berlin, a regimental comrade of Ribbentrop in World War I. "I visited Adolf Hitler and had a long discussion with him at that time," he reminisced at Nürnberg, "that is to say, Adolf Hitler explained his views ... to me." *International Military Tribunal Proceedings* (hereafter cited as *IMTP*), X, 227.

[15] Schwarz, *op. cit.*, pp. 78–79.

[16] Earlier meetings, of course, took place in the home of Baron von Schroeder, the Cologne industrialist. But Ribbentrop, in his self-composed *Wer Ist's* biography, characteristically claimed all the credit for the deal: "Through his intermediation ... the Hitler government was formed between 10 January and 30 January, 1933; the decisive meetings took place in his home in Berlin-Dahlem." *Wer Ist's* (1935 ed.).

[17] According to Hermann Rauschning, Ribbentrop was initially persuaded to join the Party by the notorious Nazi, Count Helldorf. Hermann Rauschning, *Men of Chaos*, p. 196.

[18] For one such scathing estimate, see François-Poncet, *op. cit.*, pp. 231–233.

[19] Brittanicus Viator, "Representative Men," *English Review*, LXII (April, 1936), 413–415.

[20] For a list of Ribbentrop's various offices, see his own affidavit prepared in Nürnberg, 1935: *NCA, PS* 2829.

[21] For one such estimate, characteristic of many others, see Erich Kordt, *Wahn und Wirklichkeit*, p. 91. Ribbentrop's early reports to Hitler on political questions were so filled with absurdities and patent errors that leading officials believed "he would quickly make his own standing with Hitler impossible." See also Geyr von Schweppenburg's *Erinnerungen eines Militärattachés*, p. 125, for his remarks on Ribbentrop's working methods: "He read reports only with the greatest reluctance.... Without exception the reports he personally wrote were but clumsy exercises.... His work in great measure was unsystematic, his operating procedures irregular and incalculable." Geyr was for a short time Ribbentrop's military attaché in London. He notes that following Ribbentrop's appointment there as ambassador, the ranks of experienced embassy personnel began rapidly to thin out, assuming "almost the character of a flight." Of the old and experienced personnel, only he and the Naval Attaché Admiral Wassner remained. *Ibid.*, p. 117.

[22] Kordt, *Nicht aus den Akten*, p. 88.

[23] *"Forellenzucht"*—a term used to describe the foreign service training period.

[24] Haushofer's son, Albrecht, was for several years employed by Ribbentrop in the *Büro RAM*, although his experiences there alienated him from both Ribbentrop and the Nazi party in general. He was executed by the Nazis in April, 1945. See introduction by Rainer Hildebrandt to Haushofer's posthumously published *Moabiter Sonnette* (Zürich: Artemis Verlag, 1948).

[25] Schwarz, *This Man Ribbentrop*, pp. 89–90.

[26] Peter Kleist, *Zwischen Hitler und Stalin*, pp. 11–15.

[27] Germany here acquired the right to a submarine tonnage equal in total to that possessed by the entire British Commonwealth, as long as the arrangement as to total tonnage was not violated. See G. N. Gathorne-Hardy, *A Short History of International Affairs*, 3d ed. (London: Oxford University Press, 1942), p. 398.

[28] Kordt, *Nicht aus den Akten*, pp. 61–62; also Schwarz, *op. cit.*, p. 104.

[29] Ribbentrop argued elaborately, at Nürnberg after the war, that his desire to achieve an "Anglo-German understanding" led him to turn down the state-secretary post so that he might go to London. See *IMTP*, X, 236. The same story was given by him in conversation with British officials in 1937. Winston S. Churchill, *The Gathering Storm*, pp. 222–223.

[30] London *Times*, December 10, 1936.

[31] *Ibid.*, February 7, 1938.

[32] *Ibid.*, October 22, 1936.

[33] *Ibid.*, December 16, 1936.

[34] Churchill, *op. cit.*, pp. 222–223.

[35] *NCA*, Supplement B, p. 1214.

[36] Churchill, *op. cit.*, p. 222.

[37] *NCA*, Supplement B, p. 1215.

[38] *Ibid.*, TC 75.

[39] This castle was expropriated from one Herr von Remitz, brother-in-law of August Thyssen. Remitz subsequently died in a concentration camp. The foreign minister later acquired two hunting lodges, one in Slovakia and the other in the Sudetenland. See Sir David Maxwell-Fife's cross-examination of Paul Otto Schmidt at Nürnberg, March 28, 1946. *IMTP*, X, 208–209.

[40] Kordt, *Nicht aus den Akten*, pp. 183–185. According to Kordt, Ribbentrop, upon becoming foreign minister, assembled his by then somewhat disgruntled staff to explain his unwillingness to take them into the Foreign Office with him. "It is unworthy of us," he declared lamely, "to strive for official posts and pension rights. The members of my *Dienststelle* should not think just of themselves and their families, but should think only of selflessly serving the Führer's policies." *Ibid.*, p. 183. The *Dienststelle* was not officially dissolved until February 1, 1940, however. See *NG* 1078, Hess to Rosenberg, January 30, 1940. Ribbentrop's *Abteilung Deutschland* took over its functions of handling Party–Foreign Office liaison on questions of foreign policy. Hess in his memorandum notes that only chosen Party members would be assigned to this new agency.

[41] Kleist, *op. cit.*, pp. 14–15; also Dirksen, *Moskau-Tokio-London*, p. 185.

[42] Dirksen, *ibid.*, p. 199.

[43] Weizsäcker, *Erinnerungen*, pp. 51–60. The state secretary's father had attracted public attention during World War I by his forthright opposition to Tirpitz's submarine policy.

[44] *Ibid.*, p. 145.

[45] Kordt, *Nicht aus den Akten*, p. 199. According to Bohle at Nürnberg, Ribbentrop did not conceal his displeasure about having a Gauleiter in his own office. "He told me that himself, one day, showing me at the same time several foreign newspapers in which I was mentioned as a promising young man who might some day be German foreign minister." *Case XI Transcript* (English version), p. 13504.

[46] Compare the Foreign Office organization chart of December 1, 1937, with that of June 1, 1938, found in appendices to *Documents on German Foreign Policy: 1918–1945* (hereafter cited as *DGFP*), Series D, I and II. Few changes on lower levels were undertaken in the first few months of Ribbentrop's tenure. One official, who had taken a dislike to Ribbentrop in the late 'twenties and had consequently opposed his admission to the Berlin *Unionklub*, was cashiered. Schwarz, *op. cit.*, p. 63; also Weizsäcker, *op. cit.*, p. 157.

[47] For accounts of these first few days of Ribbentrop's tenure, see Schwarz, *op. cit.*, pp. 227–237; also Kordt, *Nicht aus den Akten*, pp. 177–189.

[48] These figures include only officials with rank of legation counselor or higher in the higher service (*höherer Dienst*). They do not include officials then serving in missions abroad. Data have been derived by checking names from the Foreign Office membership list as of December 1, 1937 (*Geschäftsverteilungsplan des Auswärtigen Amtes*) found in *DGFP*, Series D, I, appendix ii, against *NSDAP* membership files located in U.S. Army Document Center 7771, Berlin.

[49] Prüfer, Wiehl, Mackensen, Bismarck, and Clodius. Bülow-Schwante, Neurath's protocol chief, had also joined in 1936.

[50] A few lower officials had, however.

[51] *SS* personnel files of Ernst von Weizsäcker, U.S. Army Document Center 7771, Berlin.

[52] *Loc. cit.*

[53] *Case XI Transcript* (English version), pp. 10859–10860. "Brueggelmeier"

presumably is Eduard Brücklmeier, a lower-echelon career official attached to Ribbentrop's staff in London and, later, in Berlin. Originally a Ribbentrop favorite, he was denounced by the Gestapo in 1940 for "defeatism," was retired on pension from the Foreign Office in May, 1940, and subsequently was arrested and executed, after July 20, 1944.

[54] Woermann testified at Nürnberg that Ribbentrop urged *SS* membership on him in order to obtain the uniform for ceremonial purposes. But the introduction of a special Foreign Office uniform in the spring of 1938 made this less necessary.

[55] The dilemma of having to choose between acting as a policy maker or administrator during periods of swift international activity has, of course, plagued democratic statesmen as well. One recalls the failure of Secretary James Byrnes, in 1946–1947, to reorganize the American State Department—a failure occasioned by his constant commutation between Washington and European capitals, giving rise to the Washington quip, "The State Department fiddles while Byrnes roams."

[56] Churchill, *op. cit.*, pp. 271–272.

[57] For German versions of this event, see Schwarz, *op. cit.*, pp. 233–237; also Kordt, *Nicht aus den Akten*, pp. 194–198. During Ribbentrop's absence in London, Hitler requested Neurath to conduct unofficially Wilhelmstrasse business. Ribbentrop was not able to leave London until given permission by Hitler to do so on March 14.

[58] *DGFP*, Series D, I, 607–609. Ribbentrop, in the British *Who's Who*, was to claim, in 1939, that the *Anschluss* had been his accomplishment as foreign minister.

[59] *Loc. cit.*

[60] Weizsäcker, *op. cit.*, p. 156.

[61] *NG 4062*, secret report of the Reich Ministry of Finance on expenditures of Reich ministries, dated July 17, 1939. Figures for Reich debt, General Finance Administration, and for Saarland are omitted.

[62] Karl Ritter, Prüfer's predecessor at the Rio de Janeiro embassy, was recalled to the Foreign Office at request of the Brazilian government, but until September, 1939, he was given no important task in the Berlin office. See Ritter's career affidavit: *NG 3589*.

[63] Kriebel died in early 1941.

[64] The rapidity of Schroeder's rise was, at the time, extraordinary for the foreign service. Until September, 1935, he had been in the so-called *gehobener Dienst* (the upper service of the Wilhelmstrasse's technical staff—a caste of the officialdom rigidly subordinate to the so-called *höherer Dienst*). At this time he passed his diplomatic-consular examination. Within three years he had attained the rank of senior legation counselor. As *Landesgruppenleiter*, Schroeder had attended the leader school Bennau in the summer of 1933, for Nazi leadership training under *AO* auspices. He succeeded Kriebel as division chief in 1941. Schroeder files in U.S. Army Document Center 7771, Berlin.

[65] According to the draft of a report prepared by Bertling for future foreign-service candidates, the training center was to be designed for both the higher service and lower administrative echelons (i.e., the so-called *gehobener* and *mittlerer Dienst*). "The primary condition" for admission was "membership in the *NSDAP* or proven service in the Party's affiliated organizations." "Only the elite of the racially most valuable elements will be admitted as candidates." See *NG 3781*, Bertling to *Amtsrat* Burgdorf of the Reich Chancellery, March 14, 1941.

[66] Kordt, *Nicht aus den Akten*, p. 389.

[67] Bertling's Foreign Office title was *Kommandeur des Nachwuchshauses des*

Auswärtigen Amtes. Information supplied by U.S. Army Document Center, Bertling files. Bertling's proposed school for diplomats was not the first Party experiment of its kind. Alfred Rosenberg and the *APA* earlier had set up, in Dahlem, a so-called *Aussenpolitisches Schulungshaus der NSDAP,* to train would-be Party diplomats. Although it had no official status in the Foreign Office, the latter did permit its graduates to take the preliminary attaché examination. See *Monatshefte für Auswärtige Politik,* IV (October, 1937), 651.

⁶⁸ According to Schwarz, *op. cit.,* pp. 71–78, Bülow neglected to inform the Führer in advance of a gala La Scala opera performance which he was to attend as guest of the Italian king, that military uniform, not civilian evening dress, was prescribed; a mortified Führer thus had been paraded before an honor guard of Italian troops alongside his minuscule but militarily resplendent host.

⁶⁹ *NG 5261* (A), a memorandum prepared by legation secretary (and later *SS-Sturmbannführer*) Schumberg, October 8, 1936. *Referat Deutschland's* competence for matters of Jewish persecution and cloak-and-dagger work did not, of course, preclude active participation by the state secretary and the Political Division when issues of high policy were at stake. Thus, for example, in the interministerial conference of November 12, 1938, summoned by Göring to discuss the "Jewish problem" after the assassination of Embassy Counselor vom Rath in Paris, Woermann, accompanied by Schumberg, represented the Foreign Office. A "fine" of RM 1,000,000,000 was levied upon the German Jewish community as consequence of this conference. Woermann deputized for Weizsäcker. See *NG 3936.* Decisions concerning Foreign Office subsidization of Himmler's subversive operations abroad were customarily handled, before 1940, by the Political Division. *NG 3325;* see also p. 126–129.

⁷⁰ Information above and following was obtained from the following sources: Martin Luther's *NSDAP* membership files and *SA* files; interview with Frau Irmgaard Luther, his widow; interview with Ernst Woermann who, as embassy counselor in London first made Luther's acquaintance. According to Woermann, Luther was taken to London at Frau Ribbentrop's suggestion.

⁷¹ Kordt, *Wahn und Wirklichkeit,* p. 373.

⁷² Martin Luther, *NSDAP* files, U. S. Army Document Center 7771, Berlin.

⁷³ Letter of Bormann to Supreme Party Court, October 4, 1938, *ibid.*

⁷⁴ Foreign Office organization chart of February 15, 1939. *DGFP,* Series D, IV, 715–721.

⁷⁵ Minutes of ministry chiefs' conference, May 24, 1933, *NG 4272.* Rosenberg, still languishing in disgrace from his London visit, and from repercussions arising from his *APA's* attacks upon American news correspondents in Berlin, was denied any participation in foreign-propaganda work at this time. An "exposé" of the Rosenberg-Goebbels feud over propaganda may be found in Kurt Ludecke, *I Knew Hitler,* pp. 611–704. For text of Hitler's decree, see *Reichsgesetzblatt* (hereafter cited as *RGB*), I (1933), 449. The directive also affected the Wilhelmstrasse's Cultural Division.

⁷⁶ For an account of this tempest in a teapot (unnoticed at the time because of the Polish crisis), see Kordt, *Nicht aus den Akten,* pp. 320–321. "Ribbentrop," noted Kordt in a letter to the author, "used his personal bodyguard as the officials of the Foreign Office were considered as little suited for the proposed action." Weizsäcker, for his part, competently defended his superior's position in this struggle in conferences with Propaganda Ministry officials. See his *aide memoire* of talks with division chief Greiner of *Promi,* August 17, 1939, *NG 5774.*

⁷⁷ *NG 2943,* Hitler decree of September 8, 1939. Both ministries fought hard

to attract foreign correspondents. Press conferences were regularly held twice daily in the Propaganda Ministry and once a day at the Foreign Office. See Sington and Weidenfeld, *The Goebbels Experiment*, pp. 101–102. For details on Paul Karl Schmidt's appointment, see Schmidt affidavit, *NG 3590*. Despite Hitler's compromise decree, the battle continued through the war. In 1940, Ribbentrop recaptured Foreign Office control over press attachés in missions abroad, who had been under the direct control of Goebbels. For several months during the war he even broke Dietrich's press-service monopoly by establishing the *Transkontinent Press* agency serving southeast European newspapers. Otto Dietrich affidavit, *NG 995*.

[78] *Case XI Transcript* (English version), p. 7595.

[79] Paul Otto Schmidt, *op. cit.*, p. 560.

[80] For a brief analysis of the Weimar experience with the German civil service, see Arnold Brecht, "Memorandum on Civil Service Reform in Germany," privately mimeographed report by the author; also, F. Morstein Marx, "Civil Service in Germany," in L. D. White, *et al.*, *Civil Service Abroad*. The testimony of Dr. Hans Peters, of the University of Berlin, in the Wilhelmstrasse Trial is also of interest. *Case XI Transcript* (English version), pp. 311–317.

[81] *RGB*, I (1933), 175; *ibid.*, p. 433.

[82] Arnold Brecht, *op. cit.*, pp. 1–2. "Those republican civil servants," writes Brecht, "who kept their jobs were held under severe control. They were in constant danger of losing their positions if they antagonized the Nazis; if dismissed they would have little chance of finding any other jobs.... [Voluntary] retirement automatically implied the loss of all pension rights, unless the retiring employee had already reached the legal age limit."

[83] Such transcendent considerations, of course, may prove *legally* decisive, if international conventions or trade agreements specify the permissible level of protection.

[84] For some suggestive remarks on this subject, see Joseph Schumpeter's *Imperialism and Social Classes* (New York: A. M. Kelley, 1951), *passim*.

[85] Carl Schmitt, *Staat, Bewegung, Volk*.

[86] *Ibid.*, p. 31.

[87] *Loc. cit.*

[88] *Ibid.*, p. 32.

[89] Franz Neumann, *Behemoth*, p. 65.

[90] Schmitt, *op. cit.*, p. 32.

[91] Hermann Neef, *Deutsches Berufsbeamtentum*, p. 87.

[92] For text of the 1937 civil-service law, see *RGB*, I (1937), 41–67.

[93] *Loc. cit.*

[94] Neef, *op. cit.*, p. 133.

[95] Quoted in Frederic L. Burin, "Bureaucracy and National Socialism," in Robert K. Merton *et al.*, eds., *Reader in Bureaucracy* (Glencoe, Ill.: The Free Press, 1952), p. 41.

CHAPTER IV

[1] Ambassador Karl Ritter, career diplomat, chief of the Division of Economic Affairs during the Weimar Republic; ambassador to Brazil, 1937–1938; ambas-

NOTES 185

sador at large in the Foreign Office, 1938–1945. For the greater part of the war
Ritter handled Foreign Office liaison matters with *OKW*. With Weizsäcker he
was tried before the American Military Tribunal at Nürnberg in 1948–1949.
[2] Kempner's interrogation of Karl Ritter, *NG 3627*.
[3] While Ribbentrop, until 1937, was exponent of an Anglo-German *rapprochement*, Göring was entrusted by Hitler with the cultivation of Italy. See
Elizabeth Wiskemann, *Rome-Berlin Axis*, pp. 71–74; 141. Göring's visits to
Rome in January, 1937, and April, 1939, were of decisive importance. Ciano, in
his diary on May 23, 1939, recounting the signing of the Axis "Steel Pact"
(when he formally bestowed upon Ribbentrop the collar of the *Annunziata*)
noted that "Göring...had tears in his eyes...von Mackensen told me that
Göring had made a scene, complaining that the collar really belonged to him,
since he was the true and only promoter of the alliance." *Ciano Diaries*, May 23,
1939.
[4] Ironic, since Gaus had been Stresemann's chief adviser in 1925 during the
Locarno negotiations. Later, Gaus played another, more active role in August,
1939, as Ribbentrop's chief assistant in drafting the Soviet-German nonaggression pact. Erich Kordt, *Nicht aus den Akten*, pp. 128–140.
[5] *DGFP*, Series D, I, chap. iv. Trautmann feared that abandonment of China
would only throw her into the arms of Russia. German military advisers in the
Chinese army were withdrawn in June, 1938, against Trautmann's advice. He
was recalled at the same time.
[6] Weizsäcker, *Erinnerungen*, p. 194.
[7] *NG 3716*, Weizsäcker memo of talk with foreign minister, July 21, 1938.
[8] Weizsäcker, *op. cit.*, p. 193. Cf. Weizsäcker's preference for the "chemical" instead of "mechanical" process in settlement of the Czech problem, *DGFP*, Series
D, I, Weizsäcker to Trautmann (Nanking), May 30, 1938, p. 864.
[9] *Ibid.*, p. 165.
[10] *NG 1822*, Woermann memorandum, August 25, 1938. Since 1935, the *Sudeten-
deutsche Partei* received RM 15,000 per month through the Prague legation; an
additional RM 3,000 were supplied in Berlin to the Party's representative. See
also *DGFP*, Series D, II, Eisenlohr to Foreign Office, May 12, 1938, p. 274,
warning of possible Czech discovery of subversive legation assistance.
[11] *NG 3605*, Erich Kordt affidavit.
[12] *Loc. cit.*
[13] See Theo Kordt's testimony, at Nürnberg, *Case XI Transcript* (German version), pp. 12020–12027.
[14] See, for example, Dirksen's cable of May 22, 1938, *DGFP*, Series D, II, 322;
also Welczeck from Paris, May 23, 1938, *ibid.*, p. 326; Fabricius from Bucharest,
ibid., p. 337.
[15] See Dirksen's account of his London mission—composed on August 19,
1939, after his retirement to his estate—in *Documents and Materials Relating to
the Eve of the Second World War*, II, Doc. 27. These are the U.S.S.R.-captured
"von Dirksen papers."
[16] *NG 3716*, Weizsäcker memorandum of July 21, 1938.
[17] *Loc. cit.*
[18] *Ibid.*, Weizsäcker memorandum, August 19, 1938.
[19] *Loc. cit.*
[20] *Loc. cit.*
[21] Henderson to Halifax, August 13, 1938, *DBFP*, Third Series, II, 91–92.

[22] *Ibid.*, (July 30, 1938), p. 24.

[23] *Ibid.*, (August 23, 1938), p. 138.

[24] *Ibid.*, (September 12, 1938), p. 297.

[25] *Ibid.*, (September 13, 1938), Appendix I, p. 654.

[26] *Ibid.*, (Sir G. Warner [Berne] to Halifax, September 5, 1938), p. 242. According to Burckhardt, when he arrived in Berne he "woke up" the British minister to give him the message. But unless Warner was given to sleeping afternoons, this would indicate that he did not rush this "highly placed personage's" message to London, for it certainly must have been given him during the night, but was not transmitted to London until 5:45 P.M. on September 5. Compare excerpts from Burckhardt's diary account of this affair in *Document Book Weizsäcker*, Ia, with the above British narrative.

[27] Skrine-Stevenson (Geneva) to Mr. Strang of the Foreign Office, September 8, 1938, *DBFP*, Third Series, II, appendix iv. Stevenson, who next year (1939) was to become private secretary to the foreign secretary, was then a Foreign Office counselor.

[28] Quoted in L. B. Namier, *In the Nazi Era*, p. 76.

[29] L. B. Namier, *op. cit.*, pp. 90–97. "... what," writes Namier, of Theo Kordt's London activities, "was there of concrete data to make a responsible statesman take crucial decisions? A message from an alleged Fronde of undisclosed composition and unknown strength, whose capacity to act at the time remains uncertain even now." *Ibid.*, p. 94. The same might be said of Weizsäcker's own enterprise.

[30] Excerpt from Burckhardt diary, *Document Book Weizsäcker*, Ia, Doc. 169a, written in November, 1938.

[31] Weizsäcker, *op. cit.*, p. 193.

[32] *Hassell Diaries*, p. 9.

[33] A former official of the Political Division.

[34] *Hassell Diaries*, p. 19.

[35] *Ibid.*, pp. 21–22.

[36] *Ibid.*, p. 20.

[37] *NG 3604*, Herbert von Dirksen affidavit, describing his work in London. See also his memoirs, *Moskau-Tokio-London*, pp. 209–235. The ambassador, in August, 1939, requested to be placed on inactive duty and held no further positions in the foreign service after that time.

[38] See *Documents and Materials Relating to the Eve of the Second World War*, II, 190–191, for Dirksen's comments.

[39] Paul Schmidt, *Statist auf diplomatischer Bühne*, p. 464.

[40] *Ciano Diaries*, entry for November 7, 1939.

[41] See pp. 134–135.

[42] Schmidt, *op. cit.*, p. 467.

[43] Organization chart of Foreign Office as of August, 1940, *NG 035*.

[44] Data have been obtained in the same fashion as those of 1938, by comparing the organizational chart of the Foreign Office (as of August, 1940) with *NSDAP* records in U.S. Army Document Center 7771, Berlin. Reasons given in Party records for rejection of membership were chiefly lack of noticeable enthusiasm or work for the Party. Werner von Grundherr, the Political Division's Scandinavian expert, however, was rejected on grounds of his "conceit and arrogance."

[45] Of the 35 *Referenten* in the Economic and Political Divisions 11 were not Party members in 1940. The highest incidence of rejection of applications was

in the Political Division, where 4 applications of 14 higher officials were turned
down.

[46] Weizsäcker in his memoirs had the following to say of his acceptance of
SS and Party membership: "It was obvious that I could not reject these two
appointments without promptly abandoning my self-chosen task. . . . They were
for me an inescapable concession to the responsibility I had assumed as State
Secretary." Weizsäcker, *op. cit.*, p. 153.

[47] For a more intimate account of this novel arrangement, see Paul Schmidt,
op. cit., pp. 467–468; Kordt, *Nicht aus den Akten*, pp. 384–388. Even when in
Berlin, the rift between the "regular" Foreign Office officials and Ribbentrop's
personal staff continued. Emulating their chief, the *Büro RAM* functionaries
arrived later than normal business hours every morning (about 10:00 or 11:00
A.M.), shared meals with Ribbentrop, and rarely left their staff quarters before
midnight. Franz Sonnleithner affidavit, *Document Book Ritter*, I, pp. 7–8.

[48] Affidavit of Andor Hencke, Woermann's successor as Chief of the Political
Division, *Document Book Woermann*, III, Doc. 92.

[49] *NSDAP, SA*, and *SS* files.

[50] Kriebel decree, May 7, 1940, *Document Book Woermann*, III, Doc. 3.

[51] This last, grotesque task of Luther's division was specifically mentioned on
the official Foreign Office organization chart of August, 1940. *NG 035.*

[52] *Ibid.*, Kriebel circular of May 21, 1940.

[53] Memorandum of Legation Secretary Werner Picot of *Abteilung Deutschland*,
August 16, 1941, *Document Book Weizsäcker*, IX (supplement), Doc. 492a,
concerning *Abteilung Deutschland's* unique distribution policy: "Insofar as
there may exist an essential competence of another [agency], *Deutschland* will
permit a copy of the communication concerned to be transmitted to it." See also
division chief Luther to *SS Obergruppenführer* Müller of *RSHA*, December 8,
1942, *Document Book Weizsäcker*, IX (supplement), Doc. 492b. Here Luther
informs Müller that henceforth all communications from his office of the Foreign
Office, including top secret ones, should be sent directly to *Abteilung Deutschland.* Müller's office (*Amt VI*) was the central Gestapo headquarters.

[54] Hans Bernd von Häften was a career diplomat in the German Foreign
Office. Implicated in the July 20 conspiracy (his brother, Lieutenant Werner
von Häften, was an aide-de-camp of Colonel Claus von Stauffenberg), he was
executed in 1944. According to an affidavit of his widow, he was transferred,
with Weizsäcker's permission, from the Personnel Division to *Abteilung Deutschland* in 1940. See *Document Book Weizsäcker*, V, Doc. 244. According to Dr.
Wilhelm Melchers, Häften almost succumbed to a nervous breakdown from his
observations of Luther's activities, "but managed to hold out, in order to make
use of this listening post." *Document Book Weizsäcker*, VI, Doc. 16.

[55] Affidavit of Dr. Herbert Siegfried, *Document Book Weizsäcker*, VI, Doc. 336.

[56] Testimony of Ribbentrop's personal secretary, Margarete Blank, *IMTP*, X,
190: "These plans did not go beyond the initial stage because of the war. In
the course of the war they were taken up again when the question of new blood
for the Foreign Office became acute."

[57] Schroeder affidavit, *Document Book Weizsäcker*, Ib, Doc. 171. Also, Kordt,
Nicht aus den Akten, pp. 388–391. The foreign minister's wrath was incurred in
this case by Hasso von Etzdorf, a young Political Division official, who, without
Ribbentrop's knowledge, had relayed to *OKW* headquarters a communication
from the United States government (charged with the protection of Belgium's

interests in Germany) notifying the German government that Brussels was to be an open city. Henceforth, Etzdorf's office (Pol. I-m) was placed in the hands of one Heinz Kramarz, a reliable Nazi Ribbentrop appointee. *NG 035*, Schroeder administrative decree of July 17, 1940. Kramarz was the only higher official in the Political Division during the war who owed his appointment to the foreign minister; he was previously a close associate of Luther in *Abteilung Deutschland*.

[58] The 1937 Reich civil-service law originally provided that civil servants could "at any time" request to be retired; compliance with such requests in all ministries was mandatory. See *Deutsches Beamtengesetz 1937*, 60, *RGB*, I (1937), 50. Shortly before the invasion of Poland, on March 25, 1939, this provision was eliminated; henceforth, ministry chiefs of civilian agencies were permitted to deny such permission for a period terminating December 31, 1941. See *Gesetz zur Änderung des Deutschen Beamtengesetzes*, sec. 2, par. 2, *RGB*, I (1939), 577–578. This amendment was renewed on October 21, 1941, and the ministers of the interior and finance (Frick and Schwerin-Krosigk) were given discretionary power to determine "the date when this limitation [of the resignation right] shall cease to be in effect." *RGB*, I (1941), 648. The limitation continued in force until the end of the war. The provision for automatic retirement of officials at the age of 65 was not, however, altered.

CHAPTER V

[1] See *Jahrbuch für Auswärtige Politik, 1943*, for particulars.

[2] One practical reason for such Foreign Office interest in these subjects was the concern evidenced by neutral protective powers over the fate of nationals of states they were obliged to protect. Thus, for example, when 660 Dutch Jews were removed by the *SS* to concentration camps in Germany between February and June, 1941, and it was discovered that 400 of them had subsequently died, the Swedish government, as trustee of Dutch interests, requested the Foreign Office for permission to inspect the German camps. As Undersecretary Luther observed, in a memorandum to the *RSHA* on November 5, 1941, such a request was difficult to reject summarily, since a rebuff might lessen Swedish vigor in representing German interests in enemy countries. For this reason, the Foreign Office recommended to the *RSHA* that such persons should not in the future be brought to the Reich, since, if they remained in the Netherlands, they would not come under the competence of the protective power. *NG 3700*, Luther to *RSHA*, November 5, 1941. This position was later abandoned by the Foreign Office.

[3] Occasionally, Foreign Office officials themselves initiated recommendations for the elimination of prominent political figures in occupied countries. Thus, for example, Otto Abetz recommended to the Foreign Office on May 13, 1944, the execution of "influential dissident leaders" in France as reprisal against the Algiers Committee's threatened execution of pro-Nazi Tunisians. "I take the liberty," wrote Abetz, "therefore to refer to my proposal ... to shoot, as reprisal measures ... French dissident personalities responsible for the outbreak of the war ... beginning with Leon Blum, Paul Reynaud, and Georges Mandel." *NG 3065*, Abetz to Foreign Office, May 13, 1944.

[4] Such as the assassination of the French general Mesny, late in the war, while "attempting to escape." *NG 037.*

[5] *NG 4652,* minutes of meeting held at the Foreign Office, June 30, 1941, of interministerial conference on volunteers for *Waffen-SS* units to be used against the Soviet Union. Representatives of the Foreign Office, the *OKW,* the *SS-Hauptamt,* the Reich plenipotentiary for Denmark, and the *APA* attended. The Foreign Office's role in such matters involved negotiation of agreements with satellite governments to facilitate such recruiting.

[6] Occasionally, the Foreign Office was excluded from such talks by order of the Führer. *NG 1508,* Lammers memorandum of January 4, 1944. The state secretary, however, did represent the Foreign Office at such meetings on occasion. *NG 1510,* Lammers memorandum, July 12, 1944. Diplomatic representation was necessary where negotation with foreign states was required.

[7] See *NG 754*—for example, memorandum on meeting of interministerial Committee on Trade Policy, September 9, 1942, in which representatives of Göring's Four-Year Plan, of the Ministry of Food and Agriculture, of the Military Commander in France, and of the Armistice Delegation participated. The meeting concerned routine demands on the French government for increased food deliveries to Germany.

[8] See, for example, *NG 3755,* report of Dr. Kieser, *Abteilung Deutschland,* to Luther, January 27, 1942, concerning interdepartmental meeting with representatives of fourteen Reich agencies participating, to discuss the problem of intercourse between German girls and foreign slave workers. The *RSHA* proposed a ban on intercourse with all foreign workers, not merely with Czechs and Poles (for whom a ban already existed). The ban, the *RSHA* representative urged, would be applied discriminately, in accordance with Nazi racial theories; more stringently for "alien" racial types, loosely for "related races." The death sentence was currently being prescribed for Polish offenders. The Foreign Office refused to give consent until the *RSHA* proposal was put in writing.

[9] Briefly, in 1942, representatives of various Reich agencies, including the Foreign Office, discussed the feasibility of holding a propaganda trial of Grynzspan, the murderer of vom Rath. Weizsäcker, in April, 1942, discussed with his subordinates the matter of Foreign Office representation at the trial which was to be sponsored by the Propaganda Ministry. For unknown reasons, the idea was finally dropped—possibly for fear Grynzspan might publicly admit homosexual relations with the German embassy counselor. See *NG 973,* minutes of meeting of January 22, 1942; representatives of the Foreign Office, Justice Ministry, Propaganda Ministry, the Gestapo, and the People's Court were included.

[10] *NG 3193,* memorandum on competence of Werner Best, January 5, 1943. Ribbentrop and Himmler, after Best's appointment, waged a continuing struggle over authority to issue directives to him.

[11] For example, *NG 3170, OKW* order of March 28, 1941, outlining functions of Foreign Office propaganda units in the Greek campaign.

[12] *NG 3167,* memorandum on interministerial conference, February 5, 1941, between Foreign Office and *OKW* experts concerning the solution of technical transportation problems for German military units. Foreign Office participation was necessary because one crucial problem was the movement of war supplies through Yugoslavia to Bulgaria.

[13] *NG 146,* Foreign Office order of June 22, 1941, signed by Kuensberg, desig-

nating detachments of Foreign Office officials in Russia; also *NG 188*, report from Belgrade to Foreign Office, May 3, 1941, on Kuensberg's capture of the personal effects of Foreign Minister Nincec in Belgrade; also *NG 3950*, Sonnleithner to Protocol Division, July 12, 1941, informing of the foreign minister's instructions to Kuensberg to proceed to both Leningrad and Moscow "in order to safeguard works of art."

[14] *NG 4634*, foreign-minister order, January 17, 1944. The Führer's order permitting the Propaganda Ministry to assist in stimulating prisoners of war to work, did in no way affect the responsibilities of the Foreign Office. According to Erich Albrecht, the Foreign Office Legal Division attempted to conceal from neutral investigators German violations of The Hague Convention in POW camps, fearing that such discoveries would lead to enemy reprisals. *NG 3353*, Robert Kempner's interrogation of Erich Albrecht, October 21, 1947.

[15] Foreign Office financial encouragement facilitated the establishment of such organizations as the Anti-Jewish World League, camouflaged as an export-import firm in its foreign work (*NG 4939*); see also *NG 3908*, *Abteilung Deutschland* correspondence concerning the establishment of an *Arbeitsgemeinschaft für europäische Völkerpolitik*, a "private" organization to work on ethnical aspects of German postwar policy.

[16] This development in fact was facilitated by the Foreign Office. Weizsäcker, representing the Foreign Office in an interministerial conference on October 23, expressed the view that "the Polish *General-Gouvernement* should not be designated nor administered in the international legal sense as an occupied area, as was Belgium in the 1914–18 war, since in that case rules of international law might apply to which we doubtless would not care to subject ourselves." *NG 4330*, Weizsäcker memorandum, October 23, 1939.

[17] See *PS 3614*, Reich Foreign Minister to Keitel (*OKW*), August 3, 1940. Ribbentrop here quotes the following Hitler decree: "The Führer has hereby expressly ordered that Ambassador Abetz is exclusively responsible for the handling of all political questions in Occupied and Unoccupied France. In so far as his functions touch upon military interests, Ambassador Abetz will act only in agreement with the Military Commander in Chief." In Denmark, Renthe-Fink's legation remained the liaison between Reich authorities and the Danish government until 1943.

[18] *Ciano Diaries*, entry for October 2, 1939. Ciano's estimates of Ribbentrop, one upstart's of another, were never favorable, but assumed great bitterness after the Nazi attack on Poland. On October 5, 1939, he wrote: "He [Ribbentrop] is an aristocrat, or, rather, a parvenu, and the shedding of the blood of the people does not worry him."

[19] See U.S. Department of State, *Nazi-Soviet Relations, 1939–1941*, pp. 330–334: a Schulenburg memorandum of his conversation with Hitler on April 28, 1941, and the Weizsäcker memorandum to Ribbentrop of the same date. Weizsäcker noted, *inter alia*: "It might perhaps be considered an alluring prospect to give the Communist system its death blow.... But the sole decisive factor is whether this project will hasten the fall of England." A German attack on Russia, the state secretary argued, "would only give the British new moral strength. It would be interpreted there as German uncertainty as to the success of our fight against England. We would thereby not only be admitting that the war was going to last a long time yet, but we might actually prolong it in this way...." It is ironic that verbal, tactical opposition to new projects of German

aggression compelled the state secretary, for the sake of argument, cumulatively
to accept the viability of prior adventures—such as the war in the West—which
he previously had opposed.

[20] Kordt, *Wahn und Wirklichkeit*, p. 304, footnote. I have not been able to
discover the document to which Kordt refers. It is not included in the above-cited
Nazi-Soviet Relations.

[21] *NG 2871*, Hitler decree of April 20, 1941. Before the invasion, Rosenberg's
office was, rather turgidly, known as the *Dienststelle für die zentrale Bearbeitung
der Fragen des osteuropäischen Raumes*.

[22] See pp. 33–37.

[23] Kordt, *Wahn und Wirklichkeit*, pp. 310–311, footnote. For information on
the moribund Council, see pp. 41–42.

[24] See *NG 4548*, minutes of *Chefbesprechung*, February 9, 1940, attended by
Goebbels, Lammers, Rosenberg, Kerrl, Ley, Heydrich (*RSHA*), and Weizsäcker.
This meeting was held to discuss the text of a proposed Hitler decree naming
Rosenberg "deputy for the safeguarding of the unity of National Socialist
philosophy." Kerrl objected to the decree on the grounds that such an official
government act would risk making the Nazi State seem an "enemy of Chris-
tianity." Weizsäcker, however, opposed Rosenberg's nomination to such a post,
because the Foreign Office insisted that "all directives and suggestions which
touch upon foreign policy require the approval of the Foreign Minister." Ribbentrop opposed any measure which might give Rosenberg opportunity to interfere in the internal affairs of his ministry.

[25] For details on this establishment, see chap. iii, n. 67.

[26] For details on Rosenberg's Norwegian activities, see *PS 004*, Rosenberg to
Hess, June 16, 1940. This report is highly critical of both the Foreign Office
and the Oslo legation (Minister Brauer), for their opposition to Rosenberg's
views about Quisling. Actually, before the invasion of Norway, only a handful
of Wilhelmstrasse officials, among them Ribbentrop, Weizsäcker, and Grundherr
(of the Political Division), were kept informed of the development of Rosenberg's and Hitler's plans with Quisling. The Foreign Office had no direct contact
with the latter until January, 1940, when it agreed to furnish him with a RM
200,000 subsidy.

[27] Peter Kleist, *Zwischen Hitler und Stalin*, p. 143.

[28] *NG 4633*, Senior Legation Counselor Grosskopf to Ribbentrop via Weizsäcker, June 4, 1941. Grosskopf's plan, which apparently was accepted in substance by Ribbentrop, initially was to involve the attachment of large staffs of
diplomats to army-group commands in the East. Later they would have been
located in Kiev, Tiflis, Riga, Minsk, and Moscow. Chief Wilhelmstrasse representatives would have been Twardowski, Dienstmann, Zechlin, Dr. Kleist, and
Tippelskirch. Hilger, embassy counselor in Moscow, was to remain with Ribbentrop as "interpreter."

[29] *NG 4990*, Grosskopf to Ribbentrop, June 19, 1941.

[30] Rosenberg's subsequent grotesque failure to impose his ministry's authority
over the brutal and ignorant *Reichskommissars* Koch and Lohse who later were
appointed by Hitler to govern the Ukraine and Baltic areas, has been sketched
by one of Rosenberg's own officials, Peter Kleist, *op. cit.*, pp. 129–229. Kleist
formerly was with Ribbentrop's *Dienststelle*, and was for a time head of Rosenberg's *Abteilung Ostland*.

[31] *Ibid.*, pp. 147–148.

[32] *NG 1690*, Rosenberg to Lammers, July 11, 1942. In this note, Rosenberg demanded from the Führer that Foreign Office diplomatic representatives be recalled, and also that the Wilhelmstrasse's Russia Committee be dissolved. Regrettably, I did not have access to the files of Foreign Office representatives' reports from Russia (now in possession of the U.S. Army) to obtain a clear picture of their activities. For Ribbentrop's complaints to Hitler, demanding on-the-spot policy-making powers for Foreign Office representatives, see *NG 1691*, foreign minister to Lammers, June 6, 1941.

[33] *NCA, L 221*, Protocol of Hitler meeting concerning basic occupation policy in the U.S.S.R., July 16, 1941. In this meeting, Rosenberg did not lose his opportunity to insist that the foreign minister's demand for a voice in Russian affairs be quashed.

[34] *NG 4556*, Gaus affidavit, January 25, 1948, regarding Ribbentrop's aims in 1941. Directly after the June 22 attack on Russia, the foreign minister embarked upon his vigorous but ill-starred efforts to draw Japan into the war against Russia. See his memorandum of June 28, 1941, regarding a conversation with the Japanese Ambassador Oshima, *NG 3437*. "Japan," Ribbentrop urged, "has been offered a unique opportunity by the present situation.... After Soviet power has been liquidated in the Far East ... Japan will find no difficulties in solving the Chinese problem in the desired way." The same sentiments were transmitted to the Japanese embassy the same day. A quick German-Japanese victory in Russia, the note declared, would serve to persuade the United States of the foolishness of going to war to aid Britain "against the most powerful combination on earth." *NG 4657*. Two weeks later, the foreign minister was even more sanguine. In a cable to the German ambassador in Tokyo, urging Ott to use "all the means at his disposal" to bring Japan into the war, he wrote: "It must remain our natural aim to join hands with Japan on the Trans-Siberian Railway before the beginning of winter." *NG 4426*, foreign minister to Ott, July 10, 1941. The foreign minister communicated the same sentiments to officials of the Foreign Office.

[35] *Hassell Diaries*, entry of August 22, 1941.

[36] *NCA*, Supplement B, p. 1229, Justice Jackson's interrogation of Ribbentrop. Erich Kordt had noted that "Hitler reportedly became so agitated during this conference that he was ill for several weeks in August." Kordt, *Wahn und Wirklichkeit*, p. 312, footnote.

[37] G. M. Gilbert, *The Psychology of Dictatorship* (New York: Ronald Press, 1950), p. 201.

CHAPTER VI

[1] *Völkischer Beobachter*, Berlin edition, May 21, 1942.

[2] *Loc. cit.*

[3] *NG 1251*, chart of the Foreign Office as of April 1, 1943.

[4] Kempner's interrogation of Dr. Fritz Hesse, formerly of the Information Division, *NG 2679*.

[5] *NG 2801*. Kempner's interrogation of Werner von Tippelskirch, former em-

bassy counselor in Moscow and member of the Russia Committee. The committee was formed in May, 1941. See *NG 142*, Grosskopf memorandum, May 5, 1941.

[6] *NG 3009*, foreign minister decree, April 5, 1943.

[7] *Loc. cit.*

[8] *Loc. cit.*

[9] Leonardo Simoni (pseudonym of Michele Lanza), *Berlino—Ambasciata d'Italia, 1939–1943* (Rome: Migliaresi, 1946), extract from Lanza's diary, May 14, 1943. Lanza was first secretary of the Italian embassy, 1939–1943.

[10] For a thorough treatment of the Foreign Office's part in the Third Reich's anti-Jewish measures, see Raoul Hilberg's study, "The Role of the German Civil Service in the Destruction of the Jews."

[11] Documents offered in evidence in the Wilhelmstrasse Trial (Case XI) by the American prosecution provide information on the role of the Foreign Office in these matters.

[12] Emil von Rintelen affidavit, June 4, 1947, *NG 3622*.

[13] *The Goebbels Diaries*, p. 512.

[14] Steengracht testimony at Ribbentrop's trial, *IMTP*, X, 108.

[15] *NG 4406* and *NG 5119*.

[16] For complete data on such Himmler agents, including their names and the posts to which they were assigned, see *NG 4852*, Geiger to Reich foreign minister, May 12, 1944. It emerges from this collection of documents that L. C. Moyzisch, author of *Operation Cicero*, was actually an *RSHA* police attaché, disguised in the Ankara embassy as "assistant to the trade attaché," and not a foreign-service officer, as his book would have us believe.

[17] Luther, or one of his immediate subordinates, represented the Wilhelmstrasse at the following characteristic conferences: the crucial Wannsee conference on January 20, 1942, concerning the "final settlement of the Jewish question," *NG 2586*; the conference on January 29, 1942, to draft a decree defining the term "Jew" in occupied Eastern territories, *NG 5035*; the conference on December 3, 1941, under leadership of *Obergruppenführer* Heydrich concerning methods of forced labor conscription in occupied territories, *NG 3347*. Weizsäcker, however, participated directly in negotiations with Heydrich on March 31, 1941, concerning regulations governing Himmler's police attachés in German missions. See *NG 4852*. Similarly, Steengracht participated in the interministerial conference on July 12, 1944, concerning conscription of foreign manpower. See *NG 1510*. As far as can be ascertained from documents presented at the Wilhelmstrasse (Case XI) Trial, preparatory planning for this infamous Wannsee conference was carried on in the *Abteilung Deutschland*, although the Legal Division raised objections to the conclusion of multilateral treaties concerning Jewish persecutions, preferring instead bilateral arrangements. See *Das Urteil im Wilhelmstrassen-Prozess*, pp. 84–86.

[18] For example, *NG 3325*, Woermann memorandum, November 29, 1938, concerning Foreign Office subsidization of Himmler's *Sicherheitsdienst* work in Slovakia. In this latter document, Woermann recommends that the *SD* be given a Reichsmark subsidy, but that future Foreign Office grants to them be made only for specific projects, and after the *SD* had made out a case for their political value.

[19] For example, *NG 4883*, Weizsäcker memorandum, July 5, 1938, concerning talk with Heydrich about the fate of imprisoned Austrian officials, political personalities, and intellectuals. The talk followed strong British representations

to the Foreign Office. Heydrich, noted Weizsäcker, expressed a willingness to divulge such information to the Foreign Office as would be necessary to refute charges contained in such diplomatic protests.

[20] *PS 2195*, Himmler memorandum, January 31, 1939, after a lengthy conversation with Oshima. A military extremist and close confidante of Himmler, Oshima first came to Berlin as Japanese military attaché, and later became ambassador to Germany. "[Oshima] has up to now succeeded in sending ten Russians with bombs across the Caucasian frontier," wrote Himmler. "These Russians had the task of eliminating Stalin. A number of other Russians whom he sent previously were shot on the border." Other imaginative enterprises of Oshima involved the employment of six Russians in a clandestine hideout at Falkensee (near Berlin), writing and printing pamphlets which were then sent, via balloon and "favorable winds," into the Soviet Union. Tracts were also smuggled into southern Russia via motorboat from Romania. The fate of this propaganda factory after the Nazi-Soviet rapprochement is not known. The Gestapo also rendered invaluable service to the Foreign Office by pilfering state documents of foreign powers. After the war, large numbers of intercepted foreign-diplomatic dispatches were found in Foreign Office files, together with covering letters from the *Geheime Staatspolizei* in Berlin. See *DGFP*, Series D, I, 486, footnote.

[21] Weizsäcker, on several occasions, had his own office discreetly searched by Canaris's *Abwehr* technicians for hidden Gestapo microphones. See affidavit of Dr. Herbert Siegfried, *Document Book Weizsäcker* V, Doc. 337. When Sumner Welles, in March, 1940, visited the state secretary's office he noticed that Weizsäcker "drew his chair toward the center of the room and motioned to me to do likewise. It was evident that . . . the German secret police microphones were installed in the walls." Sumner Welles, *A Time for Decision*, pp. 99–100.

[22] *Das Ehrenbuch der SA* and *Wer Ist's* (1935 ed.) list Killinger as *Führer der SA für Mitteldeutschland;* Jagow as *Führer der SA Gruppen Berlin-Brandenburg;* Ludin as *Führer der SA Gruppe Südwest* (Stuttgart) ; Kasche as *Gruppenführer der SA Gruppe Niedersachsen;* and Beckerle as *SA Gruppenführer Hessen.* Even Goebbels, who entertained few charitable thoughts about Ribbentrop's ministry, noted in his diary on May 9, 1943: "Our envoys in Southeastern Europe who stem from the *SA* have, in the opinion of the Foreign Office, by no means proven themselves capable. . . . That shows that diplomacy, too, must be learned. You cannot simply assign good *SA* goose-steppers to a diplomatic post, for problems cannot be solved merely by manly courage and insolence." *The Goebbels Diaries, 1942–1943*, p. 362. Hassell, in his diary, recalled meeting Killinger, one of them, at his Bucharest post late in 1941. "Wilmowsky, Dietrich and I," wrote Hassell, "called on Killinger . . . and were horrified at this brutal, uneducated, superficial sergeant major. He remarked that it would be best simply to set fire to Bucharest; it was nothing but a pigsty. He was wholly indifferent and uninformed about the problems that interested us." *Hassell Diaries*, pp. 220–221.

[23] The *OKW-Abwehr*, since October, 1933, had been authorized by a Hitler decree to carry on its foreign espionage work "independently and without the aid of other offices." Nevertheless, according to a summary report prepared by the Foreign Office Political Division in 1940, "the closest and most confidential co-operation [had] been established over the years" between the two organizations. See *NG 3494*, Heyden-Rynsch to Woermann, May 25, 1940. Contact

between the Foreign Office and the *Abwehr* was maintained through the Political Division and not, as was to be the case with liaison with Himmler's *SD*, through *Abteilung Deutschland.* Rivalry between Canaris's and Himmler's agencies was spurred by the ambition of Walter Schellenberg, intelligence (*Amt VI*) chief of *RSHA* to monopolize German espionage, and by mounting evidence of the inefficiency and political unreliability of *Abwehr.* See H. R. Trevor-Roper, *The Last Days of Hitler,* pp. 24–28.

[24] *NG 2316,* Likus memorandum to foreign minister, August 9, 1940.

[25] *Loc. cit.* A curious self-denial, since the very same report explicitly notes instances where *SD* agents already (before May, 1940) had "carried out . . . measures of foreign policy" such as "preparation for the annexation of Austria," the "dissolution of Czechoslovakia; preparation for the war against Poland; and the Venlo affair [kidnapping of British agents from the Netherlands]."

[26] *NG 3928,* Schumburg to Kotze of the Riga legation, January 3, 1940, notifying him of plans to send additional Himmler agents abroad. Reports from Himmler agents transmitted through German missions should be sent to *RSHA* via the Foreign Office's *Abteilung Deutschland.*

[27] *NG 4588,* Himmler-Ribbentrop agreement signed at Führer headquarters on August 8, 1941.

[28] *NG 4852,* Geiger memorandum to foreign minister, May 12, 1944. Sometimes, apparently, "green-envelope material" was scrutinized by mission chiefs. According to Geiger, the Himmler agent in Ankara, Moyzisch (who handled the famous Operation *Cicero*), made the habit of submitting "practically all the material going to *RSHA* . . . to the Chief of Mission [Papen]" for information. "Green" correspondence came chiefly from missions in Madrid, Stockholm, Lisbon, and Lausanne.

[29] *NG 2214,* Ribbentrop to Lorenz, chief of *VOMI,* January 18, 1941. Ribbentrop's demand in this note that Lorenz submit "all general political questions" to him for approval caused Himmler to pencil a marginal comment on it: "So the Foreign Minister now wants to lead the Germans abroad!"

[30] *NG 3981, Abteilung Deutschland* file labeled "Difficulties between the *Reichsführer-SS* and the Foreign Office, 1942." According to an organization chart, January 1, 1941, the *RSHA* controlled issuance of passports for German citizens. Later, in October, 1943, *RSHA* had a central visa office as well. See Case XI, *Prosecution Document Book,* LXXI, *L 185* and *L 219.*

[31] *NG 3334, Reichsführer-SS* to Foreign Office, May 10, 1943.

[32] See *NG 3363,* Kaltenbrunner of *RSHA* to foreign minister, denouncing Minister Veesenmayer in Budapest for "defeatism," September 6, 1944; see also similar Kaltenbrunner memorandum, September 15, 1944, *NG 3043;* also affidavit of *SS* General Karl Wolff, concerning *SS* denunciation of Ambassador Ritter in 1940, *Document Book Ritter,* II, Doc. 8.

[33] *NG 3330,* Luther to *SS* General Wolff, August 8, 1942, dealing with various squabbles of this character, such as the Hungarian Minister Stojay's "unauthorized" and "illegal" negotiations with *SS-Gruppenführer* Berger concerning drafting of *Waffen-SS* units in Hungary.

[34] Ribbentrop interrogation, August 30, 1945, *NCA,* Supplement B, p. 1182.

[35] Ribbentrop interrogation, August 31, 1945, *ibid.,* pp. 1195–1196.

[36] *NG 5036,* Steengracht to foreign minister, November 7, 1943.

[37] See *Operation Cicero,* pp. 81–97, for Moyzisch's account of this strange imbroglio.

[38] *NG 4852*, draft of telegram from Ribbentrop to Papen, June 17, 1944.

[39] See Curt Prüfer affidavit, *Document Book Steengracht*, I, Doc. 6.

[40] *Loc. cit.*

[41] Schroeder, chief of the Personnel Division, later recalled having gotten wind of Luther's scheme "around Christmas of 1943," at which time he (Schroeder) informed Weizsäcker of it. See Schroeder affidavit, *Document Book Weizsäcker*, V, Doc. 146. As far as is discernible, the state secretary took no part whatsoever in Luther's scheme. I have not come across Luther's memorandum, which easily may have been destroyed.

[42] *Hassell Diaries*, entry for March 28, 1943, p. 293.

[43] The fabric of this account is woven from various sources—Kordt's *Wahn und Wirklichkeit*, p. 373; Weizsäcker's *Erinnerungen*, p. 345—and was confirmed by Luther's widow in a conversation I had with her in July, 1951. Incarcerated in various camps, Luther attempted suicide, was hospitalized, and released just before the Russian capture of Berlin. He apparently died shortly thereafter of a heart attack. It was Hassell's view that the SS was little "interested" in Luther, but "set a trap for him in the hope of getting something on Ribbentrop." *Hassell Diaries*, entry of March 6, 1943, p. 290. According to Sir David Maxwell-Fyfe at Nürnberg, Luther had recommended to Himmler that Werner Best, a former *RSHA* official then Reich minister in Denmark, be made foreign minister; this has not been confirmed by any other sources, however. See *IMTP*, X, 213–214.

[44] For complete details of these administrative changes, see *NG 4891*, a regulation promulgated by Schroeder on March 25, 1943.

[45] *IMTP*, X, 126. "I was adjutant," Steengracht testified, "that is to say I was concerned with technical matters. At that time I never presented a political report to him [Ribbentrop]." I have discovered nothing to contradict this.

[46] *The Goebbels Diaries*, entry for May 26, 1943.

[47] Affidavit of Dr. Gerhard Klopfer, former Party Chancellery official, *Document Book Steengracht*, Doc. 13. "Bormann," wrote Klopfer, "told me of this afterwards, apparently in order to induce me to act similarly."

[48] During the Wilhelmstrasse trial, Wagner (who testified for the prosecution before fleeing from Germany) had the following to say to a defense lawyer's sarcastic assertion that Wagner had "entered the Foreign Office via [his] sports career and not because of any academic examination as is usually required for such a post": "I would like to object to this question in this form. Like many other people of all nations I believed that sports was the best basis for understanding between the youth of all nations." Wagner conceded he had begun his diplomatic career "by being attached to the most prominent guests at the Olympic Games." *Case XI Transcript* (English version), pp. 2585–2586. Upon taking up the new "sport" of liaison with Himmler and Kaltenbrunner, Wagner was pushed up the service ladder to the rank of senior legation counselor in September, 1943; on December 9, 1944, the Finance Ministry was requested to authorize his appointment as minister first class. See *NG 2894*.

[49] Schroeder decree, March 25, 1943. *NG 4891*.

[50] *Loc. cit.*

[51] Schroeder circular, May 5, 1943. *NG 1791*.

[52] *The Goebbels Diaries*, pp. 266–267.

[53] *Ibid.*, pp. 289–290.

[54] *Ibid.*, p. 539.

[55] This comment via Hassell. *Hassell Diaries*, p. 236.

[56] *The Goebbels Diaries*, p. 502.

[57] *Ibid.*, entry of July 27, 1943, p. 407.

[58] G. M. Gilbert, *op. cit.*, pp. 190–191.

[59] *Hassell Diaries*, pp. 300–301.

[60] Ribbentrop earlier, on June 6, 1942, had offered to make a deal with Himmler: for every 10,000 *Waffen-SS* volunteers the Foreign Office could round up in occupied areas, Himmler should make available 10 young *SS* men for diplomatic service. Ribbentrop complained that previous Himmler promises to turn over personnel had, "like Dr. Ley's Volkswagen, up to now remained purely platonic. Since my appointment as Foreign Minister I have not received a single co-worker from *SS* ranks." *NG 3648*, Ribbentrop to Himmler, June 6, 1942.

[61] Emil von Rintelen affidavit, *Document Book Woermann*, III, Doc. 82.

[62] Steengracht's appointment came as somewhat of a surprise to some officials since, as Erich Albrecht of the Legal Division further observed in his affidavit, "he had not followed the normal career of foreign service." See *NG 4278*. This was plausible; not since the early 'twenties had a noncareer diplomat occupied the post.

[63] An old friend of Steengracht, from university days, described the state secretary as a weak-willed man, driven by an "ambitious and unscrupulous wife." He told an American official that Steengracht "was not capable of giving orders, even to his own servants. He just could not do it." *NG 3747*, Kempner's interrogation of Philipp August von Bethmann-Hollweg.

[64] Ribbentrop's private secretary, Margarete Blank, testified at Nürnberg that when Steengracht was informed of his appointment by Ribbentrop (while on the latter's train en route to Salzburg), a vigorous clash ensued, reverberating through the train, when Steengracht tried to get out of the job. See her affidavit, *Document Book Steengracht*, I, Doc. 5.

[65] See telegram from Kaltenbrunner to *SS Personalhauptamt*, March 22, 1943, notifying it of Six's new appointment. U.S. Army Document Center 7771, Berlin, *SS* Personnel files.

[66] For Megerle's background, see Derrick Sington and Arthur Weidenfeld, *The Goebbels Experiment*, p. 130.

[67] Rühle's Party activities since 1925 were nothing short of monumental. Before joining the Foreign Office about 1939, he held no less than 26 active posts in various Party apparatuses. Rühle files, U.S. Army Document Center 7771, Berlin.

[68] *NG 3512*, Steengracht memorandum for foreign minister, July 19, 1944.

[69] *Loc. cit.*

[70] *Loc. cit.*

[71] Hilberg, *op. cit.*; for illustrative examples of *Inland*'s exterminative work, see *NG 8424*, memorandum from Paul Karl Schmidt, of Press Division, to the state secretary, May 27, 1944; also *NG 2952*, Thadden of *Inland II* to Wagner, June 8, 1944.

[72] *NG 5015*, Steengracht to German missions abroad, April 28, 1944. Rudolf Schleier, in an affidavit, ascribed the *Aktionsstelle*'s establishment to Hitler's wish to "influence" the forthcoming American presidential election, through anti-Semitic propaganda. The Führer offered this job to Ribbentrop, threatening that if Ribbentrop declined it he would give it to Goebbels. *Document Book Steengracht*, I, Doc. 69.

[73] *NG 2952*, Thadden to Wagner, June 8, 1944. One consular secretary, Hez-

inger, deserved a promotion. He had done much of the spade work for the inter-ministry Jewish-specialist conference at Krummhübel, and most of the editorial work on *Tagesspiegel*, an anti-Semitic journal.

[74] Thus, for example, *Inland* officials urged on June 6, 1944, that large-scale violence against Budapest Jews scheduled for some time that month be so timed as to coincide with Allied landings in France; thus news of the former would be drowned out by the latter. *NG 2260*, Wagner memorandum. Paul Karl Schmidt, of the Press Division, anticipating "violent reactions" abroad after the Budapest action, urged in another memorandum that pretexts for it be "arranged," such as "discovery of explosives in Jewish clubs or synagogues, unearthing of sabotage organizations." *NG 2424*, Schmidt to state secretary, May 27, 1944.

[75] See Hans Schroeder affidavit, *Document Book Steengracht*, VII, Doc. 118. According to Schroeder, Ribbentrop refused to consider Steengracht competent to deputize for him. "It was on account of that decision and on account of other fundamental questions that Herr von Steengracht...requested the Foreign Minister in my presence to release him from his position. The Foreign Minister abruptly refused his request....I know that Ribbentrop feared that another change of State Secretaries within so short a period might result in personal disadvantages for him, and that it was quite possible that he might be forced to appoint as State Secretary one of Himmler's agents."

[76] *NG 1251*, organization chart of the Foreign Office as of April 1, 1943, prepared by Dr. Friedrich Gaus.

[77] Erich Albrecht affidavit, *NG 4278*.

[78] Franz Six's affidavit, *Document Book Steengracht*, I, Doc. 11.

[79] *NG 1251*, Gaus's April 1, 1943, organization chart. The higher officialdom, by April 1, 1943, was almost totally Nazified. Of the 63 officials appearing on Dr. Friedrich Gaus's (incomplete) organization chart of that date, 51 were, by then, Party members. Two had been rejected by the Party after application. Information on four is unavailable.

[80] *Hassell Diaries*, December 5, 1943. Goebbels also described the raid. "The government quarter," he wrote, "is nothing short of an inferno. One can hardly recognize the Wilhelmplatz." *Goebbels Diaries*, November 24, 1943. For newspaper accounts of these raids, see New York *Times*, November 24 and 25, 1943.

[81] Schmidt, *op. cit.*, p. 558.

[82] For a brief account of this bureaucratic evacuation see *DGFP*, Series D, IV, x–xi.

[83] *NG 3703*, interrogation of Legation Counselor Eduard von Selzam, July 18, 1947.

[84] Testimony of Albrecht von Kessel, June 21, 1948, at Nürnberg, *Case XI Transcript* (English version), pp. 9553–9556; also Allen W. Dulles, *Germany's Underground, passim*. The "nexus" between Foreign Office and army conspirators seems to have been provided by familial relationships of Häften, Kessel, and others.

[85] Weizsäcker, *op. cit.*, p. 177.

[86] See Kessel testimony, *Case XI Transcript* (English version), pp. 9553–9556. Also Dulles, *op. cit.*, pp. 125–146.

[87] Weizsäcker was not held in high esteem by some of the more important July 20 conspirators. The full story is not clear; until early 1942, Hassell had viewed the state secretary as a useful informant. But Weizsäcker, evidently fearful of Hassell's extreme intentions and his indiscretions, broke with him. In a conver-

sation between the two on April 29, 1942, at Weizsäcker's home, "he proceeded [Hassell wrote] to heap reproaches on me as he paced excitedly up and down. I had been unbelievably indiscreet, quite unheard of; as a matter of fact, 'with all due deference,' so had my wife. This was all known in certain places (the Gestapo), and they claimed to have documents. He must demand, most emphatically, that I correct this behavior. . . . I should certainly burn everything I had in the way of notes which covered conversations in which one or another had said this or that. Apparently he meant himself. . . . Finally he said: 'Now, auf Wiedersehen, but please not too soon!' " *Hassell Diaries*, entry for April 27 (*sic*), 1942. Immediately thereafter the state secretary evidently warned his subordinates to shun Hassell, instructing them under no circumstances to tell Hassell of this. *Hassell Diaries*, entry for May 1, 1942. Hassell would have none of him after this, nor, apparently, would General Beck, one of the principal underground leaders. Discussing possible post-Nazi cabinet leaders in December, 1943, Hassell wrote: "Goerdeler thinks Popitz would be suitable for the embassy to the Vatican. Not bad, for Beck would reject Weizsäcker for this post, and, indeed, for any post, especially because of Weizsäcker's speech to the diplomats . . . returning from America in May, 1942." *Hassell Diaries*, entry for December 27, 1943. See p. 121.

[88] Hans Schroeder affidavit, *Document Book Ritter*, IV, Doc. 44. Also Gustav Adolf Sonnenhol affidavit, *Document Book Weizsäcker*, V, Doc. 43. For a partial transcript of Judge Freisler's McCarthy-like *Volksgericht* proceedings against Schulenburg, Hassell, Trott zu Solz, and others, see *NG 1019:* transcript from a recording of the Nazi propaganda film, "Proceedings against the Criminals of 20 July 1944." A total of eight martyred diplomats are listed by Rudolf Pechel in his *Ehrentafel der Toten des 20. Juli*. Pechel, *Deutscher Widerstand*, pp. 339–343.

[89] *NG 4972*, Bohle to Himmler, September 25, 1944.

[90] Bohle testimony, *Case XI Transcript* (English version), p. 13510.

[91] *NG 3876*, Lammers memorandum, December 13, 1944.

[92] Ribbentrop interrogation, August 30, 1945. *NCA*, Supplement B, p. 1182.

[93] *NG 3341*, Rintelen memorandum, September 30, 1944.

[94] *Loc. cit.*

[95] Trevor-Roper, *The Last Days of Hitler*, p. 32.

[96] *Ibid.*, p. 52.

[97] Count Folke Bernadotte, *The Fall of the Curtain*, pp. 13–19.

[98] *Ibid.*, p. 18.

[99] Trevor-Roper, *op. cit.*, p. 52.

[100] Schmidt, *op. cit.*, p. 584.

[101] New York *Times*, June 17, 1945.

CHAPTER VII

[1] Some characteristic reflections on this problem may be found in Gordon Craig, "The Professional Diplomat and His Problems," *World Politics*, IV (January, 1952), 145–158; George Kennan, *American Diplomacy, 1900–1950* (Chicago: University of Chicago Press, 1951); Harold Nicolson's two works: *Lord*

Curzon: The Last Phase (Boston: Houghton Mifflin, 1934) and *Diplomacy* (New York: Harcourt, Brace, 1939) ; Sir Victor Wellesley, *Diplomacy in Fetters* (London: Hutchinson, 1944) ; and Sir Robert Vansittart, "The Decline of Diplomacy," *Foreign Affairs*, XXVIII (January, 1950), 177–188. All of these works approach the problem in a fashion sympathetic to the professional diplomat.

² Quoted by A. F. Whyte in his introduction to De Callières, *On the Manner of Negotiating with Princes* (English transl., Boston: Houghton Mifflin, 1919), p. xi.

³ Nicolson, *Curzon*, p. 387.

⁴ Robert Nightingale, *The Personnel of the British Foreign Office* (London: The Fabian Society, 1930), *passim.*

⁵ David Thomson, *Democracy in France*, p. 59; also Frederick L. Schuman, *War and Diplomacy in the French Republic* (New York: McGraw-Hill, 1931), *passim.*

⁶ Robert Bendiner, *The Riddle of the State Department* (New York: Farrar and Rinehart, 1942), p. 112.

⁷ *Ibid.*, p. 111.

⁸ An observation of Sir John Simon, in his introduction to John Tilley and Stephen Gaselee, *The Foreign Office* (London: Putnam, 1933), p. ix.

⁹ *Proposals for the Reform of the Foreign Service*, Cmd. 6420 (London: H. M. Stationery Office, 1943), p. 2.

¹⁰ An American official recently estimated that, in the 1947–1948 fiscal year, "only 25 per cent of the U.S. representatives in 394 international meetings were from the Department of State." George McGhee, "Coordinating Foreign Aid," *Department of State Publication 3392* (January, 1949), p. 8.

¹¹ Craig, *op. cit.*, pp. 147–148.

¹² Vansittart, *op. cit.*, p. 186.

¹³ Nicolson, *Curzon*, pp. 48–49.

¹⁴ *Ibid.*, p. 60.

¹⁵ "Lord Curzon," Nicolson wrote, "used to complain bitterly that, of all Government Departments, the Foreign Office was the only one which was never permitted to conduct itself." *Ibid.*, p. 60, footnote.

¹⁶ *Ibid.*, p. 56.

¹⁷ Vansittart, *op. cit.*, p. 186.

¹⁸ Craig, *op. cit.*, p. 153.

¹⁹ Sumner Welles, *Seven Decisions That Shaped History*, pp. 215–216.

²⁰ James F. Byrnes, *Speaking Frankly* (New York: Harper, 1947), p. 23.

²¹ William Langer and S. Everett Gleason—in their study of American diplomacy, *The Challenge to Isolation* (New York: Harper, 1952), pp. 8–9—observe that the president "felt that the Department and more particularly the Foreign Service contained ... many men who had been appointed for social rather than for more practical considerations, who were unfriendly to his foreign as [sic] to his domestic policies, and who were not beyond making unauthorized disclosures to opposition circles."

²² The all-time mileage record for transoceanic diplomatic hopping seems to have been set by former Secretary James Byrnes, of the United States. In the fifteen months between July, 1945 and October, 1946, the secretary of state crossed the Atlantic no less than 14 times. Byrnes's travels are proudly and graphically mapped on the cover pages of his recollections, *Speaking Frankly*.

²³ For Kennedy's views, see Langer and Gleason, *op. cit.*, pp. 481–482: "Church-

ill ... certainly sensed the Ambassador's skepticism and must have feared its effect on Washington. Happily, as a 'Former Naval Person,' the new Prime Minister had been in direct though only occasional communication with the President."

[24] Jules Cambon, *The Diplomatist* (London: Philip Allan, 1931), p. 3.

[25] Nicolson, *Curzon*, pp. 402–403.

[26] Vansittart, *op. cit.*, p. 179.

[27] *Loc. cit.*

[28] Bendiner, *op. cit.*, p. 109.

[29] Kennan, *op. cit.*, pp. 93–94.

[30] Hannah Arendt, *The Origins of Totalitarianism*, pp. 380–381.

[31] The nadir of such incongruous diplomatic affability is recorded in the memoirs of Paul Otto Schmidt, chief of Ribbentrop's *Büro RAM*. When the American chargé d'affaires in Berlin, on December 11, 1941, appeared before Ribbentrop to receive from him Germany's declaration of war on the United States, Schmidt recalls how he himself afterwards "accompanied the American diplomat—with whom we in the Foreign Office had good reason to sympathize— to the door, gave him my hand, and smiled at him. Outside, the Protocol Chief awaited him, and to my satisfaction assumed the same demeanour as I, and did his best to lighten these painful moments for the American chargé." Schmidt, *op. cit.*, p. 542.

[32] Hitler himself was conscious of the benefits of such administrative chaos. "German diplomacy," he once remarked during the war, "was so alienated from reality that it never placed confidence in the German colonists abroad, nor did it cultivate and direct them. What German consulate now goes out of its way to help German colonists? For this reason he had had to create the *Auslands-organisation*, to the great displeasure of the Foreign Office." Picker, *Hitlers Tischgespräche im Führerhauptquartier*, pp. 60–61.

BIBLIOGRAPHY

DOCUMENTARY SOURCES

The major primary sources of materials for this study are located in the documentation of the so-called Ministries Trial, *The United States of America against Ernst von Weizsäcker, et al.*, conducted under Military Tribunal IV of the U.S. Army under Control Council Law No. 10. This was the last of a series of American military war-crimes trials and was concerned with German diplomats and other officials. It was held at Nürnberg between January 6, 1948, and April 14, 1949. The material consisted of about 6,000 documents—chiefly the so-called *NG* Series—assembled by the Office of Chief of Counsel for the Prosecution of Axis Criminality, only a small part of which was offered in evidence; approximately 15,000 mimeographed pages of trial transcript; and document books prepared by counsel of each of the 21 defendants (seven of whom—Ernst von Weizsäcker, Gustav Adolf Steengracht von Moyland, Ernst Woermann, Karl Ritter, Ernst W. Bohle, Otto von Erdmannsdorff, and Edmund Veesenmayer—were former officials of the German Foreign Office).

Original documents of the *NG* Series are deposited in the U.S. Army Document Center in Alexandria, Virginia. I chiefly used mimeographed copies of them, together with staff evidence analyses and the trial transcript, deposited in the International Law Library of Columbia University. I also used the mimeographed defense document books now in the Law Faculty of Heidelberg University.

NG materials used consisted primarily of extracts from the captured archives of the German Foreign Office, covering the period 1938–1945, and, to a lesser extent, the preceding five years of Nazi rule; interrogations by prosecution staff members of former Foreign Office officials; affidavits prepared by former German diplomats; and extracts from various German newspapers, official journals, and other publications. Defense document books were mostly composed of affidavits by former German diplomats; diary extracts; and affidavits by non-German diplomatic, ecclesiastical, and other personalities.

Other document series (*PS, D,* and *L*) cited as sources are materials prepared for evidence in the trial of the major war criminals, and may be found either in *Nazi Conspiracy and Aggression* or in *Trial of the Major War Criminals* (fully cited below.

For official German materials on the legal basis and structure of the Foreign Office, I consulted the *Proceedings of the Weimar Constitutional Assembly* (*Verhandlungen der deutschen Nationalversammlung,* 1919), the *Proceedings of the German Reichstag* (*Verhandlungen des Reichstags,* 1920–1932), and the official *Reichsgesetzblatt* (1933–1943).

For biographical data and information of Party membership of members of the German Foreign Office, I made use of captured membership files of the Party, *SS,* and affiliated Nazi organizations, in possession of the Army Document Center 7771, Berlin. Lists of higher German Foreign Office officials stationed in Berlin between 1937 and 1943, prepared by me from official organizational charts of the Foreign Office, were submitted to the Document Center, which checked them against its files. The files of some selected leading officials I checked myself, in the Document Center.

Other biographical data were drawn from the German Who's Who, *Hermann Degeners Wer Ists* (1922, 1928, and 1935 editions), and *Das Ehrenbuch der SA* (Düsseldorf: Friedrich Flöder Verlag, 1934).

Other Official Publications

International Military Tribunal. *Trial of the Major War Criminals Before the International Military Tribunal, Nürnberg, 14 November 1945–1 October 1946* (Nürnberg: International Military Tribunal, 1947–1949), I–XLVI. Transcript of trial, and documents offered in evidence by American, British, French, and Russian prosecution staffs.

United States. Office of Chief of Counsel for Prosecution of Axis Criminality, *Nazi Conspiracy and Aggression* (Washington: U.S. Government Printing Office, 1946), I–VIII, 2 supplements. Documentary evidence and guide materials prepared by American, British, French, and Soviet prosecution staffs for presentation before the International Military Tribunal in the trial of the major war criminals.

United States. Department of State. *Documents on German Foreign Policy: 1918–1945,* Series D, I–IV. Extracts from German Foreign Office archives, edited jointly by teams of American, British, and French scholars. The materials thus far published in this series cover the period 1937–April, 1939.

United States. Department of State. *Nazi-Soviet Relations: 1939–1941. Documents from the Archives of the German Foreign Office.* Edited by Raymond James Sontag and James Stuart Beddie (Washington: Government Printing Office, 1948).

United States. Department of State. *National Socialism: Basic Principles, Their Application by the Nazi Party's Foreign Organization, and the Use of Germans Abroad for Nazi Aims.* Prepared by Raymond E. Murphy, *et al.* (Washington: Government Printing Office, 1943).

United States. Army Headquarters, Army Service Forces, *Civil Affairs Handbook Germany, Section Z: Government and Administration* (M 356-2) (Washingington: 1944).

Great Britain. Foreign Office. *Return showing the Conditions of Entry into the Austro-Hungarian, German and Other Diplomatic and Foreign Offices* (London: H. M. Stationery Office, 1913).

Great Britain. Woodward, E. L., and Rohan Butler (eds.), *Documents on British Foreign Policy: 1919–1939.* Third Series, I–III. (London: H. M. Stationery Office, 1946–1950).

Union of Soviet Socialist Republics. Ministry of Foreign Affairs, *Documents and Materials Relating to the Eve of the Second World War* (Moscow: Foreign Languages Publishing House, 1948), I, II. German Foreign Office files and papers of former Ambassador Herbert von Dirksen, captured by the Soviet Union.

BOOKS AND ARTICLES

Arendt, Hannah. *The Origins of Totalitarianism* (New York: Harcourt, Brace, 1951).

Bernadotte, Folke. *The Fall of the Curtain* (London: Cassel, 1945).

Blücher, Wipert von. *Deutschlands Weg nach Rapallo* (Wiesbaden: Limes Verlag, 1951).

Carr, Edward Hallett. *The Twenty Years' Crisis: 1919–1939*, 2d ed. (London: Macmillan, 1946).

Churchill, Winston S. *The Gathering Storm* (Boston: Houghton Mifflin, 1950).

Ciano, Gallazeo. *The Ciano Diaries, 1939–1943.* Edited by Hugh Gibson. Garden City: Doubleday, 1946.

Craig, Gordon. "Military Diplomats in the Prussian and German Service: The Attachés, 1816–1914," *Political Science Quarterly*, LXIV (March, 1949), 65–94.

———, and Felix Gilbert, eds. *The Diplomats: 1919–1939* (Princeton: Princeton University Press, 1953).

———. "The Professional Diplomat and his Problems, 1919–1939," *World Politics*, IV (January, 1952), 145–158.

Curtius, Julius. *Sechs Jahre Minister der Deutschen Republik* (Heidelberg: Carl Winter Verlag, 1948).

Dirksen, Herbert von. *Moskau-Tokio-London: Erinnerungen und Betrachtungen zu 20 Jahren Deutscher Aussenpolitik, 1919–1939* (Stuttgart: W. Kohlhammer Verlag, 1949).

Dodd, William E., Jr., and Martha Dodd, eds. *Ambassador Dodd's Diary* (New York: Harcourt, Brace, 1941).

Dulles, Allen Welsh. *Germany's Underground* (New York: Macmillan, 1947).

Fischer, Ruth. *Stalin and German Communism* (Cambridge: Harvard University Press, 1948).

François-Poncet, André. *The Fateful Years: Memoirs of a French Ambassador in Berlin, 1931–1938.* Translated from the French by Jacques Le Clercq (New York: Harcourt, Brace, 1949).

Germany Speaks. With a preface by Joachim von Ribbentrop. (London: Butterworth, 1938).

Gerth, Hans. "The Nazi Party: Its Leadership and Composition," *American Journal of Sociology*, XLV (January, 1940), 517–541.

Geyr von Schweppenburg, Freiherr. *Erinnerungen eines Militärattachés, London, 1933–1937* (Stuttgart: Deutsche Verlags-Anstalt, 1949).

Gilbert, G. M. *Nuremberg Diary* (New York: Farrar, Straus, 1947).

Goebbels, Paul Joseph. *The Goebbels Diaries.* Edited by L. P. Lochner (New York: Doubleday, 1948).

Hallgarten, George W. F. "General Hans von Seeckt and Russia, 1920–1922," *Journal of Modern History*, XXI (March, 1949), 28–34.

Hassell, Ulrich von. *The von Hassell Diaries, 1938–1944.* With a preface by Allen Welsh Dulles. (Garden City: Doubleday, 1947).

Heiden, Konrad. *Der Führer* (Boston: Houghton Mifflin, 1944).

Henderson, Nevile. *Failure of a Mission* (New York: Putnam's, 1940).

Hilberg, Raoul. "The Role of the German Civil Service in the Destruction of the Jews," unpublished master's thesis, Columbia University, 1950.

Hindenburg, Herbert von. *Das Auswärtige Amt im Wandel der Zeiten* (Frankfurt am Main: Societäts-Verlag, 1932).

Hintze, Otto. "Die Entstehung der modernen Staatsministerien," *Historische Zeitschrift*, IV-3 (1908), 53–111.

Hitler, Adolf. *Mein Kampf* (New York: Reynal and Hitchcock, 1940). Edited and annotated by John Chamberlain, *et al.*

Kleist, Peter. *Zwischen Hitler und Stalin* (Bonn: Athenäum Verlag, 1950).

Kordt, Erich. *Nicht aus den Akten* (Stuttgart: Union Deutsche Verlagsgesellschaft, 1950).

———. *Wahn und Wirklichkeit* (Stuttgart: Union Deutsche Verlagsgesellschaft, 1948).

Kraske, Erich. *Handbuch des Auswärtigen Dienstes* (Halle an der Saale: Max Niemeyer Verlag, 1939).

Kühlmann, Richard von. *Thoughts on Germany* (London: Macmillan, 1932). Translated from the German by Eric Sutton.

Lang, Serge, and Ernst von Schenck, eds., *The Memoirs of Alfred Rosenberg.* Translated from the German by Eric Posselt. (Chicago: Ziff-Davis, 1949.)

Ludecke, Kurt G. W. *I Knew Hitler* (New York: Scribner's, 1938).

Mackay, B. L. *Die Moderne Diplomatie* (Frankfurt am Main: Rutten und Loening, 1915).

Martienssen, Anthony. *Hitler and his Admirals* (New York: Dutton, 1949).

Mendelssohn-Bartholdy, Albrecht. *Diplomatie* (Berlin-Grunewald: Dr. Walter Rothschild, 1927).

Morstein-Marx, Fritz, "Civil Service in Germany," in White, Leonard D., *et al.*, *Civil Service Abroad* (New York: McGraw-Hill, 1937).

———. *Government in the Third Reich*, 2d ed. (New York, McGraw-Hill, 1937).

Moyzisch, L. C. *Operation Cicero* (New York: Coward-McCann, 1950).

Muncy, L. W. *The Junker in the Prussian Administration under William II, 1888–1914* (Providence: Brown University Press, 1944).

Namier, L. B. *Diplomatic Prelude: 1938–1939* (London: Macmillan, 1948).

———. *In the Nazi Era* (London: Macmillan, 1952).

Neef, Hermann. *Deutsches Berufsbeamtentum* (Berlin: Verlag Beamtenpresse, 1942).

Neumann, Franz. *Behemoth: The Structure and Practice of National Socialism* (New York: Oxford University Press, 1942).

Nicolson, Harold. *Diplomacy* (New York: Harcourt, Brace, 1939).

———. *Lord Curzon: The Last Phase* (Boston: Houghton Mifflin, 1934).

Norton, H. K. "Foreign Office Organization," *Annals of the American Academy of Political and Social Science*, CXLIII (1929), supplement.

Pechel, Rudolf. *Deutscher Widerstand* (Zürich: Eugen Rentsch Verlag, 1947).

Picker, Henry, ed. *Hitlers Tischgespräche im Führerhauptquartier, 1941–1942* (Bonn: Athenäum Verlag, 1951).

Pollock, James Kerr. *The Government of Greater Germany*, revised printing (New York: Van Nostrand, 1940).

Poole, De Witt C. "New Light on Nazi Foreign Policy," *Foreign Affairs*, XXV (October, 1946), 130–154.

Rahn, Rudolf. *Ruheloses Leben: Aufzeichnungen und Erinnerungen* (Düsseldorf: Diederichs Verlag, 1949).

Rauschning, Hermann. *Hitler Speaks: A Series of Political Conversations with Adolf Hitler on His Real Aims* (London: Butterworth, 1939).

———. *Men of Chaos* (New York: Putnam, 1942).

Richthofen, Hartmann Freiherr von, Dr. Friedrich Berber, et al., eds. *Jahrbuch für Auswärtige Politik* (Berlin: Brückenverlag, later A. Gross, 1929–1943). In 9 annual vols.

Rogers, Lindsay, et al. "Aspects of German Political Institutions," *Political Science Quarterly*, XLVII (Sept. and Dec., 1932), 321–351, 576–601.

Rosenberg, Arthur. *The Birth of the German Republic, 1871–1918*. Translated from the German by Ian F. D. Morrow (New York: Oxford University Press, 1931).

Schifferdecker, Otto R. *Die Organisation des Auswärtigen Dienstes im Alten und Neuen Reich* (Heidelberg: privately printed, 1932).

Schmidt, Paul [Otto]. *Statist auf diplomatischer Bühne: 1923–1945. Erlebnisse des Chefdolmetschers im Auswärtigen Amt mit den Staatsmännern Europas* (Bonn: Athenäum Verlag, 1949).

Schmidt-Pauli, Edgar von. *Diplomaten in Berlin* (Berlin: Mauritius Verlag, 1930).

Schmitt, Carl. *Staat, Bewegung, Volk* (Hamburg: Hanseatische Verlagsgesellschaft, 1935).

Schrameier, W. *Auswärtiges Amt und Auslandsvertretung: Vorschläge zur Reform* (Berlin: Verlag von Karl Curtius, 1918)

Schuman, Frederick L. "The Conduct of German Foreign Affairs," *Annals of the American Academy of Political and Social Science*, CLXXVI (November, 1934), supplement.

Schwarz, Paul. *This Man Ribbentrop: His Life and Times* (New York: Julian Messner, 1943).

Seel, Hanns. *Das Neue Beamtengesetz* (Berlin: Junker u. Dünnhaupt Verlag, (1937).

Sington, Derrick, and Arthur Weidenfeld. *The Goebbels Experiment* (New Haven: Yale University Press, 1943).

Taylor, A. J. P. *The Course of German History: A Survey of the Development of Germany Since 1815* (New York: Coward-McCann, 1946).

Taylor, Telford. *Sword and Swastika: Generals and Nazis in the Third Reich* (New York: Simon and Schuster, 1952).

Trefousse, Hans L. *Germany and American Neutrality, 1939–1941* (New York: Bookman Associates, 1951).

Trevor-Roper, H. R. *The Last Days of Hitler* (New York: Macmillan, 1947).

Das Urteil im Wilhelmstrassen-Prozess: der amtliche Wortlaut der Entscheidung im Fall Nr. 11 . . ., with introductions by Dr. Robert M. W. Kempner and Dr. Carl Haensel (Schwäbisch-Gmünd: Alfons Bürger Verlag, 1950).

Weber, Max. *From Max Weber: Essays in Sociology*. Translated from the German, edited, and with an introduction by H. H. Gerth and C. Wright Mills (New York: Oxford University Press, 1946).

Weizsäcker, Ernst von. *Erinnerungen* (Munich: P. List, 1950).

Welles, Sumner. *The Time for Decision* (New York: Harper, 1944).

Wheeler-Bennett, John. *Munich: Prologue to Tragedy* (New York: Duell, Sloan and Pearce, 1948).

White, L. D., *et al. Civil Service Abroad* (New York: McGraw-Hill, 1935).

Wiskemann, Elizabeth. *The Rome-Berlin Axis: A History of the Relations between Hitler and Mussolini* (London: Oxford University Press, 1949).

Zechlin, Walter W. *Diplomatie und Diplomaten* (Stuttgart: Deutsche Verlags-Anstalt, 1935).

Zorn, Philipp. "Deutsches Gesandtschafts- und Konsularrecht," in *Handbuch des Völkerrechts*, III–1. Edited by Dr. Fritz Stier-Somlo (Stuttgart: W. Kohlhammer Verlag, 1920).

INDEX

Secret Cabinet Council, 41, 115
"Secret diplomacy," 9, 151 ff.
Seeckt, General Hans von, 23, 45
Selzam, Eduard von, 142 f.
Seyss-Inquart, Dr. Artur von, 66, 114
Sicherheitsdienst, 128, 130, 138, 193 n.
   18
Simon, Hugo, 30
Simon, Sir John, 37, 176 n. 8
Simons, Walther, 17
Sitzkrieg, 100 f.
Six, Dr. Franz Alfred, 137
Skrine-Stevenson, R. C., 96
Slave labor, 124, 189 n. 8, 193 n. 17
Social Democrats, 9 ff., 16, 22, 28 f., 80,
   174 n. 33. See also individual
   Social-Democratic leaders
Solf, Dr. Wilhelm, 21
Sonderkommando, 113
Sonderzug Heinrich, 104
Sonderzug Westfalen. See Ribbentrop:
   railroad car of
Sonnleithner, Franz, 106
Soviet Union
   anti-Soviet propaganda, 194 n. 20
   art looting in, 113
   diplomacy of, 28
   German diplomats with army in, 113
   invasion of, 114–118
   nonaggression pact and collaboration
      with Hitler, 23, 45, 114, 185 n. 4
   rejects Socialist as German ambassa-
      dor, 174 n. 33
   slave labor from, 124
   technicians sent to, 23
   See also Russia Committee

Spain, 43, 45, 57
SS, 44, 50, 108, 126 ff.
   admission of Weizsäcker, Woermann,
      63 f.
Stahlhelm, 30
Stahmer, Heinrich, 52
Stalingrad, 140
Steengracht, Baron Gustav Adolf von
   Moyland, 52, 106, 124, 126, 130,
   134, 136 ff., 140, 193 n. 17
Sthamer, Friedrich von, 16, 18
Stöcker, Walter, 174 n. 33
Stresemann, Gustav, 21, 23, 155, 157

Studentenkorps, 8
Sudeten crisis, 76, 92–99
Supreme Command of the Armed
   Forces, 42, 103, 113. See also
   Abwehr
Sweden, 178 n. 42
Switzerland, 96

Talleyrand, 97
Teheran Conference, 131, 141
Le Temps, 48
Thomsen, Dr. Hans, 121
Thoiry, 155, 157
Tiefenbacher (SS-Obersturmführer),
   64
Times (London), 37, 48, 55, 151
Tippelskirch, Werner von, 191 n. 28,
   192 n. 5
Tirpitz, Grand Admiral Alfred von, 83,
   181 n. 43
Totalitarianism, xii f., 162–170
Transkontinent Press, 184 n. 77
Trautmann, Oskar P., 18, 91, 99
Trevor-Roper, H. R., xiii
Trotsky, 29
Trotha, Thilo von, 178 n. 42
Trott zu Solz, Adam von, 142 f., 144 f.
Turkey, 130
Twardowski, Dr. Fritz von, 103, 137,
   191 n. 28

Ukraine, 116
United States
   airmen, trial of, 138
   Department of State, 153, 157, 160
   fear of war with, 92
   foreign service, 152 f., 157 ff.
   loyalty of diplomats, 172 n. 6
   Nazi repatriates from, 120
   political duress in, 170
   troops in Sicily, 140
   Trott as U.S. specialist, 143
   war declaration received, 201 n. 31
Union of Soviet Socialist Republics.
   See Soviet Union

Vansittart, Lord, 57, 155, 156, 160
Veesenmayer, Edmund, 167
Versailles peace treaty, 12, 23, 31, 38,
   43